Scotland's Road to Socialism:
Time to Chooose

Scottish Left Review Press

scottish left
review press

Published by Scottish Left Review Press
The Jimmy Reid Foundation, PO Box 8781, Biggar ML12 9AG

Scottish Left Review Press is a trading name of Left Review Scotland Ltd.,
741 Shields Road, Pollokshields, Glasgow G41 4PL

www.scottishleftreview.org

First published 2013

Edited by Gregor Gall

British Library Cataloguing-in-Publication Data are available

ISBN 978-0-9550362-5-5

Printed and bound in Great Britain by:
Martins the Printers
Sea View Works
Spittal
Berwick-upon-Tweed
Northumberland TD15 1RS

Contents

Contributors

John Aberdein is a novelist and activist, who has worked as herring fisher, English teacher and outdoor instructor. His first novel, *Amande's Bed*, is a revisiting of working-class Aberdeen in 1956, with particular focus on the crisis in the Communist Party over Hungary. His second, *Strip the Willow*, is a simultaneous take on the liberations of 1968 and on the threat of corporate takeover in 'Uberdeen'. He has been a democratic republican green socialist since he can remember, and has campaigned widely both within and outwith parties of the left.

Cat Boyd is chair of Coalition of Resistance in Scotland. She is a Youth Officer in the Public and Commercial Services union and a member of the International Socialist Group (ISG) Scotland. She writes here as an ISG member.

Pauline Bryan is editor of *The Citizen*, the magazine published by the Scottish Campaign for Socialism (a current with the Scottish Labour Party). She is also convenor of the Red Paper Collective which is campaigning for a labour movement alternative to both the demands for independence and retaining the *status quo*.

Maggie Chetty is currently chair of the Communist Party of Scotland (CPS), has been since 2000, and writes in this capacity. She was a member of the Communist Party of Great Britain from 1973 until its dissolution in 1991 and the CPS thereafter. She was previously a teacher, secretary of the Scottish International Labour Council and director of Strathclyde Racial Equality Council. She was active in the anti-Apartheid Movement (now ACTSA) as well as in the EIS, NUT and Unite unions until her retirement.
Maggie is currently the treasurer of Glasgow Central Citizens' Advice Bureau.

Jim Cuthbert lectured in statistics at Glasgow University then joined the civil service in 1974, and worked in statistics in the Scottish Office and the Treasury. He was latterly Scottish Office Chief Statistician. His research is particularly in the areas of Scotland's public finances and the Scottish economy, in certain aspects of purchasing power parities, and in aspects of Irish history. Particular interests have been in the analysis of government expenditure and revenues in Scotland (GERS), the performance of PFI schemes, and developing alternatives to current models for utility charging.

Margaret Cuthbert lectured in economics at several Scottish universities: she has spent most of her career as an economics and business consultant. Her major area of research has been public expenditure in Scotland. She edited and contributed to *Public Expenditure in Scotland*, one of the few economics texts on Scotland written in the period after the first Devolution referendum. Specific interests include GERS, and the improvement of the GERS data and analysis: critiques of the private finance initiative: the analysis of devolved and reserved spending: and research into the basis of the costings of the policy of free care for the elderly.

Neil Davidson is the author of *The Origins of Scottish Nationhood* (2000), *Discovering the Scottish Revolution* (2003), for which he was awarded the Deutscher Prize, and *How Revolutionary Were the Bourgeois Revolutions?* (2012). Neil is member of the Socialist Workers Party (SWP) and sits on its Scottish Steering Group and UK-wide National Committee. His contribution expresses a personal take on the SWP's position of support for Scottish independence.

Neil Findlay is a former bricklayer and teacher. He was a Labour Councillor for 9 years before being elected to the Scottish Parliament as a member for the Lothian Region at the 2011 election. Neil is a member of UNITE and the EIS. He is currently a shadow Minister for skills and learning, and writes here in a personal capacity.

John Foster is emeritus professor of social sciences at the University of the West of Scotland and his contribution has the approval of the Scottish Committee of the Communist Party of Britain. He is the CPB's International Secretary and has written on Scotland's economic and social history.

James Foley is researching a PhD at Edinburgh University on Scottish financial capitalism. He is the author of *Britain Must Break: the internationalist case for independence* (ISG, 2012) and a member of the International Socialist Group (ISG) Scotland. He writes as member of the ISG.

Colin Fox is the joint national spokesman of the Scottish Socialist Party. An SSP MSP for four years from 2003 to 2007, his Bill to abolish NHS prescription charges was picked up and implemented by the Scottish Government.

Gregor Gall is professor of industrial relations at the University of Bradford. Previously, he held the same post at the universities of Stirling and

Hertfordshire. He was the editor of the original *Is There a Scottish Road to Socialism?*, has been a columnist for the *Morning Star* since 2005 and is author of *Tommy Sheridan: from hero to zero? A political biography* (Welsh Academic Press, 2011). He has been a member of the editorial board of the *Scottish Left Review* since 2003 and the editor of *Scottish Left Review Press* since 2007.

Lynn Henderson is the Scottish Secretary and National Officer for Northern Ireland and Northern Region of the Public and Commercial Services Union. She is a member of the STUC General Council, Red Paper Collective, Scottish Living Wage Campaign Steering Group, People's Charter Scottish Co-ordinating Committee and the Campaign for Socialism. Lynn has been a member of the Labour Party since 1984 and is a member of Scottish CND. She writes here in a personal capacity.

Tommy Kane is a member of the Red Paper Collective, parliamentary researcher to Neil Findlay MSP and completing a PhD into the Scottish Water industry at the University of Strathclyde. He has contributed to *Scottish Left Review* on a number of occasions.

Bill Kidd MSP represents Glasgow Anniesland for the SNP and although the Scottish Government Chief Whip he is writing in a personal capacity. Bill is Co President of PNND (Parliamentarians for Nuclear Non-proliferation and Disarmament) and is a Global Council Member of Abolition 2000. He says: 'If there isn't a Scottish road to socialism, there isn't one at all.'

Richard Leonard is GMB Scotland's Political Officer, a former chairperson of the Scottish Labour Party, and the longest serving member of its elected Executive. He is the Secretary of the Keir Hardie Society and stood for Parliament in 2011 in the Carrick, Cumnock and Doon Valley constituency. For over twenty years, Richard has been a regular writer and campaigner on the Scottish economy, firstly as an Assistant Secretary at the STUC responsible for economic affairs and then as an Organiser for the GMB representing manufacturing, commercial and public service workers across Scotland. He is a founding member of the Red Paper Collective.

John McAllion is an executive member of the Dundee and Scottish Pensioners' Forums. He was formerly the Labour MP for Dundee East (1987-2001) and Labour MSP for Dundee East (1999-2003). He left the Labour Party in 2005 to join the SSP. He remains a member of the SSP but is writing here in a personal capacity.

Mhairi McAlpine, from Glasgow, currently lives in Athens, Greece. She is a former member of the Scottish Socialist Party, and has been a Marxist and radical activist for over 25 years. Most recently she has been involved with Radical Independence Conference and the Glasgow Coalition of Resistance as well as various initiatives in Greece. She takes a particular interest in anti-colonial movements, including the campaign for Scottish independence, and feminism. She writes for a variety of radical publications, and blogs at *Second Council House of Virgo*.

Robin McAlpine is Director of the Jimmy Reid Foundation, Editor of the *Scottish Left Review* and author of *No Idea: Control, Liberation and the Social Imagination* (Scottish Left Review Press, 2005).

Dr Conor McCabe is a researcher with the University College Dublin's School of Social Justice. He is the author of *Sins of the Father: Tracing the Decisions That Shaped the Irish Economy* (History Press, 2001) and is a frequent contributor to the *Irish Left Review*. He is writing here in a personal capacity.

Peter McColl is a writer and activist, living in Edinburgh. He is a member of the Scottish Green Party and is a co-editor of the Bright Green Blog. He was voted top Green blogger in 2011 and was in the top 10 left bloggers. He is also Rector of the University of Edinburgh. This chapter is written in a personal capacity.

Gordon Morgan has been active in socialist parties and campaigns for over 40 years. He is presently treasurer of Solidarity, on executive of the Scottish Independence Convention and an editorial board member of the *Scottish Left Review*, but writes in a personal capacity.

Mike Small is an activist, writer and publisher originally from Aberdeen. He is a social ecologist, Scottish socialist and republican. He was co-founder of *Product* magazine (first launched as *Red Herring* in 1998) as well as one of the group behind Indymedia Scotland. He has written for *Lobster* and *Variant* magazines, is currently a columnist for the *Guardian's* Comment is Free website. He is currently co-editor of *Bella Caledonia* with Kevin Williamson. He writes in a personal capacity in this edited book.

Dave Watson is the Head of Bargaining and Campaigns with UNISON Scotland. He manages its bargaining, legal, equalities, communications, research and political functions, and is a past Chair of the Scottish Labour Party and a member of its Scottish Executive Committee. He is the Secretary of the Scottish Trade Union Labour Party Committee (STULP) and Secretary of the Socialist Health Association (SHA) Scotland. He is also a member of the Red Paper collective and the Keir Hardie Society Committee. He edits the Journal 'Healthier Scotland' and the blogs Revitalise Scottish Labour, SHA and Utilities Scotland as well as regularly contributing to the print media and other publications. He has been a full- time union official for 32 years.

Acknowledgements

Thanks are to Nadia Lucchesi for the cover design and to Robin McAlpine for typesetting and production.'

Chapter 1

Scene setting for the scenario of socialism in Scotland and Scottish socialism

Gregor Gall

Seven years ago, Scottish Left Review Press (SLRP) published the original *Is There a Scottish Road to Socialism?* Its purpose was to examine how a road – maybe *the* road - forward to socialism in Scotland might be mapped out. Would it be a Scottish, British, European or global road? Or, a mixture of some or all four? The feeling at the time on the pro-independence left was that while the issue was still of importance, it was no nearer in reach given the implosion of the Scottish Socialist Party (SSP) and a minority SNP government. But by 2011, the tectonic plates of Scottish politics had moved considerably. An unexpected SNP landslide in the May Scottish elections of that year began a process which we now know will lead to a referendum in late 2014 on 'should we stay or should we go' – indeed, Saturday 18 October 2014 is the date, given that Alex Salmond told the new Sunday edition of the *Scottish Sun* this on 18 February 2012 when welcoming the successor to the defunct *News of the World*. The tectonic plates of Scottish politics were also moved by developments elsewhere - most obviously, the return of the Tories to government in Westminster, the economic depression in the global north and the age of austerity. Such momentous events cannot but help shape how any road or roads to socialism come about even if the desired end point remains unchanged whatever one's perspective. So in late 2012, the Scottish Left Review Press decided that it was more than high time to return to the question of 'Is there a Scottish road to socialism?' Again, we wanted to look at how a road can be mapped out and what obstacles are faced to doing so.

So when the contributors were approach in the summer of 2012, the main question posed to them was: 'how do we move forward to a socialist Scotland?' The supplementary to this was:

> *Following from this, can Scotland achieve socialism on its own? Is socialism a real prospect in contemporary Britain? Which dynamics in Scottish and British politics give reason for optimism and which*

give reason for pessimism? Where do the necessary powers lie and how realistic is the hope that they will be used in the right way? What concrete steps and reforms can be put forward as a realistic means of moving towards a socialist Scotland?

So, is an independent Scotland more or less likely to achieve socialism? If you believe that the independence option offers a way to achieve this, outline what kind of society you envisage after a 'yes' vote, how this will come about and what political forces will lead this development.

If you believe that independence does not offer this way possibility, please outline what other arrangement - most obviously within the union of the four nations - will deliver upon your vision for social and economic justice as well as how this will come about.

In addition to those that contributed a chapter, STUC assistant secretary Ann Henderson, Scottish Left Review's chair Bob Thomson, Plaid Cymru AM Bethan Jenkins, writer Gerry Hassan, Joan McApline MSP, writer Andy Wightman, journalist Joyce Mcmillan, Plaid Cymru leader Leanne Wood AM and Caroline Lucas MP were also asked but constraints on their time meant they were unable to contribute. A number of others were also asked to contribuute but failed to respond. Contributors were sought across the axes of being pro- or anti-independence and across gender as well as outside the borders of Scotland. Although no one was able to make a contribution from the STUC (but with permission from the STUC), in the appendix its document on the outcome of its consultation meetings called *A Just Scotland* is published. The document was published at the end of 2012 after a series of public meetings in the major towns and cities of Scotland.

The original *Is There a Scottish Road to Socialism?* contained chapters from 14 contributors. We deliberately sought widen the net and canvass more and wider opinion for this current version. We are grateful to those who again contributed a chapter as well as those that did so for the first time. As before, socialism was defined as the search for social justice, whether in its forms of social democracy or revolutionary socialism, or anything in between. Social justice is primarily concerned with fair and equitable economic and social outcomes for the vast majority of its citizens. Each contributor was given the freedom and leeway to respond in his or her own way to these same, standard aforementioned questions. The process of editing was a light touch one whereby a house style was used to standardise the presentation of each chapter. No attempt was made to say to each or any contributor that such and such a question was not answered or the answer was not very convincing. Consequently, readers can - with some certainty

- compare and contrast where different writers and political perspectives stand on their answers to the questions of the day over independence and social justice as well as how strongly and convincingly they stand on their answers. Equally well, where contributors do not focus upon answering particular questions, it is up to readers to draw their own implications about what this means. Despite some variety in the way of responding to the key questions, it is clear where the fault lines in the debate within and across the left lie. We hope then that this collection can make a significant contribution not only to the dialogue amongst the left on the issues at hand but also can help inform the public debate on the issues. It is the case that conversation between both sides of the left is not a dialogue of the deaf and this bodes well, especially because come the referendum and its outcome both sides will need to continue such a dialogue (albeit one side might be in a stronger political position than the other). As will become apparent, no order of priority is given to how the chapters are ordered. They were simply presented alphabetically by the author's last name. Where references to material are used, they are either in text ones or contained in a brief list after the last chapter. The remainder of this introduction sketches out some of the major themes and issues which are germane to the debate and the following chapters.

To a man and a woman, it is obvious that the contributors believe in a broad form of socialism that transcends existing and future national boundaries. If a schism exists at this meso-level, it is not one of simple 'internationalism' versus 'nationalism' then. Of course, what weight they give to the importance of various national cultures and the like before and after the achievement of socialism varies. There is no sense of either competitive nationalism or aggressive nationalism, and very little that there are entirely national solutions to national problems, i.e., 'socialism in one country' or autarky. The debate is about where and how to start - or continue - the battle for socialism in the context of the approaching referendum and the existing hegemony of neo-liberalism and austerity. Can developments in Scotland kick start a wider process or must they merely be part of a wider flowering? How does the internal relate to the external? In this sense, it would be more accurate to see the common and major thread running the contributions as one of the search for social justice and social liberation as of a fraternal *trans*-national nature, that is across and over nations (as opposed to inter-national meaning *between* nations). It is for this reason that most contributions quite rightly focus upon the economic and social rather than political and constitutional. Yet the danger is this is that the 2014/2016 dichotomy is underplayed. The referendum is entirely - at the formal level - about a constitutional relationship. In no political sense will Scotland be different the day before and after a 'yes' vote (if that is what happens). However, to gain a 'yes' vote or to substantially alter the social terms of the existing union, political and other arguments will have to be used. For example, the SNP's heavily neo-liberal influenced vision of independence does not – indeed, cannot- address pressing social questions in a way that will compel a majority of citizens to support independence. So for those favouring a radical vision of independence, radicalism needs to have influence not just in regard of the reasons of voting for independence but on the voting to determine the composition of the fifth parliament that begins in 2016. Equally for those favouring the continuation of the union (albeit under different terms) requires that not only is a no vote is successful but that the 2015 Westminster election provides for a Labour government which is considerably more radical than Ed Miliband and Ed Mills will allow for, and that promises for devo-max – and the use of those new powers for progressive ends – are kept. Again, radical political and other arguments will need to hold sway for this particular outcome to be realised. It becomes clear that both tasks are quite Herculean and that not only do the contending arguments of the left need to hold sway but that this means having a level of influence that is a complete step change from where we are at the moment, a moment of the left labouring under the yoke of continued neo-liberalism. Thus, both sides of the left here must urgently address not just issues about the internal cogency of their arguments but critically how they will also gain credibility amongst the mass of citizens for these arguments. If you like, the battle is win hegemony inside their respective camps and then with the public at large outside these camps.

In these processes, the radicals for independence must set out what they want independence from as well as what they want independence for. Ironically, the radical yes vision is actually a *no* vision – *no* to NATO, no to Trident, no to austerity, no to imperialism and no to neo-liberalism. But even that does not go far enough because there must also be a wholly positive version of the vision of what an independent, radical Scotland will look like under independence. Here the pounds and pence of the economic and social questions must be set out. For the radicals for the union, the key task is to differentiate the type of union desired, otherwise – again ironically, they will be saying *yes* to NATO, yes to Trident, yes to austerity, yes to imperialism and yes to neo-liberalism.

There are important tactical matters to be considered along the way. The clamour of the 'cultural nationalists' just before the close of 2012 over the alleged domination of the English in the world of the administration of Scottish art and culture indicates that the debate has to be intelligent and cute enough to say that if there is an issue with English people managing Scottish arts, then it is an issue of what political values the managers from England hold and not that they are English *per se*. Otherwise, we will enter dark and dangerous territory. Also towards the end of 2012, Nicola Sturgeon gave a talk at the University of Strathclyde outlining that there were two cases for independence, namely, the existential (self-determination as an end itself) and the instrumental (self-determination as way to gain social justice). She favoured the latter but this marked a conversation with the commentariat, and not the proletariat. This pattern continued with her essay in *Scotland on Sunday* in late January 2013. Even if Sturgeon's message is more likely to resonate with the mass of citizens, like the Yes Scotland campaign in general, the message remains a rather passive one with little direct connection because it is not as yet part of a campaign or movement that springs organically from the collective grievances of working people (as the anti-poll tax campaign did). In other words, not only is independence not yet seen as the answer to solving poverty and inequality whereby it springs organically from the current struggles of working people and their families but it also has to be part of a transitional approach whereby struggling for one demand opens up and augments the desire for more fundamental change and the capacity to achieve it. A third matter concerns that of experience and memory. In living memory, Scotland has never been an independent nation, state or nation-state. To this extent, it is untried and untested. But that also may present opportunity to ask the 'what if' questions in an untainted way. By contrast, the British road to socialism has had a long period of existence as a living project. Its highpoint was the period of the 1945-51 Labour governments. Is that a strong enough memory to cling on to – as well as to constitute a springboard to another and better chance to go down the British road? Some may say it has had chance enough and new ways and means are now warranted.

If politics is the art of the possible, then it is incumbent upon those in favour of a yes vote to presage a radical reconfiguration of society in Scotland to also work out the *probabilities* of such a change being able to occur. And, of course, to be open and honest when they do so. This is the key message from those who argue in this collection for a different type of union to that which currently exists. But the boot is on the other foot too because it is also incumbent upon those that argue for a radical configuration of the union to also work out the *probabilities* and to stop talking about just the *possibilities*. Citizens will be better off with hard-nosed and realistic assessments rather than flights of fancy. All this is because what is desirable is not necessarily possible or probable because gaps exist between means and ends.

Chapter 2

Up for It!

John Aberdein

I am retired, though not retiring by nature, and a pensioner of my profession, which was teaching. I am currently a novelist, fictionalising the joys and travail of folk who work for a living rather than exploit others. And, like millions upon millions, I have had enough, far more than enough, of the effects of the outrageous neo-liberal, anti-human lies that currently sweep the UK and much of the world in order to strengthen capital's desperate grasp.

Nor can I see much hope of succour from the mainstream parties that occupy Westminster. All parties of size are thirled to neo-liberalism, kowtowing to major banks and to subjugation of the world's people and resources to short-term lust for profit. Disgracefully supporting that agenda are the Westminster parties, Tories and LibDems, both of whom clapped together would barely form a rump in Scotland. As for Labour, its offers no clear declaration of principle that would encourage people to follow its banner. When Clause 4 was ripped up by Blair and co in 1994, any residual principle was shredded with it. Labour is, at best, the least worst party - a pitiful position to inhabit.

Westminster is a handmaiden of reaction, and so we must seek to raise our dream elsewhere and by other means. I have never been a 'Wha's like us?' nationalist. Along with enormous feeling for the languages, technology and culture we have in Scotland, I have huge respect for the languages, technology and culture of the rest of the world. Yet now, as economic, social and environmental crises deepen by the day, what I do want for Scotland, extremely urgently, is to achieve independence as a small, self-propelled, shape-able, principled country. Let us try to create - not just for ourselves, but as encouragement to the peoples of England, Wales and Ireland, and as a beacon to many in the world - a society that takes its stand on human decency.

First, we have to win the referendum on independence in 2014. It is very possible to do this if each of us already committed to voting Yes persuades at least one other person. That referendum won, would a Scottish road to social human decency open up? How about we think less of a road, which sounds a bit grand, and instead think of two other kinds of route: the path and the track. Obviously many contributory Scottish paths to social human decency would remain tread-able, or become more tread-able, after independence: not easy trails, but stony paths up the side of a steep mountain. Many of these paths are already known to us, though some are better marked than others. They include union action for wages and conditions; maintenance through general taxation of health and education services universally provided and free at the point of need; development of common land ownership and resource access; building of cooperatives in all spheres and of all sizes; rebuilding of public ownership of major banks, utilities and enterprises; and insistence - not only in the civic but also in the economic sphere - on governance by principles of participative democracy, environmental sustainability and international peace.

The referendum won and these paths freshly attempted, there would, of course, still exist the same enemies as we have now, blockading and ambushing: that set of practitioners, agents and infiltrators who include filthy warmongers, selfish privateers, lying rhetoricians of neo-liberalism, destructive 'developers', cynical promoters of rampant consumerism, divisive fomenters of hate and discrimination, subverters of human solidarity, and eroders of the intrinsic value of each one of our souls and beings. Social human decency will not be won without a war! To scale the mountain and approach our summit of human potential, we would need to challenge and change the whole political climate.

Yet it has to be acknowledged that there persists the risk of atomisation, of being off doing our own thing and meanwhile being divided, diverted and ruled by our enemies. So therefore, flanked by those various upward paths, there will surely need to be a central track, a common track, a popular coalition position that allows agreed candidates to be put up without opposition from progressive forces, so that it is then the neo-liberals who land up dividing their vote, and so that lasting office and latent power can be obtained for the cause of social human decency. Let's give that coalition an interim title: Up for It! What might the basis for such a coalition be?

I would submit that the basis for the 'Up for It!' position cannot be the views of any single party, group or platform merely because it has a trusty historical record of being elected in Scotland and/or marches and campaigns loudly and/or claims the best Marxist analysis and/or knows how to pitch to the media and/or is adept at stitching up a majority behind the scenes and/or is currently in possession of a charismatic leader. All of those are well-tried approaches, we've seen them come and we've seen them go, and all are compromised, whether through inherent divisiveness, inertia, emotionalism or temporariness, when we consider how desperately strong the enemy currently is.

No, the basis for a coalition position on social human decency must be scientific: and only because of its scientific nature will it have the right to command the widest possible assent. There must be one idea that is proven beyond doubt to be not just sectionally helpful, but credibly beneficial right across society. Tough call? Up until four years ago we had no such idea. We have now. The idea is this: societies with greater equality of income have better social outcomes for everyone. Here it is not just better social outcomes for the unemployed, or for those on benefits, or for the working-class, or for the middle-classes, or for the relatively rich but for all of those classes together. How can this possibly be?

The scientific position is set out in *The Spirit Level* by Wilkinson and Pickett (2010). Their incontrovertible finding is that societies with wide disparity of income breed unbridled consumerism and consumer envy, poor self-esteem, despair, distrust, illness, social dissolution and crime. By contrast, peoples in societies with greater income equality thrive far better. They do better at school, live longer, feel healthier, are less obese, trust each other more, form more cohesive communities, are less likely to experience mental illness, use illegal drugs, be imprisoned, be violent or kill. An extra bonus is that the people in these more equal societies are able to lift their eyes: they are more likely to actively support moves for peace, overseas aid, and public measures on global warming.

These findings were not arrived at on the basis of wishful thinking. They are the result of the collection and collation by two UK epidemiology professors of publicly available data stretching back decades across 25 developed nations, and all their resultant analyses and graphs have been rigorously peer-reviewed. The data is so strong, and so revolutionary in its implications, that Wilkinson and Pickett have felt compelled to travel far and wide, giving over 350 lectures and seminars since the book came out, an average of one every three days. Their position has been attacked, but survives intact. Their position stems from the fact that countries like Japan, Sweden and Norway, with greater levels of income equality, do far better across a range of social outcomes, compared with places like Singapore, the US and the UK where gross levels of income inequality has been ramping up over the last thirty years.

One of the main reasons for the right-wing attacking them is that, in arguing for better distribution of income as the key plank of socio-economic policy, Wilkinson and Pickett have had no truck with trickledown theory, or with any notion that redistribution of income can be achieved only on the back of future growth. In fact a corollary of their position is that economic growth has now reached such a level in developed economies that growth itself, as a variable, has no impact on improving social outcomes. (Underdeveloped societies patently lack that basis of wealth, largely due to exploitation from outside, and this situation has to be addressed first. *The*

Spirit Level analysis does not apply to them, and that is made clear by the authors.)

The core of Wilkinson and Pickett's position, then, is that an unequal, very hierarchical society like ours -with obscenely rewarded CEOs and abysmally paid service workers, with vacuous celebrities on telephone number salaries yet countless graduates unable to find work and contribute their skills - places its members in intolerable economic and psycho-social positions. In such a society, everyone to maintain or improve their status is expected to take part in endless rabid scuttling after the latest consumer goods. For those unable to assert their place in society by means of the latest phone, pad, designer-wear, fancy postcode and frequent foreign holiday, significant loss of self-esteem and various self-harming behaviours are likely to follow. Such behaviours have lamentable costs to the individual, but also make heavy charge on the health, social services, and law and order budgets, and those latter costs then bear upon everyone. Those public budgets, though, are often no better than sticking-plasters that barely adhere over running and continually aggravated wounds. Personal diminishment, social dislocation, and huge but often futile stopgap provision go hand-in-hand. That is what neo-liberalism has done - and is doing - to us.

So back to our post-independence 'Up for It!' position on social human decency. Adopting as its central plank not economic growth but the reduction of income inequality, what measures could the coalition promise if elected?

1. Greater income equality could be achieved by better pay in the first place. Union membership should be encouraged and repressive UK labour laws repealed. Without the relentless historical commitment and effort of unions, we would be in a very poor place. In EU countries, 70 per cent of employees are covered by collective agreements, but in the UK the figure is a wretched 35 per cent. That has to change.

2. Greater income equality could be achieved by reforming company structures. The coalition could commit through targeted tax allowances to helping companies transform themselves, not just towards employee share-ownership but crucially to elected employee participation in the boardroom. There already exist such companies like John Lewis, with its £8.7bn turnover. John Lewis is owned by a trust on behalf of all its employees - known as partners - who have a say in the running of the business and who receive a share of annual profits, which is usually a significant addition to their salary. In general, it can be noted that employee-owned and directed companies are unlikely to countenance stratospheric CEO pay, and are likely to flatten pay differentials.

3. Greater income equality could be achieved by the growth of

cooperatives. The Mondragon federation of cooperatives in the Basque country has 83,000 workers, who collectively determine the company pay structure, with senior manager to semi-skilled worker often at a ratio lower than five to one, and who pursue a humanist business approach while at the same time managing to be the seventh largest company in Spain. The coalition should commit to studying such examples, and to promoting cooperative practice in all sectors of the Scottish economy. A major cooperative in the renewables sector is much needed, for example, and would broaden the income-share from our vital struggle to arrest global warming.

4. Greater income equality could be achieved through tax reform. Tax and insurance loopholes should be closed, thus increasing take from the better-off. If, for example, an oil group wants to remain in Aberdeen to benefit from the concentration of industry-related skills, it would have to pay national insurance in Scotland, not use the loophole of a Guernsey company registration to avoid this. And crucially a land-value tax - replacing both business rates and council tax - is long overdue to release private land for productive use and to reduce severe inequalities in the housing market.

These four approaches might be enough for 'Up for It!' at the outset. There is plenty room for debate. But what we can surely agree on is that there is stunningly little point in Scotland becoming independent if we do not immediately make major strides towards income equality. For, if we were only to have the clarity and courage to make these strides, then we would help all classes of folk - and indeed all progressive campaigners - to reach far higher up the difficult mountain of social human decency towards those longed-for peaks of human fulfilment and achievement.

Chapter 3

Out of the ghetto - why detoxifying the left is the first step to revival

Cat Boyd and James Foley

A socialist strategy in Scotland must necessarily involve two parts. The first is a consideration of the objective possibility of - and the need for - an anti-capitalist party in Scotland. This is the question of 'political space': how much room do we have for an alternative at the ballot box when we are squeezed between SNP and Labour? The second is about our own behaviour, the trust we have for each other and our legitimacy with social movements and working class communities. This may be called the subjective factor.

Our position is that there is space for a radical left alternative in Scotland. There is a crisis in Scottish society, lying somewhere between the nationalisation of RBS/HBOS (economic crisis) and the referendum of 2014 (constitutional crisis). This Scottish crisis presents definite opportunities. To anticipate and shape this process, we must face up to our own need for reform. Due, in part, to the SSP split, the left in Scotland has a toxic reputation that extends far beyond our own ranks. We do not think our own crisis can be resolved by the final defeat or victory of any sector of the left: what is required is a three step detoxification process.

In the short term, we must achieve *left unity*. This is not just about united action with the Greens, union activists and so on. It means active steps to restore working relations in the post-SSP left. In the medium term, we must regain the trust of protest movements and the wider radical left currents in society: we may call this *left renewal*. Lastly, there is the broad task of winning the leadership of society in the battle to transfer wealth from the rich to the poor. This hegemonic task clearly requires winning over 'reformist' voices in the SNP, Labour, and the unions. We call this *left realignment*. These steps, we wish to argue, depend on each other, but stem from a reading of objective difficulties in maintaining existing Holyrood alliances.

Space for the left?

Scottish politics is often thought of as a 'village' in which 'everyone who is anyone knows everyone else who matters'. Few will deny that there are elites who shape the policy framework in Holyrood. But we also need to remember that Scotland is a capitalist, class society with staggering inequalities of wealth and power. One study, in 2003, showed that two Edinburgh districts have more millionaires than anywhere in Britain other than Hampstead in London. 'Blackhall is better heeled than Belgravia and Morningside is more upmarket than Mayfair' reported the *Telegraph* (6 February 2003). Contrast this to the figure that men in the Calton ward of Glasgow live to an average age of 54. With these facts in mind, we dispute any idea that Scotland has a distinctively 'collectivist' civil society. The neo-liberal trajectory in Scotland, like elsewhere, has led to extreme polarisations of income.

Reversing these trends is the goal of the anti neo-liberal left. The size of this group may be disputed. At the higher end of estimates, 43 per cent of Scotland favours government action to redistribute wealth from the rich to the poor. In practice, this is unlikely to form part of the platform of either Scottish Labour or the SNP. Yet, this should not lead to the conclusion that this grouping is liable to switch allegiances to the left anytime soon. Winning this layer of Scotland to the left is the long-term goal. In the short term, we must seek to win back those who have deserted anti-capitalist politics in recent elections.

It is over-simplistic to attribute the decline of the radical left in Holyrood to the SSP split alone. Clearly, there are objective socio-economic and political factors to account for. Some argue that the left was always liable to get squeezed in the battle between the SNP and Scottish Labour, and thus view recent results as inevitable, irrespective of contingent factors. Conveniently, this 'objective' account draws attention away from our own flaws. But there are, certainly, good reasons to look at objective circumstances.

Firstly, the fact that Scottish Labour is consistently positioned to the right of the SNP government puts the nature and identity of union politics into question. Unions will not 'jump ship' to SNP; such an arrangement would suit neither. But their current link with Labour is not feasible so long as the neo-liberal turn continues. The left could, and should, play an active role in resolving Scotland's crisis of working class representation. Secondly, there is lasting evidence of anti-capitalist and left-of-Labour sentiment in Scotland. A decade ago, the Scottish Socialist Party (SSP) was able to command 130,000 votes and six MSPs. The Greens secured a similar vote, roughly seven per cent, gaining seven MSPs. The Iraq factor played a strong role in these results. However, it is also evidence that there is a significant part of the Scottish electorate that can be won to leftist ideas. Anti-war sentiment in Scotland did not emerge from nowhere. It built on frustration with the 'village' atmosphere of Scottish politics, especially the failings of Scottish Labour to tackle poverty and class inequality. Recently, these frustrations have only intensified. While we may disagree on the actions of the SSP in

Holyrood, we can surely agree that it had some success in tapping into this current of anger. Thirdly, the last few years have seen a significant revival of the extra-parliamentary radical left in Scotland. The student movement against fees and cuts was the precipitating factor. However, this has helped to reinvigorate other currents as well, such as feminist, environmental, and international solidarity campaigns. Many of the people involved with these campaigns will strongly disagree with us on the need for political organisation. We ignore them at our peril. Our belief is that they can play a strong role in revitalising the left, but only if the existing left is ready to change its own habits and routines. We have as much to learn from the movements as they have to learn from us.

A crisis of radical left politics is not peculiar to Scotland. All across Europe, the victories of anti-capitalist forces after Seattle and during the Iraq war have been pushed back for a decade. The organised left has failed to offer a coherent challenge, system-wide, to the crisis, the bailouts, and the cuts post-2008. We note that the defeats of the organised left have not been even. In some nations, the left has positioned itself well to present a challenge to the dominant austerity narrative. If Syriza in Greece is at one end of the spectrum of left-wing success, Britain has most definitely been at the other end. Given this, we believe there is no reason for fatalism. We are a victim of contingent events, largely of our own making. By contrast, there is a much more protracted, structural crisis of Scottish politics. Qualitatively new forms are likely to emerge from these conditions. We can help to shape this process, by putting poisonous recriminations aside, by participating in grassroots campaigns, and by leading the battle for a break with Britain in 2014.

The perverse glocalization of Labour

Scottish Labour is at the centre of the Scottish crisis. Accusations of 'machine politics', of 'negative campaigning', and of 'tribalism' are common in all accounts of Scottish Labour. It was widely accepted that Labour had to learn from its Holyrood electoral hammering in 2011. Iain Gray, a 'flop' as a leader, was replaced by Johann Lamont in December 2011. Lamont conceded that Labour had an image problem, coming across as 'a tired old politics machine which was more about itself than it was about them.' This dour public face is, ultimately symptomatic of deeper factors. Adapting factional local politics and 'patronage networks' to demands to 'think global' is a particular challenge. Hardly a month goes by without new reports of a hornet's nest of factional antagonisms and interest group politics in Labour, often, but not always, grouped in the west coast. Most recently, Labour's chief Scottish spin doctor, Rami Okasha, was suspended amid allegations of 'insubordination'. This exposed east-west coast divisions, and also divisions been the Holyrood and Westminster arms of politics. These often express themselves as divisions within groupings, as the recent debacle over candidate selection for the Glasgow Council elections exposed.

At the same time, Scottish Labour is open for business when it comes to the amorphous benefits of 'globalization'. It has proved far too intellectually timid to challenge Blairite norms. Gordon Brown summed up this new spirit in his 2006 Mansion House speech: 'The message London's success sends out to the whole British economy is that we will succeed if like London we think globally ... advance with light touch regulation, a competitive tax environment, and flexibility'. A consensus held that London was a 'model' to imitate for other urban economies. Glasgow City Council, in any case, had long been at the vanguard of neoliberal 'urban boosterism' and place-marketing strategies. Thus, when Jack McConnell implored Labour to act as 'the party of enterprise' in 2004, he was merely stating conventional wisdom and long-established practice. It is telling that Scottish Labour has not produced critical figures like John McDonnell MP and Jeremy Corbyn MP. They would almost certainly find other political homes in Scotland, perhaps even in the SNP.

There has, thus, emerged a perverse 'glocalization' effect in Scottish Labour. On the one hand, there is a far more ingrained policy consensus in Labour than in any other organisation. The 'race to the bottom' in regulation and the virtues of competition were accepted with little resistance. The only qualification was the need to preserve the 'cherished values', lying somewhere between 'British-ness' and 'social democracy' of the Labour movement. A very British and very 'global' consensus, thus, prevails. The monetarists won the intellectual debate; but social democracy still has 'the right values'. There is no dissent from this flimsy intellectual framework. However, imposing neo-liberal demands in practice needs a party machine built on a tough local fabric of council housing, local council employment, and unions. Gerry Hassan and Eric Shaw in their recent book, *The Strange Death of Labour Scotland* (2012) refer to a (mythologised) 'Labour Scotland' that services Scottish Labour in this regard. These factors are still largely responsible for Labour's core base of support in Scotland, despite decades of appeals to 'professional' middle class voters through 'modernization' policies. Unions, to take one key example, are still by far the biggest funders of Scottish Labour. The result is that loyalty to Labour is corrupting local representation with intellectual complacency and widespread factionalism. Although working class voters may be less inclined to vote Scottish Labour, the tissue of representation is still poisoned by its local feuds and its superstitious respect for 'global market forces'.

The Lamont moment

It might be argued that these factors culminated with the diabolical election performance of Iain Gray's Labour in the Scottish elections in 2011. We wish to extend this a step further. The apogee of Labour's factional-intellectual crisis has arrived only this year, with Lamont's attacks on universal benefits and Scotland's supposed 'something for nothing culture'. Two factors have been identified here. The first is a lack of vision about Scottish taxation that Hassan calls 'block grant conservatism'. The result of thinking of Holyrood in terms of fixed fiscal parameters is to regard funding as a zero-sum game between 'middle class benefits' and tackling poverty. Of course, there is no intellectual wriggle room in this straightjacket, since any leeway is likely to lead to further calls for 'fiscal autonomy', a slippery slope to independence.

A second issue is that Lamont is trying to massage internal disputes between roving bands of councillors, MPs and MSPs. The attack on 'freebies' like free education and prescriptions may satisfy the need for daylight between the SNP and Labour in policy terms, but how will the public respond? The problem is that these 'freebies' are inexpensive and highly popular. The assumption that universal benefits are primarily a tax-break for the middle class, and a distraction from fighting poverty, is also highly dubious. Certainly, there is a problem of poverty in terms of direct material deprivation in Scotland - but often the deepest impact of poverty is the humiliation and stigma of it. Means-testing benefits, to save very meagre sums, will do what it always does: pile up bureaucracies and pile on degrading poverty exams for the most vulnerable in society. Even if Labour can successfully mount a defence of this policy, which seems unlikely, there is little prospect of any minor 'cost savings' getting used to fight a war on poverty, in any sense of the word. Scottish Labour finds itself on the right of the Scottish government on almost every social issue, never mind Trident and war. At the same time, Labour's roots and its funding base remains in the unions. This settlement is surely unstable and hence, fundamental revisions in Scottish politics are possible.

The many hats of nationalism

While the Lamont factor has forced Labour further to the right, it has reined in some of the more neo-liberal tendencies in the Scottish government, at least temporarily. So when Education Secretary, Mike Russell, used his co-authored 2006 book, *Grasping the Thistle*, to claim that Scotland should scrap universal benefits, as part of a sweeping set of cuts to the public sector, he was forced to retract these claims under pressure: 'I am more than prepared to say today that my experience of the recession and the loss of 25,000 university places south of the border makes me believe I was wrong' (*Herald* 4 October 2012). It would be foolish to read into this a change of heart from the SNP's small, but influential, free market wing. What it represents is an attempt to unify the shifting imperatives between Scottish government, SNP party organisation, and the Yes campaign for 2014. How these tensions play out will shape the future alignments of Scottish politics.

With a more or less fixed income from Holyrood's block grant, Salmond's team will be under pressure to make cuts as part of the Britain-wide austerity squeeze. There is no escaping this, all things being equal constitutionally. On the basis of its defence of the NHS, opposition to tuition fees, and defence of universalism, the SNP government has a legitimate claim to the identity of 'real Labour' against 'new' Labour. But this political manoeuvring does not change the social base of Salmond's power amongst elements of the new middle class, small businesses, unorganised sections of the working class, and nouveau riche 'entrepreneurs'. This clash between collectivist 'values' and social structure was dramatised over the 30 November 2011 strike (N30) in which SNP ministers happily crossed picket lines. The idea that N30 was an act of London-based 'vested interests' with no relevance to Scotland was uncritically accepted in some sections of the Scottish broad left.

Since the SNP membership is not, and cannot be, built out of the unions, breaches like this are inevitable. However, this does not mean the SNP is a right-wing wolf in sheep's clothing. It is a party built on the class fault lines of a nationalist platform. There is clearly a very genuine enthusiasm for anti-war and anti-nuclear politics in the SNP ranks. This has been qualified by a sad oversight on Afghanistan, where leaders have stuck to mainstream complacency. This is a telling contrast with Labour, where any anti-war politics is a dirty secret. The debate on NATO clearly reveals the fractures of trying to win the public to independence. Yes Scotland repeats the official line: let us not talk about the precise details of a future nation, let us unite for today and all issues can be democratically agreed after 2014. But all the while the media and 'civil society' demands answers about 'security' after independence. The British establishment is adept at manipulating the politics of fear, and Yes Scotland has no basis to tackle this. Thus, the SNP is buying time with the left using Yes Scotland's sterile optimism, while shifting its own positions to make ground to the right in practice. This has already led to a humiliating public spat with the Scottish Green leader, Patrick Harvie. This wrangling has resolved itself, at least for the time being, but serious divisions remain over the function of Yes Scotland.

Today, the SNP is still clearly to the left of Scottish Labour. Only the most dogmatic determinist would pretend otherwise. In a peculiar twist, the SNP gained a majority of working class votes in 2011. It even managed to break Scotland's Catholic community away: 43 per cent voted SNP against 36 per cent for Labour, testament to its break with a poisonous perception of pro-Orange politics. These factors cannot withstand the elements forever. Surely after the 2014 referendum, the SNP's contradictions must start to unravel (as Stephen Noon intimated in *Scotland on Sunday* 30 December 2012), or it will move back to the right of Labour under pressure from the pro-market wing of the party.

The movements

No consideration of the future of the left can leave aside the question of the extra-parliamentary movements. There are two aspects to consider in this respect, namely, unions and protest groups. We would defend the decision to consider these forces separately. Sadly, the evidence of surveys has suggested that these rarely crossover. While there are many honourable counter-examples, we feel these are two separate strands. It goes without saying that it is incumbent on union leaders, at the top and the bottom of organisations, to change this.

Union adaptation to devolved Scotland has been very uneven. The apparatus of the major, Labour-affiliated unions have been reluctant to acknowledge a Scottish dimension to politics. Many still deny that any substantial changes to the 'united British working class' are worthy of consideration, or constitute anything more than a distraction. Labour tribalism is deep rooted in many unions and a huge proportion of union officials belong to Labour. Attitudes to devolution have, thus, often fallen into the same complacent, business-as-usual mode. However, the STUC has a somewhat different approach. It has a long record of campaigning for devolution, and to some degree has shown willingness to work to engage with 'Scottish civil society'. This has led, in practice, to a tendency towards 'popular front' mobilisations, which are often accused of defining 'broadness' by how many priests they can put on a platform. A more radical case is the Fire Brigades' Union (FBU), which at one stage considered affiliation to the Scottish Socialist Party. The RMT did affiliate, through some of its branches in Scotland, to the SSP (before the split). Sadly, these openings have been the exception, not the rule, and the left has failed to capitalise on disenchantment with 'new' Labour.

Not surprisingly, union officials have been awkward and stilted when responding to the approaching referendum in 2014. They have not given direct material support to Better Together, an openly reactionary coalition of interests which has been startlingly uncritical of the British *status quo*. An explicitly pro-British line would be difficult to maintain for the unions. Their core supporters are divided, and the most likely supporters of independence are the manual and routine working class. Thus, the unions have instead played a peculiar game of brinksmanship, flirting with devo-max while claiming to 'facilitate debate'. Anecdotally, it is often claimed that many union leaders actually support independence, and privately they will vote for it. Of course, they can never state this publically, for fear of breaches with London HQs. Undoubtedly, many are keeping their options open in this fluid Scottish conjuncture.

By far the most inspiring recent challenges to Scottish neoliberalism have come from outside the organised left. There is a broad, confused eco-system of protest movements that has become a significant factor in its own right. The catalyst for this was a highly successful student-led movement against cuts and fees in Scottish universities. This took its momentum from England, but unlike the English movement, it was ultimately successful in forcing the SNP into a dramatic policy U-turn prior to the election. The context of anti-cuts protests was, undoubtedly, a huge factor in Labour's heavy defeat in 2011. A noteworthy consequence has been the radicalisation of a layer of young people against the violent arm of the Scottish state, as campaigns have been mounted to defend student protesters against victimisation. The youth-led protests have reinvigorated other dormant leftist trends: Palestine solidarity, feminism, and anti-racism to name but a few. Perhaps, the most inspiring example was the sight of young activists from Coalition of Resistance and the Hetherington Occupation joining with community campaigners to save the Accord Centre for those with special learning needs in east Glasgow. Meeting the organisational and intellectual needs of this sort of 'movement from below' is precisely the reason for rethinking old habits on the left.

What needs to happen on the left?

Ironically, both the union and the protest movements have reached a similar dead end after the concessions post-N30. It is at a time like this when an organised left is most needed. Sadly, its authority has been badly tarnished by the aftershock of recent splits. Only an unreasonable optimist would claim that the post-SSP left in Scotland has clarified anything about socialist strategy or tactics. The split has generated a volcano of heat and precious little light. Electoral programmes of post-SSP groups have been nearly identical. Any promise that the split would bring new opportunities for the left to relate to political movements have surely been refuted in practice.

We believe that restoring the health of the left in Scotland requires three components. Left unity, namely, the restoration of working relationships in the post-SSP fragments, is a logical first step. It is very difficult to build trust in wider society when paranoia and suspicion is rife within our own ranks. Some will object that any future moves towards unity, however desirable, must be made Britain-wide. But this does not take full account of the territorial changes in British governance. The Holyrood system offers far greater opportunities for the left to gain a purchase in parliament. This may not be the end goal of revolutionary politics but it is surely desirable to have a permanent voice of opposition to cuts, war, racism, and sexism in public focus.

The referendum in 2014, whatever the result, is another reason for restoring working relations in Scotland without waiting for support for such a project to break out in the rest of the UK. The last thing we want is to end up like Scottish Labour, belatedly forced into accepting the need for Scottish organisation after years of pummelling defeats. Left renewal needs to happen. It is our job to ensure that left dis-unity is not a roadblock to the organisational needs of the movement from below. At present, the organised left has a toxic reputation. Only unity can solve this. The subjective factor - the modification of habits and 'behaviour'- is, thus, highly important. Objective factors do count. But when opportunities open up to shape the debate, the left's intervention will be lacking if we put our own bad blood above the needs of the movement. Even if we profess good intentions like an end to sectarianism, we must prove it in practice. A last factor is that the wider, societal left (i.e. those concerned with fundamentally changing the existing patterns of wealth and power in society) is fragmented across various organisations. Indeed, many belong to no group. To win the respect of this milieu is contingent on left unity and left renewal. That is to say, union members who wish to see a radical left-of-Labour force will not take us seriously until we have won the right to represent the needs of the movement.

In Holyrood, the centre cannot hold, and things - as they stand - are liable to fall apart. One way or another, this is the trajectory towards the 2014 referendum. The issue of the SNP's credibility as a moderate party of government will come to a head with its credibility as a force of constitutional change is questioned. Labour's base of financial support from nurses, school teachers, and cleaners will conflict with the needs to make Westminster the hub of pro-market politics in Europe. We are not claiming to offer any sort of blueprint for the kind of party or organisation we need in the future. It is merely our intention to say that the patterns of the last five years do not have to recur forever. We can choose to put an end to this. Another five years in the ghetto is unforgiveable. The renewed radical left current in Scotland is already emerging from below, and there is space for it to grow. Unity is about ensuring that the toxic waste of past splits does not poison the future.

Chapter 4

Socialism, social democracy or at least resisting austerity

Pauline Bryan

As this chapter was being written, Alex Salmond and David Cameron have signed the formal agreement giving the Scottish Parliament the power to hold a binding referendum. One could sense a nervous excitement developing that the momentous event is actually going to happen. For SNP members, there must be a sense of unreality. There are not many political activists who actually get to the point where their dearest held beliefs are put to the public in a democratic vote. The polls, however, have regularly indicated that there is a majority against independence. The Panelbase poll conducted towards the end of October 2012 for the *Sunday Times* and *Real Radio Scotland* found 37 per cent of Scots agreed the country should be independent, with 45 per cent opposed. When it asked voters what they would do if they felt the 2015 UK general election would result in either a majority Conservative government at Westminster or another Tory-Liberal Democrat coalition, 52 per cent said this would make them likely to vote in favour of Scotland leaving the UK. With two years to go there is everything to play for and the Better Together campaign would be foolish to think that they can spend two years rubbishing the SNP without offering an alternative vision for Scotland.

Many independence supporters would see themselves as socialist or social democrats. It is hard to put a figure on how SNP membership would divide, but the recent vote on whether an independent Scotland would seek to be a member of NATO indicates it could be over one third. Other issues, such as retaining the monarchy, membership of the EU and the leadership's plans to make an independent Scotland a low corporation tax economy, will have tested some members' trust in a socialist future for Scotland to the limits. As with most other nationalist parties it must, by its very nature, appeal across the political spectrum. William Wolfe (1973:160) described the SNP as 'a genuine movement for social justice ... which avoided 'left' versus 'right' arguments'. Supporters from the left will argue that once independence is achieved the fight for socialism can begin. Even assuming this is so, can Scotland achieve socialism on its own?

There have, of course, been countless words written about the problems and possibility of socialism in one country. Without getting into questions of Marxist theory, I will instead simply look at the practical questions. Firstly, Scotland will have its referendum at a point of extreme economic difficulty. Should there be a vote for independence, there will be many years of negotiation and untangling of Scotland from the UK. It will adopt a constitution which will, most likely, be based on the SNP's current positions. We now know that it intends to seek membership of NATO. We also know that it intends to retain the monarchy, Sterling and remain in the European Union. We can expect that these commitments will find a place in a new constitution. When the state of Kosovo was established in 2008, it adopted a constitution that included a commitment to a 'market economy', that it be 'in membership of NATO' and that it would 'meet the criteria required by European Union'. These issues are not policies open to change through normal political channels, but embedded in the country's constitution. It is important to remember that a constitution is not a set of neutral rules and regulations, but serves to mould the new state in a particular way. Whoever drafts the constitution gets to put their stamp on the future development of the country.

The first step to creating a socialist Scotland may, therefore, have to include a fundamental challenge to its constitution. This is not an easy thing to do as it would probably require a two thirds majority in Parliament and it would not be welcome in the early stages of a 'new nation'. Experience tells us that the party that brings a nation into being often continues to shape its destiny for a long time after. Even supposing that there is sufficient public support for a socialist Scotland, could it be established and continue to exist in isolation? I will lower my sights somewhat and explore whether we can realistically establish social democracy in one country.

George Foulkes (1981) made a much quoted claim that 'there is an inherent socialist bias in devolution ... favouring high taxation, public spending and public intervention in the economy...'. Though they may find him an unlikely bed fellow, many people contributing to the discussion on independence share this view. Even if we accept that there is something inherent in the devolution of power, or within the Scottish people, that makes higher taxation and greater public spending more acceptable how would this be brought about? SNP strategists are compiling a 'prospectus for independence' which they hope to use to sell the idea of separation to Scots ahead of the referendum in 2014. The document is not due to be published in full for another year but SNP insiders have disclosed key extracts. They reveal that SNP leaders want an independent Scotland to look north and east in Europe for partnerships, trade and key defence relationships (*Independent* 5 December 2011).

Following in Scandinavian footsteps

The SNP makes great play of its similarities to Denmark, Sweden and Norway and senior nationalists, including Alex Salmond, have made several trips to Scandinavian countries to pave the way for greater co-operation if Scotland becomes independent. There is a particular focus on energy and initial plans have already been drawn up for an electricity super-grid between Scotland and Norway. The Scandinavian approach has been supported by Angus Robertson, the SNP's defence and foreign affairs spokesman in Westminster who is quoted as saying that Scotland's relationship with its Scandinavian neighbours had suffered because of a southern bias since the Act of Union in 1707.

We could be lulled into thinking that in Scandinavia some countries have achieved social democracy and have established a model that Scotland could follow. Göran Therborn (2000) argue that social democracy had, at one time, been achieved in one country, but went on to add that single country social democracy has failed to become international. There is not, he argued, a shared Scandinavian approach, but instead four or five separate countries finding their own separate ways forward and where each is feeling the impact of globalisation. Since Therborn's article the breakdown in social democracy has continued to the extent that neo liberal policies have gained an even greater hold. Scandinavian countries slashed government budgets after the financial crisis of the early 1990s. In the aftermath of the crisis, Sweden systematically cut public provision through a combination of cuts and monetary policies. Other Scandinavian countries followed suit, and began the process of reducing public services and lowering taxation. Besides downsizing the state, Scandinavian governments have privatised railways, airports, air-traffic control, motorways, postal services, fire departments, water systems and schools. In Sweden, Carl Bildt's cabinet in the early 1990s made it possible to privatise health care at the county level and its introduction of school vouchers led Michael Gove, in 2008, to state: 'We have seen the future in Sweden and it works' (*Guardian* 9 February 2010).

Meanwhile, Denmark enjoys one of the most flexible labour markets in the world. Hiring and firing can occur at a very low cost and within one day. It is known as 'flexicurity' because it is supposedly based on being able to find an alternative job relatively quickly. The concept is explained in the *Employment in Europe Report 2006* (European Commission 2007) which tells us that the use of stringent methods to protect employment is slowing down the movement of workers between jobs. This EU Commission calls on the Member States to find a common approach to combining flexibility and employment security in the labour market. They may produce more flexible workforces, but cannot deliver on the security element of alternative jobs.

And, Dalibor Rohac (2012) of the London-based neo-liberal Legatum Institute states: 'Nordic countries demonstrate that in order to make the welfare state work, we need a large dose of free-market economics. The left is right: the UK should indeed aspire to be more like Scandinavia - in liberalising its markets and bringing public spending under control.'

Can one country social democracies withstand the pressures of neo-liberal globalisation? The power of globalisation is clearly asymmetical, creating vastly more resources and opportunities for capital than for people. It would suggest therefore than in most cases smaller countries are more at the mercy of global market forces and easier to exploit. What it would certainly require is a population committed to the project and which is prepared to make sacrifices to achieve it. And remember, social democracy is not an attack on capitalism but an accommodation to it. Yet even social democracy was deemed to be too egalitarian in its effects since the rise of the neo-liberal hawks under Thatcher and Reagan.

Resisting the neo-liberal consensus

Perhaps I need to set my sights lower still, and ask 'is there a real possibility of fighting back against austerity?' Currently the fight back lacks political leadership. There is no major political party that clearly stands against the austerity agenda. Nicola Sturgeon, the SNP's depute First Minister, may suggest that austerity would not be necessary in an independent Scotland, but there is little evidence of how they would turn the economy around, except by using the model of attracting inward investment with low corporation tax. The strategy of inward investment has been a continued series of failures. Who can forget the high-profile failure of Chunghwa, Scotland's largest inward investment project, opened by the queen and then First Minister Donald Dewar in 1997? It closed in 2001 having cost the public more than £20m. Vion's Halls of Broxburn is but the latest example. Just one year before the announced closure of the Brockburn plant, First Minister Alex Salmond said: 'Securing 1,250 jobs through the new Centre of Excellence at Halls in Broxburn is fantastic news. Vion's investment in their new training centre - supported by Training Plus funds of £1.45m from Scottish Enterprise and up to £500,000 from Skills Development Scotland - is a major vote of confidence in the Scottish workforce and Scotland's economic future' (*BBC Scotland news online* 27 September 2011).

Unfortunately there is no evidence of any real alternative in Westminster. Ed Miliband is more concerned to be tough on unions (and, thereby, demonstrate his independence) than on those who caused the financial disaster. Only an extreme optimist would predict significant change within the Labour Party in the foreseeable future. So the case for remaining in the UK is not based on the premise that it will produce socialism; rather it offers a more realistic basis of a long-term strategy to combat the power of global capitalism because of its size and comparative wealth. If it chose to, the UK would be better placed to withstand the attacks on its economy that would inevitably follow any introduction of even social democratic policies.

Better still would be a European Union that took such a stand, but since there is no democratic means of achieving this currently or in the near future, it is a strategy based on wishful thinking. Peter Gustavsson (2005), of the Centre for a Social Europe, argued:

> *To understand this strong Left opposition [to the EU], we need to take a short look in the mirror. During the 1980s, the left wasn't able to formulate an alternative and the European right succeeded in making a shift and turning the tide. From the post-war era's development towards increased equality, the development was now towards decreased equality. The EU was a powerful tool in the hands of the right wing. Since the early 1980s, the ERM/EMU project has been the cornerstone of the neo liberal monetarist policies that has devastated country after country.*

We have subsequently seen the vicious nature of the attacks the EU has made on the citizens of weaker member countries who are being made to pay dearly for an economic crisis that they had no part in making.

Unions leading a class response

We are, therefore, obliged to identify how we can begin to fight back in such difficult circumstances and, of course, we must look to those organisations of working people that were set up to combat exploitation at its most fierce - in the workplace. The unions remain the most effective defence against the interests of global and local capital and they have learned that industrial power is not enough. Only political change can alter the balance of power between the exploited and the exploiters.

In current conditions, the choice before the unions is stark: they must either reclaim the Labour Party as a party of and for working people or find an alternative means of expressing working class interests in the political process. Some unions have already begun. Unite the Union has established a community membership section open to people who are not in paid employment. The idea is to put in place an infrastructure that will allow activists to place organising at the centre of local communities. Dave Quayle, chair of Unite's national political committee, caused something of a flurry in the media when he stated in an interview: 'We want a firmly class-based and left-wing general election campaign in 2015. We've got to say that Labour is the party of and for workers, not for neo-liberals, bankers, and the free market. That might alienate some people, but that's tough' (*Solidarity* 11 July 2012). In Scotland, UNISON plays a leading role in organising Labour Party members to ensure that policies are made by members in a democratic way. It also seeks to involve public service users alongside its members in resisting cuts and for improved quality of care.

Any union-led strategy has to be based on an accurate analysis of the sources of power in Scotland the Britain. Richard Leonard has written a clear and chilling account of who owns Scotland (Red Paper Collective 2012). He details that 87 per cent of Scotland's manufacturing industries turnover is in companies owned outside Scotland and that has grown by 16 per cent since 2002. He states 'But the importance of this pattern of ownership to any democratic socialist is that it first illuminates then determines the level we need to intervene at. Economic power does not lie in Scotland. It still predominantly lies at a UK level.' He goes on to quote Nye Bevan who wrote in the opening to his seminal work, *In Place of Fear*, 'that the fundamental question for socialists was simple 'Where was power and which the road to it?'

Multi-national organisations, as clearly demonstrated by the Starbucks experience, are global money making machines with no regard for nations, customers or products. According to the Reuters investigation, Starbucks generated £398m in UK sales last year but paid no corporation tax. It found Starbucks had made over £3bn in UK sales since 1998 but had paid less than one per cent in corporation tax. Kris Engskov, managing director, Starbucks Coffee UK has justified this on the company website by saying: 'The truth of the matter is, the one tax that has been debated in the media, corporation tax, is based on the profits we make in this country - and regrettably we are not yet as profitable as we'd like to be.' The UK Government does not have the will to resist these companies and, unfortunately, it appears that neither does the SNP government. Neither acknowledges the conflict of interest between democracy and the power of corporations. The truth is that 'the state cannot be regarded as a neutral arbiter among all interests: the business corporation wields disproportionate influence over the state and, therefore, over the nature of democratic outcomes' (Dahl 1989)

Democracy has to mean more than what happens in Parliaments and local councils - it needs to include what happens in the economy and in the workplace. We need to exert democratic control at both a global and more local level. We do need the power to bring to account those global, multinational, forces that operate outside effective democratic control. None of the main parties of power will take a lead in this process so we are obliged to build opposition through the growth and exercise of people power and to recreate political power that will challenge neo-liberal orthodoxies and unite people on the basis of class struggle rather than national identity, however heterogeneous that identity may be:

> *It was precisely the singularity of the working class challenge to*
> *the rights of industrial capital and property that local elites feared*
> *most in the immediate post-war period [1919] ... the danger to the*
> *established order lay neither with orthodox trade unionism, however*
> *militant, nor parliamentary socialism, but in the continuation of*
> *politicised industrial struggle.* (McKinlay and Morris 1991)

When we look back in Scotland to the momentous struggles of the working class, the most effective have been those that included unions and communities, whether that be the rent strikes, or the UCS, they created a shared sense of outrage that, however, angered people are by the austerity measures, is not being replicated today. It should be stressed that in many of these struggles, there was a mobilisation on British scale.

Creating democratic federalism

Are there, then, any constitutional reforms that could make a difference? Now that we are definitely faced with a single question referendum, we have a choice between two options both based on a neo-liberal model of economics which in their own ways prevent even a classical social democratic approach to fiscal policy and the stimulation of economic growth. If, however, the labour movement's response is simply to run a negative campaign in alliance with Tories and other reactionary forces, not only is there an increasing chance they could lose but they will have wasted an opportunity to involve people in a discussion about the kind of society we want to achieve.

The object of this alternative should be to create the conditions where the power of capitalism and the use of markets can be brought under democratic control. The purpose of achieving democratic control would be, firstly to enable a variety of forms of social ownership to build a sustainable economy and secondly to redistribute wealth from the superrich to the rest of the population and geographically, from areas of greater wealth to areas of need.

Neither an independent Scotland nor the *status quo* can deliver this. It will require a fundamental transformation of our democratic structures. The devolution of power to Scotland and Wales and the structure of the Northern Ireland Assembly have, for good or bad, broken the centralised grip of Westminster on policies, but we need a mechanism that does not turn the UK into four neo-liberal economies vying with each other to be the lowest taxed and the lowest paid. We need to turn the diversity into a means of strengthening the power of working people.

The STUC, founded in 1897, first formally adopted a policy of support for a Scottish Parliament in 1914. The Independent Labour Party from its inception in 1893 had a commitment to Home Rule and played a prominent role within the Scottish Home Rule Association. Their demands were for a federal arrangement rather than for independence. The terms of The Scottish Home Rule Bill, introduced in 1924 were that the Westminster Parliament have responsibility for the Post Office, the military, Customs, Foreign Affairs and Tax Collection. There would to be no reduction in the number of Scottish MPs in the House of Commons, but Scottish Members would abstain from voting on English matters. A joint Exchequer Board would allocate finances allowing for redistribution.

The labour movement's position, unlike the nationalist one, acknowledged the bonds the British working class had forged in two centuries of political struggle and recognised shared class interests over and above the shared interest of living in Scotland. Far from wanting to separate from the English, they wanted to join with working people across the Islands in creating a socialist alternative. While campaigning for the devolution of powers the early pioneers adopted internationalism as their ideal. Now that we have the Scottish Parliament, Welsh and Northern Irish Assemblies, we have the basis for a federal arrangement with power devolved within the UK, but with the strength of a single Parliament dealing with macro-economic issues and international relations. This dual approach will allow variations in policy within the constituent parts, but retain the combined strength to operate within the global economy.

What might a democratic federalist arrangement mean for Scotland? For a start it would resolve the 'West Lothian' question. Scottish representatives would have the right to vote on issues that impacted on the UK as a whole and on Scotland in particular. They would not have the right to vote on issues that relate only to England or other parts of the UK. It would, however, safeguard the ability to redistribute wealth within the UK and allow the labour movements in the whole UK to collaborate in resisting attacks on working people. It would lessen the likelihood of a race to the bottom in making Scotland a low pay, low corporation tax economy. It would reduce the extent of the London centric nature of the Westminster Parliament which is as damaging to Lancashire as it is to Lanarkshire.

Enhanced tax raising powers should enable a Scottish government to redistribute wealth within Scotland, but also allow for redistribution within the UK. The power held by the Scottish Parliament could be used more flexibly to create a fairer tax system both nationally and locally that can improve public services and the pay and conditions of public employees and make requirements on private sector employers to pay a living wage.

We should support the extension of the capacity to borrow for capital and revenue purposes that go well beyond the limits set out in the Scotland Act. This should be used to end the Scottish Parliament's dependence on PPP, PFI or the Non-profit Distributing Projects of the present Scottish

Government. A Scottish Parliament should, in appropriate situations, have the right to take land and enterprises into public control. These rights could be used to safeguard jobs and industries or where the best interests of those dependent on the land or the enterprise are in jeopardy. A Scottish government should be able to create publicly owned enterprises to rebuild Scotland's industrial base on green technology, renewable and high value manufacturing, addressing unemployment black sports and creating a more prosperous future for the people, especially the young people, of Scotland.

We can look to Labour in Wales for some innovative ideas. The Welsh Labour Party, unlike Scottish Labour, went into the assembly election with a left manifesto and won a majority. Welsh Labour promoted social ownership of the utilities including the rail franchise. What we acknowledge is that since the establishment of the Scottish Parliament and greater powers going to the Welsh Assembly, there will inevitably be change at Westminster. The Tories are dodging the West Lothian Question, but it will not go away. Carwyn Jones, leader of the Welsh Assembly, has called for a Constitutional Convention for the UK. He commented on the *Unlock Democracy* website on 12 July 2012 that: '... for me, devolution is not about how each of Wales, Scotland and Northern Ireland are separately governed. Rather it is about how the UK is governed, not by one but by four administrations, and which are not in a hierarchical relationship one to another.' He also stated 'representatives of all the states should come together and agree amongst themselves what limited range of powers should be conferred 'upwards' on the federal authority.

Putting class over nation in a federal framework would enable working people to unite to fight for the highest levels of public services, employment rights, pay, fair taxation and so on, and to use the best examples from other parts of the UK as the benchmark. This can create a levelling up, rather than creating a climate of competition in which, to win, you must race to the bottom. We may be a long way from achieving socialism, but at least it will not have taken us in the opposite direction.

Chapter 5

A nudge in the right direction

Maggie Chetty

Identity is not only a story, a narrative which we tell about ourselves, it is stories which change with historical circumstances. And identity shifts with the way in which we think and hear them and experience them. Far from only coming from the still small point of truth inside us, identities actually come from outside, they are the way in which we are recognised and then come to step into the place of the recognitions which others give us. Without the other there is no self, there is no self- recognition. Stuart Hall, 'Negotiating Caribbean Identities' in *New Caribbean Thought: A Reader* (2001)

In ideological struggles, language is everything. It can be a tool to fashion ideas in specific ways that shape popular attitudes. It can distort views of objective conditions and it can ignore or lie about the historical process. In the current debate about independence, the use of the terms 'separation' and 'break-up' are produced as evidence of a negative and hostile process organised by pro-independence forces. They are used by parties at either end of the political spectrum from the Conservative/Liberal Democrat (Con/Dem) Alliance to the Communist Party of Britain (CPB). In the case of the Con/Dem Alliance, the emphasis of 'separation' is the destruction of a successful economic, social welfare and taxation system that works to the benefit of all the nations of Britain. The argument produced by the Labour Party and the CPB is that the strength of the working-class movement in Britain is the status quo, that inequality is best addressed by the framework of the United Kingdom with its Westminster Parliament and its (mainly) London-based headquarters.

A difficulty for those of us who support the idea of a socialist, republican, independent Scotland is that there are complex cultural, and political issues embedded in the history of the Union that need to be brought to light in the debate and it is difficult to do this when there is a barrage of hostile propaganda that keeps the argument at a duplicitous and trivial level. The cultural imperialism that had pervaded the debate for centuries has used all its powers in the media, in the arts and in literature, to promote the idea that the Union was 'a good thing', that it was entered into freely by the Scottish people and that it continues to be beneficial to the health and wealth of the people Scotland despite all evidence to the contrary. At the heart of the republican, socialist argument is the idea that the Union of the Parliaments in 1707 was part of England's process of Empire building and was against the wishes of the majority of Scottish people. The reversal of this process would bring about the destruction of the final bonds of Empire and the capacity to unite Britain in a federation of equal and independent nations, including a united Ireland.

In the case of the Con-Dem government, the argument is put forward that that the current *status quo* will provide an economic base, taxation and welfare benefit system that meets the needs of all the nations of the United Kingdom. This is immediately contradicted by the proposals that are laid out on a daily basis for the dismantling of the NHS in England and the destruction of the post-war consensus that helped to get Britain back on its feet in the 1950s and 1960s. The present Conservative government has revealed a ferocious ideological commitment to the destruction of anything that smacks of social democracy. This is hardly surprising given the social make up of most of the Cabinet and the elitist circles in which they move. Perhaps, more disappointingly the Liberal Democrats have displayed a hunger for power that has shocked even its own supporters. The Lib-Dem leadership horrified student supporters by their U-turn on their commitment to free tuition fees , leading to leader Nick Clegg's apology satirised in the musical version of 'I'm sorry'.

The claim that Scottish independence will divide and weaken the working class movement requires serious consideration. The views of trade unionists are influenced by union leaderships who are largely based in London. Like the London-based Labour Party, there is a little self–interest in the need to maintain the support of Scottish trade unionists and Labour Party members who traditionally have provided loyal workers and leaders to maintain the movement's prestige and vigour, not to mention the funding of the increasingly expensive headquarters and infrastructure. However, one of the key markers for any definition of socialism is the extension of democracy. If the workers of Scotland were organised under a powerful and re-vitalised Scottish Trades Union Congress, with the officials, powers and finances based in Scotland, does this mean that democracy has been weakened or strengthened by such a process? If the unions in the respective nations of Britain operated more locally and concentrated more on local communities, is this a positive or negative feature? I am not imagining the small- minded, parochial kind of organisation that cares only for its immediate constituency, but rather a process that ensured that workers and communities who were well organised at the grassroots would be better able to support their colleagues elsewhere who required their solidarity on the issues that affected all.

An interesting letter in the *Morning Star* (26 September 2012) from Unite member, Elaine Jones, highlighted Unite's policy of staying within the EU to maintain working class unity against the depredations of capitalism in Europe. She made the point that 'a campaign now to withdraw from Europe would not help that unity. It would be dominated by the right whipping up xenophobia and nationalism. … It mis-educates people into thinking the main threat we face, is from Europe rather than our own ruling class.' The CPB has the contradictory position of campaigning to come out of Europe in order to reclaim national and political sovereignty but is opposed to the efforts of pro-independence Scots to do the same thing in the UK. Incidentally Unite, my own union, is one of the few to set up a Community Membership scheme, at low cost, to attract unemployed, unorganised workers and community members-a positive effort to begin the essential process of better grassroots organisation.

The recent scandals about MPs' expenses, including those of all the major parties, are a demonstration of the political distance of MPs from their constituents and their communities. The widespread public disgust for the laxity and abuse of the rules governing expenses has exposed the corrupt nature of Westminster and its governance and, despite all the claims about the changes made to the process, MPs continue to produce high levels of expenditure in contrast to the Government's demand for an austerity budget for the majority of the working population. Added to this, we have witnessed the near collapse of the economic system in the West due to the illegal and unregulated practices of bankers who have not been made to answer for their reckless behaviour but have been bailed out with public money. Public fury about such unaccountability has reached levels never seen before and has impacted upon populations in Greece, France and Spain who have reacted, in turn, with huge public demonstrations. In England, where the monarch's Diamond Jubilee and the London Olympics have provided a backcloth for much John Bull jingoism, the anger has been more muted. But, nevertheless, the culture of deference has been dented and the London riots of the summer of 2011 revealed simmering discontent in areas where opulence and destitution rub shoulders.

Lord Leveson's inquiry has exposed the hidden processes whereby huge multi-nationals like News International (NI) and a handful of individuals, unduly influence the politics and skew the democratic process. The closeness of MPs of all the major political parties to NI and its journalists and lobbyists has been a cause for further public disgust and signals the need for major efforts to be made to challenge political cynicism on a scale never seen before:

> *The evidence to the Leveson inquiry is a sobering reminder of the*
> *nature scope and scale of lobbying and that this form of politics*
> *routinely avoids scrutiny and is therefore unaccountable. The mooted*
> *private members bill on lobbying at Holyrood is to be welcomed if it*
> *promotes transparency and accountability.* (Will Dinan 'Who needs
> democracy when you've got money?' *Scottish Left Review,* issue
> 71, 2012)

Here's where we come to the how-to!

What needs to be done to clean up the state of politics in Westminster, democratise the process and persuade people that politics has improved for the better and requires our participation and commitment? How can we energise the trade union and working class movement and convince the Labour leadership that the Party needs to be seen to belong to the workers of the UK, those who set it up and those who finance it. It is not the temporary possession of those who have achieved power although it might have seemed so at various points in its recent history. Is the Green Party the new people's party? Is there space for a new workers' party?

The Scottish political framework is different from Westminster as are the Welsh and the Northern Ireland assemblies, given their different cultures, histories and political influences and priorities. But they are linked to each other nevertheless by their Celtic heritage. What develops in Scotland must inevitably impact on the other nations of Celtic heritage and on Westminster.

The Union of the Parliaments in 1707 was agreed and brought about by a corrupt set of Scottish nobles who saw their opportunities in the burgeoning Empire and were willing to collude in the process for their own gain. As Rabbie Burns, republican and democrat commented: 'Bought and sold, for English gold. Sic a parcel o' rogues in a nation'. The decision was not widely admired and there were riots in the main towns and cities. A century later in the revolutionary uprisings for the right to vote for working people and the right to lawful assembly, the Scottish Radicals, John Baird, James Wilson and Andrew Hardie, attempted to mobilise under the banner *Scotland Free or a Desert* and were hanged and beheaded for their efforts in 1820. Twenty thousand people turned up to the execution of James Wilson, deemed to be Leader of the Uprising. He turned to the executioner and said casually: 'Did you ever see sic a crowd?'

A century after that sees revolutionary ferment on the Clyde during World War One, John MacLean being appointed the Soviet Consul by Lenin and Winston Churchill sending tanks into George Square Glasgow to pre-empt any attempt to emulate the Bolshevik Revolution. In 1923, just before he died, MacLean said that if Scotland had to elect a Parliament to sit in Glasgow - rather than send representatives to Westminster - then it would 'vote for a working class Parliament.' Such a 'Parliament would have to use the might of the workers to force the land and the means of production in Scotland out of the grasp of the brutal few who control them and place them at the full disposal of the community'. He was sure also that 'a social revolution was possible sooner in Scotland than in England. Scottish separation would be part of a process that would lead to disintegration of the Empire and help towards the ultimate triumph of workers world-wide' (in Alan Stewart, *Independent Scotland: A Left Perspective,* 2009).

From the fourteenth century onwards, Scotland's struggle for independence and freedom from English dominance has been a feature of Scottish politics. The seven hundredth anniversary of the Battle of Bannockburn when Robert the Bruce defeated the English King Edward II falls in the referendum year of 2014, of which Alex Salmond, as a scholar of medieval history, is mindful. The brutal repression that took place after the unsuccessful Jacobite Rebellion in 1746 is retained in folk myth and the sight of the Union Jack to many Scottish patriots is a reminder of the efforts of 'Butcher' Cumberland, George II's man in Scotland, to crush the rebelliousness of the Scottish clans and their Gaelic culture. Thus began the trickle of Scottish exiles to the New World either as indentured labour or as outlaws. The powerful Scottish culture of folk song and ceilidh music passes on historical and cultural reference points from one generation to the next. During the Highland Clearances, thousands of people from island communities and Northern villages were forced into mass emigration by extreme poverty and landlordism to the United States, Canada, Newfoundland Australia and New Zealand. They took this cultural knowledge with them and it was passed on to successive generations. A visit to the annual World Pipe Band Championships on Glasgow Green gives a sense of how powerful these links are. This rich legacy would have been in mind when the Scottish Government set up Tartan Day in America and the SNP Government set up The Homecoming Year which will also be celebrated in 2014.

In addition, there is a strong tradition of historical societies who keep alive the memory of heroes like William Wallace and the 1820 Radicals. All of these feed into the Scottish sense of identity and culture which includes empathy with those oppressed and sympathy for the underdog. Rabbie Burns, Scotland's premier poet and writer of songs, drew strongly on all these traditions and made reference to them particularly in the world famous statement of independent thinking and equality 'A man's a man for a' that' sung at the inauguration of the re-assembled Scottish Parliament. The annual Burns Suppers that take place from Greenock to Russia and China proclaim friendship, comradeship and love of life. Those who view the campaign for independence and national sovereignty without an understanding of these underground tributaries in Scottish life and thinking will have some difficulty in making sense of the current political situation in Scotland.

The World Heritage Site of the New Lanark mills, school and model village in Lanarkshire were set up by an enlightened entrepreneur, David Dale in 1786 and run along progressive lines by his son-in-law, Welshman Robert Owen. He believed in the worth of individuals and the impact of environment and education in the development of character. Their early expressions of cooperative and socialist principles in the way New Lanark was run, attracted many famous visitors who very impressed by the healthy and educated children who were brought up in this environment- an early humanistic experiment that looks modern to contemporary eyes today.

Perhaps what differentiates Scotland from England in terms of its ideological base is a desire for fairness and justice that has permeated mainstream culture. This was aided by a belief in the 'man o' pairts', an idea that literacy was important and that village lads could go to university and become scholars. The fierce democratic traditions of Presbyterianism also supported the idea of literacy (to read the Bible) and the idea of the individual relating to God without any intercession from priests or bishops. Unfortunately, this has also left other, more unwanted, traditions of bigotry and rigidity! The traditions of the autodidact are well known and were widespread in the glory days of the Scottish Labour Party and the Communist Party of Great Britain. Activists and progressives who went to 'night school' or were self- taught or educated through Marxist classes run by the CPGB or the unions.

It is significant that important figures such as Keir Hardie and Jimmy Maxton and the Clydeside MPs had influence in the ILP and the Labour Party and Willie Gallagher and later Mick McGahey were very influential in the CPGB and the labour movement as a whole. Considering the size of the Scottish population - about 10 per cent of the United Kingdom - a high proportion of major Labour movement figures have been Scottish. This is not to strike a triumphalist note but simply to explore contributory factors of political development. It might, of course, relate to the way in which Scotland has been used by the British ruling class to develop the Industrial Revolution and the Empire with the three 'S', namely, ships, steel and soldiering.

The depopulation of the Highlands in the eighteenth and nineteenth centuries has left a legacy of chronic underdevelopment and poverty and an economy which focusses on the Central belt. The historian, James Hunter, highlighted the links between the impoverishment created by the landlords of these times who cleared the land for sheep and the high numbers of young men who went to war from those areas:

> *While most landed proprietors of the Highlands and Islands were undoubtedly anxious to foster sheep-farming and while the United Kingdom politicians had no desire to frustrate that ambition, neither the Regions landlords nor their political backers wished at the start of*

*the nineteenth century to empty the Highlands and Islands of people.
(History of the Clearance, two volumes, 1982-1985, p202)*

*The British Government's interest in the maintenance of a substantial
population in the Highlands and Islands stemmed from that
population's role as a reservoir of military manpower-manpower
which was badly needed during the years on either side of 1800
as a result of the United Kingdom's wars with revolutionary and
Napoleonic France. (Last of the Free, 2010, p244)*

This has created an uneven spread of development in Scotland and
its economy and politics have been similarly skewed. The coal mines,
steelworks and shipbuilding of the Central Belt created a proletariat that
quickly organised itself into unions and political parties that espoused the
politics of industry. Engels' ideas about labour aristocracy were to quickly
manifest themselves in the opportunism and reformism of sections of
working class organisation such as the boilermakers. There has developed
in Scotland a very well-worn path in the labour movement from full-time
union organiser to MP and this has impacted on the labour movement as a
whole. It has created political cynicism at the grassroots and to some extent
held the more left wing elements of the movement in the grip of right-
wing moderation. Interestingly, Johann Lamont in her major speech to the
Labour Party Conference 2012, made an approving reference to Scotland as
'the engine of Empire', an observation with which thoughtful interpreters
would agree but perhaps emphasise differently. This, on the same day that,
Labour-led Glasgow council, in these times of austerity, was found to have
spent almost £150,000 on a morning visit by the Queen (uncovered by
Republic on a Freedom of Information request).

Working class political organisation in Scotland has concentrated
on the Central Belt and largely neglected the areas of the Highlands and
Islands which make up one sixth of Scotland. The particular issues of under-
population and unemployment in the Highlands and Islands cannot be
separated from their particular history. Unfortunately, the Labour movement
in its heartland has failed to demonstrate much consistent interest in the
problems of the North, unlike the SNP who have paid serious attention
to the problems of the fishing communities, crofting, land use, under-
population and underemployment. The result has been that the Liberals
and Conservatives have traditionally dominated the Highlands and Islands
and the Borders until the Thatcher era when the Conservatives were almost
wiped out. The growing popularity of the SNP has shown a shift in support
and it is likely that the current unpopularity of the Con/Dem Government
will remove a few more Lib/Dem MPs/MSPs from their hitherto safe seats.

The SNP Government was elected for the second time in 2011 with a landslide victory. This was done on the platform of support for the NHS; protection of the public sector; free university fees; free personal care for the elderly; removal of Trident nuclear weapons system; and no foreign imperial adventures. The SNP promised to hold a referendum on independence in the autumn of 2014. Their strategy has been that they will move towards this date with an optimistic approach and good governance as ways of winning electoral support. This election programme - with its mix of social democratic and anti-imperialist pledges - has found favour with many of the Scottish people. The SNP's ambition for and commitment to the development of renewable power, particularly in the Highlands and Islands, has created the vision of a new industrial revolution that will perhaps, in the future, replace the oil boom. An example of this is the transformation of the Nigg yard that used to make oil rigs and which has been sold to Global Energy Group, a company that will transform the site into a multi-use energy park for gas, oil and renewables with £1.8 million investment from Highlands and Islands Enterprise and the promise of 2000 jobs in 2015.

The current campaign for Yes for Independence has seen a visible growth of grassroots activity including Trade Unions for Independence, Women for Independence and Labour for Independence initiated by Allan Grogan. The Yes demonstration in Edinburgh in September 2012 brought out about 12,000 people from all corners of Scotland. The campaign has attracted the supported of many well-known journalists and actors like Ruth Wishart and Elaine C. Smith who might in the past have supported the Scottish Labour Party. The local groups of the campaign bring together members of the Scottish Green Party, the Scottish Socialist Party, the Scottish National Party and socialists, Communists, republicans and members of no party. The setting up of Labour for Independence is likely to have shaken up the Scottish Labour leadership. It appears to be in the throes of an internal battle. This apparently centres on how far to support Ed Miliband's 'one nation' slogan to capture 'Middle England' for the Labour Party in England. The new slogan dreamt up, no doubt, by the Labour Party advisers, is a disaster for the Scottish Labour Party as it instantly up conjures an image of an English-dominated Tory Britain. By contrast, Allan Grogan, a Labour Party activist from Inverness received a whole-hearted welcome from the crowd in Edinburgh when he spoke against the renewal of Trident, no foreign wars and the need to protect the NHS and all the social benefits achieved by working people in the last few decades.

We in the Communist Party of Scotland have been predicting these developments for some time and welcome them as a beginning of the cracks in the dyke that has shored up the neo-liberalism of Blairite politics. This is an exciting time and the political situation is moving very fast indeed. It seems that change is in the air and people sense that the possibilities are many. As part of this process, the Communist Party of Scotland is discussing the setting up of *Scottish Socialists for Independence* with republican socialist organisations and individuals with whom we have been working as a way of broadening and strengthening the diversity of the Scottish left. Republican socialists and Communists have argued that in a post –independence Scotland, the SNP may no longer operate as its goal has always been independence. Or the possibility exists that its left-wing elements may push the SNP to further develop its social democratic credentials and make a bid for a continuing hold on power. Will we see the development of a breakaway Scottish Party of Labour that will uphold traditional Labour values? Or will we see regrouping taking place in the nascent Yes for Independence organisations where the main independence parties will come together and form new parties? Decisions about NATO, the relationship with the EU or the decisions about the nature of the currency or the type of banks will not be taken by the SNP but by the post-Independence government with the agreement of the Scottish people. Whatever happens, the evidence is there for all to see, that the possibility exists for the people to nudge their ancient nation in the direction of a peaceful, republican, socialist Scotland.

Chapter 6

Is there a road for Scotland towards fundamental improvement in society?

Jim and Margaret Cuthbert

This chapter is concerned with the question of how to achieve social progress in the face of opposition from key vested interests. In our first section, we review just some of the facts which illustrate the need for fundamental change in Scottish society. We are not primarily concerned, however, with arguing the need for change: the need for change is obvious. Rather, our starting point is an observation which amounts to little more than a truism: namely, that any fundamental change in society must threaten, and probably displace, some or all of the vested interests which currently hold sway.

Our main purpose is to identify key vested interests standing in the way of change in society, and to consider whether change is possible, whether in the UK, or in an independent Scotland. Our conclusion is that serious change is vanishingly unlikely within the UK, but is potentially achievable within an independent Scotland. Paradoxically, however, the vision of an independent Scotland being put forward by the current SNP leadership in anticipation of the coming referendum seems to have been designed as far as possible to avoid confronting the existing structure of vested interests. As we shall argue, this has profound implications.

What we do not do in this contribution is to set out any detailed template for what the desired end structure of society should actually be - whether called socialism, social democracy or anything else. This is because we regard the fundamental decisions involved as being matters for the democratic will of the Scottish people. However, we are absolutely clear in our minds that the economic and social model which finally emerges should address the following key issues:

- There must be much greater equality of opportunity in education and employment as well as equality of access to the major public services like health.

- There must be a much more equitable distribution of income.

- Key resources should be held and managed in such a way that the benefits are equitably shared between the different members of the present cohort of society, and also in such a way that inter-generational equity is respected.

- And somehow, all this has to be achieved in conjunction with the development of an economic model which generates an adequate surplus in an inevitably competitive, and potentially hostile, international economic environment.

The need for change

Anyone who doubted the need for change need only consider the following facts about Scotland:

- 24.3 per cent of young people aged 16 to 24 are unemployed and 44.2 per cent of 16 to 24 year olds in work are working part-time.

- 13 Scottish councils have wards where more than 30 per cent of children live in pockets of severe poverty, seriously harming their future life chances, and around 220,000 children in Scotland live in low income households: one of the most important tools to address this problem, the tax and benefits system, lies outside the control of the Scottish parliament.

- Local authorities now only have a stock of 319,384 homes, with only 7,847 vacant, and 157,700 households are on waiting lists for them. So unmet demand for council social housing is more than half the total stock. Note too, that some of the stock is below acceptable standards.

- Young adults coming from households where the head of household is in manual employment are much more likely than their peers to lack qualifications higher than standard grade. Among 16 to 19 year olds, while less than 12 per cent of those from higher managerial and professional homes have standard grade as their highest qualification, 57 per cent of those coming from homes of routine/semi-routine employment have standard grades as their highest qualification.

- It is extremely difficult to determine the actual owners of large tracts of Scotland; some are held by 'brass plate companies' in offshore tax havens; and around 13 per cent of land is held in Trusts, so avoiding inheritance tax, capital gains tax, and stamp duty, and potentially minimising income tax payments, while at the same time enjoying EU farm subsidies.

• A total of nearly £600m was paid out to almost 20,000 farmers in 2009 under a series of different EU subsidy schemes. But while subsidies might be justified as a means of keeping down the price of food, and while most farmers received only small amounts, a few farmers, some already extremely privileged and wealthy, received very large amounts. Four farmers received more than £1m each.

We could go on.

The key vested interests

In 1921, Lenin in his collected works, stated in just two words one of his basic principles: namely, 'Who whom?' This is to be understood as 'Who controls whom?', and emphasises the importance of understanding just who the controlling interests actually are. Or, in our terminology, just who are the key vested interests. Another statement of basically the same idea was given by the spy novelist, Alan Furst, in his book, *The Foreign Correspondent* (2006), set in the run up to World War II. One of the characters in the book, a senior British intelligence officer, described the key areas the intelligence service targeted when it set out to win influence over a foreign state. These were the three Cs: namely, crown, capital and church. It is interesting that when we set out to write a short-list of some of the key vested interests who will affect Scotland's future, two of our selections, crown and capital, were among Furst's three Cs.

So who are the key vested interests on our short-list? Here are our top five candidates: namely, the crown; the landed interest; what can be called finance capitalism; the interests associated with globalisation; and the EU. There are, as we will see, degrees of overlap between these categories, and there are other important interests we have left out. But this group is plenty to be getting on with. Let's look at them in turn.

By the crown, we mean the institution which fulfils the function of head of state in the UK - but whose powers and influence go much further than would be implied by a strict interpretation of the head of state role. Witness the obsequious reportage of the BBC; the grip of the honours system, which, while politically administered, is ultimately an expression of royal favour;: the adoration and deference which royalty commands - even more in England than in Scotland; and the way in which, in a manner which is virtually Orwellian, public discourse almost lacks the language to contemplate serious alternatives to monarchy. Look too at the privileges: the flunkeys; the vast wealth; and exemption from taxes, like inheritance taxes. All of these are overt signs of status and power. But in many respects we do not know the full power of the crown. We do know that the Queen and Prince Charles have the right to be consulted in advance on any legislation which might harm their hereditary revenues, personal property, or private interest. And we do know that this right is exercised in a way which goes beyond any legitimate interpretation of private interest (which is not to imply, of course, that the head of state or their relatives should have any more right than any other private individual to be consulted on their private interests). For example, we know the Queen has been consulted on Holyrood legislation relating to salmon conservation; planning; the rights of relatives of mesothelioma victims to compensation; and the Bill to introduce a minimum price for alcohol in Scotland. But the public has no information on how it is decided which Bills are deemed to require consultation with the royal family, nor on what influence the royal family has actually had on Scottish or Westminster legislation.

Further, recent changes to the *Freedom of Information Acts* in both England and Scotland gave an absolute exemption as regards any correspondence between the royals and government departments. So we have now also lost any chance of knowing what informal lobbying the royals are carrying on. And then, on top of all that, is the influence the crown wields without any need for formal or informal direction. Potential recipients of honours or other preferment know what they need to do to obtain favour, without any need for a direct nod from the establishment.

The interests of the crown merge seamlessly into that of our second group - the landed interest. Andy Wightman (*The Poor Had No Lawyers - Who Owns Scotland (and how they got it)*, 2010) has done a brilliant job of exposing who controls the land in Scotland, and how they got it. We are not going to revisit his findings here. Suffice it to say that it is hardly possible to go anywhere in Scotland, once one's eyes are opened, without realising that the whole landscape and demography, and to a large extent, the economy, are determined by land ownership. This is most obviously true in the vast depopulated sporting estate wildernesses and Sitka spruce deserts of the Highlands. But even in the well-tended lowlands, we come to recognise that vast tracts have a tenant farmer uniformity imposed by landowners like the Buccleugh and Roxburgh estates. This kind of uniformity can be oppressively stifling for local enterprise and initiative. So much of Scotland is not only owned by so few but by a few who ruthlessly exercise their own prerogatives and agenda.

Now let's consider capital. Since the 1930s, when Alan Furst visualised the controlling influences as the three Cs, there has been a profound change in the way in which the power of capital is exercised - which is why we have called our third vested interest finance capital, rather than simply capital. In modern western capitalism, the colossi are no longer the Henry Fords and

Andrew Carnegies. They are the more anonymous figures on the boards of financial institutions epitomised by Goldman Sachs. Of course, control of finance often equates to control of key physical assets. Yet, there is a major difference. The modern finance capitalist is more concerned with financial engineering, rather than real engineering. The underlying industries, factories and assets are reduced to the level of chips, to be exchanged in high stakes games of risk - games in which the deck is often stacked against the ordinary public. Finance capital has little or no loyalty to any community, or industry, and this is much to the detriment of long-term economic wellbeing.

Finance capitalism is deeply influential in the UK state. This really needs no illustration - but to give one curious example, the City of London's Remembrancer has the right to sit behind the speaker in the House of Commons, to see that the interests of the City are not threatened (see George Monbiot *Guardian* 31 October 2011).

Unfortunately, finance capital has a huge stake in the present state of affairs in Scotland. Look at the scale of the net outflow of private finance from Scotland. This, it is estimated, could be approaching £20bn pa in some years. Yet, it can be said, it leaves the Scottish economy almost without touching the sides. This outflow is largely post-tax hydro-carbon profits, secured by those who have purchased from the UK government the 'right' to exploit Scotland's oil reserves. Look at the ownership of the Scottish whisky industry, which has largely been bought over by Diageo and other foreign companies. The result here is minimal jobs in Scotland, and an outflow of profits, and tax, not just from Scotland, but also from the UK. Consider also how Scotland embarked on PFI much more readily than the rest of the UK, in itself a proof of the hold of finance capitalism in Scotland. And, then look at who owns these PFI schemes now - almost all the owners are multinational banks or finance companies, many of whom minimise their tax by using offshore tax havens. The conclusion is inescapable. Finance capital profits so much from the *status quo* in Scotland that it will be a formidable barrier to change.

This brings us to our fourth vested interest, namely, those interests associated with globalisation. There is, of course, a big overlap here with the finance capitalists. But while the finance capitalists are basically financial institutions, the interests associated with globalisation are likely to be states. A cynic would say that the legal underpinnings of globalisation - the General Agreement on Trades and Tariffs (GATT) rules and the Word Trade Organisation (WTO) - were set up primarily by the US to provide a framework within which it planned to continue to exercise control over most of the world's resources. The UK bought into this system equally enthusiastically. It is within this framework that the finance capitalists have been able to achieve such great power. However, it must have been a very nasty surprise to the authors of the globalisation framework that other states, notably China and Germany, were able to game the currency rules within the system, ultimately to the huge cost of the founding powers. But the US and UK have invested so much in the globalisation model that they are likely to remain fully committed for the foreseeable future.

Finally, we come to our final, and perhaps surprising, vested interest, the EU. The EU is important for two reasons. First, because to an extent which is little appreciated in the UK, sovereignty on the key issue of Scottish independence has been transferred from the UK to the EU. This is not for a moment to deny Scotland's ultimate right of self-determination. But in terms of practical politics, unless Scotland was going to make a complete and unilateral break from both the UK and the EU, the terms of any final accommodation would require unanimous approval from all EU member states. (The same is true for any accommodation between the rump of the UK and the EU.) The second reason the EU angle is important is that at least some EU members are likely to resist any move to Scottish independence:. These are the countries, like Spain and Italy, which have embryonic states with strong independence movements within their own borders, and for which Scottish independence would provide a damaging precedent.

What can be done about these vested interests?

We want to look at this question, not from the point of view of what could be done to achieve Scottish independence in the face of opposition from these groups, but from the converse point of view. Namely, what powers are necessary to achieve general social progress - and is it likely that progress can be achieved without independence, or with independence.

The solution to the undue influence of the crown should be relatively simple. There are two basic elements: openness, and democratic decision. Among the questions which need to be addressed are: should the head of state have power to influence legislation: should the head of state, acting in a private capacity, have any priority over any other citizen: should the head of state play a role in awarding or bestowing any honours: should the communications of the head of state, other than those made in a completely private capacity, be secret: should the family of the head of state have any special privileges: should the head of state and their family be exempt from major taxes: should land and assets which are owned by the state be held in an undemocratically managed form in the name of the head of state: or should the head of state automatically get a percentage of any profits from such land? Clearly, in these last two points we are thinking of the Crown Estate. In a better world, all these questions would be democratically addressed and decided. And in each case, we might hope the answer would be 'no'.

The question of the landed interest is linked to the more general question of natural resources, and ultimately that comes down to what is meant by ownership. There would be much to be said for a system where all land, and other key natural resources, were either owned outright by the state, or were held in trust from the state. Where land or natural resources were held in trust from the state, the terms would recognise the right of access to land for all: would prevent undue exploitation, profiteering, or degradation, safeguarding the rights of future generations in fragile or non-renewable resources. There would also be much to be said for a system where land could only be held by a natural person, rather than a trust or corporation, and where holding was restricted to a natural person resident in the country. This would solve the problems of absentee landlords, and of avoidance of taxation on death. Clearly, in order to encourage investment and improvement, it would have to be possible to hold land for an extended period, including passing to the next generation under appropriate conditions.

As regards finance capitalism, the fundamental requirement is to alter the terms of the discourse between the state and financial institutions - putting the state much more back in charge. This should be relatively straightforward in relation to the provision of basic public infrastructure assets. The present system of privately financed public capital infrastructure is based on a number of claims, all of which can now be seen to be false. For example, that the private sector could provide long-term finance almost as cheaply as the state can borrow; that the private sector had effectively solved the problems of risk management; that there was no long run disadvantage in the public paying for the basic infrastructure of the state as if they were renters, rather than owners; and that the private financing of capital assets removed the associated liabilities off the state's books. Recognition of the falsity of all these claims opens the way for the state to finance its own capital assets by long term state borrowing - with the private sector being allowed in on those specific parts of the process where they can demonstrate real expertise.

In relation to the problems posed by finance capitalism in the wider economy, there is also much that could be done. Again, the concept of ownership plays a crucial role. It should be recognised that other agencies have stakes in companies, and should have rights, as well as the owners of the equity capital. Workers have rights, and - as in some other European countries including Germany - should have a say in the future of the company they work for. But the state itself has important rights, stemming from its role in providing the basic legal and economic framework within which the company operates, and also since the state, ultimately, should be able either to grant, or to withhold, permission for the company to operate within the state's boundaries. Formalisation of state and worker rights would provide a powerful constraint on the excesses of finance capitalism.

A possible approach to the problems of globalisation would involve increasing the rights of individual states, to give the state tools it could use, either on its own, or in concert with other states, when globalisation was causing demonstrable distortions. This does not mean the introduction of mercantilist tariff barriers. One measure, for example, would be to give states the right to refuse to be supplied by other states who were clearly gaming their exchange rates. Other measures already advocated in this chapter would also have important effects. For example, once it is established that a country's natural resources cannot be owned outright by private or foreign agencies, but can only be held in trust, then this would remove the potential for international capital to buy up a country's resources of land, water, or minerals.

Finally, there is the problem of the vested interests implicit in the EU. The issues here are rather different. Once in the EU, an individual state has little say - other than to threaten to veto major change - which, as David Cameron found, may have little effect. But that is to neglect the potential power which a state has at the moment of accession. Imagine if Scotland exercised its right of self-determination, and was poised to leave the EU as a result: taking with it its oil, fish, and strategically important waters. The question for the EU then is: if you don't want this to happen, what very favourable terms can you offer to persuade us to accede? This approach would be the direct opposite of the current negotiating stance of the SNP leadership, which appears to be: 'We want to be in the EU whatever you say or do, and we have a right to be in.' Both in terms of a feasible negotiating position and political realities, the current SNP position appears incomprehensible.

Is change possible: UK, or independent Scotland?

We argue that there are two reasons why fundamental improvements in society within the context of the existing UK state are so unlikely as to be virtually impossible.

First, key vested interests are so entrenched within the very fabric of the UK that it is difficult to see them ever relinquishing control. It's not just that the monarchy and the landed interest appear more firmly embedded than ever. More fundamentally, the UK has staked all its economic chips on the success of the finance capital economic model. In the process, it has allowed its manufacturing base to fatally fragment. The UK is now so far down this particular road that UK politicians and policymakers will see little alternative other than to stick grimly to the finance capital model, and to uphold the tenets of globalisation - during what promises to be a protracted period of decline.

Second, there is the nature of the democratic process itself. As we have already stressed, the kinds of progress we envisage inherently involve the operation of democratic consent. In other words, they can only take place in a nation which is sufficiently cohesive that it is possible to arrive at courses of action which are accepted by all as representing the settled will of the people - even though specific groups may be disadvantaged by these actions. It appears unlikely that the UK will ever again command the required degree of cohesion. It is not just the geographical disparities within the UK which are relevant here - though it is worth recalling that in the 2010 election, the Conservatives won 56 per cent of the seats in England, but only eight per cent of the seats in the rest of the UK. Over and above this, there now appears to be an unbridgeable gap between the 'haves' and 'have nots' in the UK.

By contrast, we argue that Scotland pre-eminently does have sufficient cohesion so that, if it was an independent state, it could achieve a consensus behind the need for change. Evidence for this is the success of the Scottish parliament, in rapidly establishing itself as being the legitimate body for expressing the will of the people. It is already far from the parish council that Tony Blair envisaged. So our conclusion is - do not look to the UK for fundamental change and an independent Scotland might, just might, be able to move forward.

The referendum paradox

Which brings us to a paradox: if fundamental change in society involves challenging key interest groups, and if this is only feasible from a platform of independence, then strategy *vis-à-vis* key interest groups must be a fundamental part of any independence campaign. And yet, both the vision of independence put forward by the SNP leadership, and their policies in government, are noteworthy by the way in which the key interest groups are flattered and reassured, and their positions protected.

Here are some examples. We will, it is proposed by the SNP leadership, keep the crown. Further, Richard Lochhead, the responsible SNP Cabinet Secretary recently wrote: 'Our priority for securing a more equitable and sustainable basis for delivery of the Crown Estate Commissioner's functions in Scotland will be to ensure that there is no detriment to the financial arrangements for the Royal Household under the Sovereign Grant Bill.' We will keep sterling, with the Bank of England as financial regulator and lender of last resort. There is not a whiff of challenge to the landed interest. The current policies of the Scottish government on procurement, and their Scottish Futures Trust, are very much in the big business/finance capitalism mode. There is no talk of altering hydrocarbon taxation, or stemming the outflow of private finance from Scotland. We may even keep NATO.

Something here does not add up. If Alex Salmond were to win a 'yes' vote in the referendum, what he would have would be a mandate to negotiate for the establishment of something far short of any meaningful concept of independence. Further, in these negotiations Westminster will not even go as far as the current limited vision of independence. If Scotland wants to have the Bank of England as lender of last resort, then Westminster could not possibly agree without binding up Scotland in fiscal ties which would radically limit its right to borrow, or to pursue an independent taxation policy. So it is just not feasible that anything approaching independence can emerge from the current referendum.

Does this mean the referendum is irrelevant? Far from it. In fact, the referendum is important both because it poses a danger - and also because it does present opportunity. The danger is that a 'no' vote, if that were the result, would be used by the unionists to attempt to shut down the movement towards independence for a generation. It has to be made absolutely clear that, since real independence is not on offer in the referendum, then likewise a 'no' vote settles nothing. The opportunity is that the referendum campaign represents a chance to have a meaningful debate about the issues surrounding independence. By that we mean real independence, where Scotland actually has control over the important levers of state, rather than the token version which is the best that could emerge from the present referendum. This chapter is meant to be a contribution to this wider, and very necessary, debate.

Chapter 7

What is Scottish independence for?

Neil Davidson

The most decisive changes to have occurred in relation to the question of independence since 2007 is that we now know that there is definitely going to be a referendum, that it is going to take place in autumn 2014, and that it will consist of one question, with the electorate being asked to vote for or against Scotland becoming a separate country from Britain. On this basis the outcome will, at any rate, have the virtue of clarity. For those on the left in Scotland, the significance of the Edinburgh Agreement signed by Cameron and Salmond on 15 October 2012 is, therefore, that what had once been a relatively abstract argument is now an absolutely concrete one upon which we have to take up positions, for or against. It is worth emphasising this point. Socialists may wish they were not faced with this issue, which many clearly regard as a diversion from more serious matters. But then we are rarely granted the luxury of deciding the terrain upon which we have to fight - humans being unfortunately condemned, as one moderately well-known text has it, to make history in conditions not of their own choosing. To evade the issue by affecting abstention between independence and the *status quo* is, in effect, to opt for the latter while pretending to be hostile to both.

Nor will it do to claim that this is simply a clash of national identities: there are good socialist (and indeed, capitalist) reasons for supporting either position which do not depend on possessing any nationalist feelings at all. It is possible to support the continued existence of the United Kingdom without being a British Unionist, just as it is possible to support secession from Britain without being a Scottish Nationalist. But for socialists, as opposed to British Unionists or Scottish Nationalists, independence can only ever be a tactical question. So, however contrary it may be to the ingrained habits of the left, let us at least start from the assumption that whatever the nature of our respective answers to this question, we are motivated by a common desire to strengthen the position of the working class.

Since I am going to argue that socialists should argue for a yes vote, I should emphasise from the outset that I remain as sceptical as I did in 2007 about claims that independence will *automatically* lead to the creation of a socialist, or even social democratic society north of the border. There is nothing intrinsically progressive about Scottish statehood - otherwise it would not be supported by the likes of Brian Souter or Sir George Mathewson, people who are perfectly aware of their class interests. But given that the majority of working class people are currently opposed, or at least unconvinced, by the case for independence, the most urgent task is clearly to engage with these concerns rather than dispelling magical thinking about conditions in a post-independence Scotland.

Left-wing and labour movement opposition to independence

One difficulty is that the entire issue of independence still feels slightly alien to most socialists and trade unionists, as if it were an irrelevance or distraction from our proper role of fighting austerity and expressing solidarity with the oppressed, such as the inhabitants of Gaza who are being bombed yet again as I write. In capitalist societies, however, all politics are by definition 'bourgeois' unless working class politics are forcibly pushed onto the agenda. And working class politics is not a specific set of activities like, say, union organising or anti-fascist campaigning, but a perspective from which any aspect of political life - even such terribly non-revolutionary ones as participating in bourgeois referenda - can be opened up to the possibility of revolutionary intervention.

Beyond a general feeling of disquiet about the issue, there are also two more concrete reasons for left opposition to independence, both of which have perhaps most clearly articulated in the publications of the Red Paper Collective: one is that it would change nothing in economic terms for working-class people - a position which also involves a strong element of distrust for the politics of the SNP; the other is that is that it would divide the British working class. Neither reason is absurd or unreasonable, but I believe both are, nevertheless, mistaken. Worse, both assume complete passivity and a campaign for independence which is devoid of positive content. The point is that socialists do not abandon our struggles against neo-liberalism and imperialism while participating in the referendum debate, since the outcome of these struggles will determine the kind of Scotland which emerges from the referendum, whatever the outcome. We must rather see what connections exist, or which can be made, between our day-to-day activities and the debate over independence. We cannot simply wait until 2014 before raising socialist arguments but must campaign to break with UK government policy now, in relation to both austerity and imperialism. Without this, the left will simply provide left cover for an SNP which is increasingly arguing that independence will mean no real change, to assuage both capital and the Labour supporters whose votes it needs.

It is true, of course, that short of a revolution an independent Scotland would still be dominated by capital, much of it external in origin; but who, apart from the most hopelessly naïve ever imagined otherwise? And the idea that there is something particularly pernicious about 'foreign' capital of course depends on how you see the socialist transformation of society being accomplished. If you look forward to a revolutionary overthrow of the system then the question of whether ownership is internal or external is irrelevant, since the means of production can be seized regardless of where corporate headquarters are located. What I suspect lies behind this argument is an alternative position - the truly phantasmagorical one that a future Labour government at Westminster will institute a state capitalist programme of controls, nationalisations and re-industrialisation on a UK basis. We should not underestimate how influential these arguments can be since, as T. S. Eliot once observed, human capacity for self-delusion is almost infinite, but the answer is obvious: Labour never challenged international capital even in the classic era of post-war social democracy and is unlikely to do so now. It would be foolish to rule out opportunistic moves to the left under pressure from the affiliated unions, but Labour has not seriously deviated from its rightward trajectory since 1983: it not only accepts the neo-liberal agenda in its 'social' form, but was been responsible for implementing it in Britain between 1997 and 2010.

It is also true that, in economic terms, the SNP is committed to the neo-liberal agenda - but a vote for independence in the referendum is not the same as a vote for the SNP in the next Scottish parliamentary elections: it is conceivable that independence might be won and the SNP still lose the election, or vice-versa. Support for a national demand such as Scottish independence is quite distinguishable from support for a party which advocates it: it depends on what your reasons for supporting the demand are. People who reject independence on the grounds that one SNP council here is implementing the austerity programme, or that another SNP council there has formed a coalition with the Tories, or that SNP conference has voted to remain part of NATO are simply changing the subject; in philosophical terms, they are committing a category mistake.

Reference to the NATO vote does, however, suggest one of the reasons why the SNP cannot be simply dismissed as another neo-liberal party. The debate was intense and the vote ultimately very close. One reason for this is because, unlike the Tories or Liberal Democrats, there are actual socialists in the SNP and those of us outside that party need to find ways of allying with them. Moreover, although the SNP is not a social democratic party in the way that Labour still is as a result of the union connection, it does claim to be governing in the social democratic tradition. Consequently, our demands should be for them to prove it, by carrying out their manifesto programme, refusing to implement the cuts, remaining opposed to student fees, removing Trident from Scottish soil, etc. The contradictions for the SNP are already enormous, but as long as sections of the working class regard them, however wrongly, as a viable reformist organisation, we should take that as our starting point: to do otherwise would be self-defeating sectarian stupidity. But unless there is pressure from outside in terms of real campaigns on specific issues related Scotland breaking with UK government policies, then they will be used, in many cases against their own best instincts, as foot soldiers for the neo-liberal agenda of the leadership. Once again it will be crucial to combine campaigns against UK government policy with a 'yes' for independence vote.

What of working-class unity? This is not secured by the constitutional form of the state or by the bureaucratic structures of union organization; but by the willingness to show solidarity and take joint collective action, across borders if necessary. Workers in Ireland can belong to the same unions as workers in Britain, workers in Canada can belong to the same unions as workers in the USA; there is no reason why workers in Scotland could not belong to the same unions as workers in the Rest of the United Kingdom (RUK). Workers across southern Europe have recently demonstrated the possibility of coordinated action across borders in the magnificent strikes against austerity on 14 November 2012.

Finally, if Scottish independence is so unthreatening to capital, so divisive of the working class, why then are most sections of the British - and indeed, the US - ruling class so opposed to it? The changing positions of *The Economist* - always the most reliable bellwether of neo-liberal ideology–give some sense of this. During the glory days of globalisation, it was forever insouciantly recommending that the Scots be granted independence so that they would be compelled to become more competitive by cutting wages and welfare; now it runs cover stories bewailing the fate of 'Skintland' were its inhabitants to opt for a constitutional option that the magazine had previously regarded as necessary to impose market disciplines. One suspects this change of heart is not prompted by a concern for the conditions of the Scots, but rather by a fear of the consequences for the British state, and consequently for British capital - or more precisely, capital invested in Britain from whatever source. In other words, the problems posed by independence are not directly economic, but are related to the capitalist economy through a series of mediations. This, in turn, suggests that socialists have to approach the issue by foregrounding the primacy of politics.

Socialist arguments for independence

I wrote above about the question being whether independence strengthened the working class or not. But the working class with which we should be concerned is not only British, still less only Scottish, but international.

Furthermore, the question cannot be posed in a purely economic way: strength comes from ideological and political clarity as much as from organisational capacity. So what then are socialist arguments for independence that would meet these requirements? The first and most obvious is the possibility of breaking-up the British imperialist state, or - to put it in language that might be understood by those uninitiated into the arcane vocabulary of the radical left - the possibility of preventing any further wars like those in Afghanistan and Iraq to which so many Scots were opposed. This has both ideological and practical implications.

The ideological implications are clear in the terms on which the debate is going to be conducted. Cameron has helpfully given us an indication of them with his references to commemorating British participation in the First World War during the centenary of August 2014 - a date which conveniently precedes the expected date of the referendum by two months. This suggests the occasion will be used to promote a reactionary and militaristic notion of British-ness: Danny Boyle's Olympian celebration of the NHS is unlikely to be repeated. (The rejection of British-ness does not of course involve an embrace of Scottish-ness, not least because so many aspects of Scottish identity since 1707 have been equally shaped by the Empire.) The practical implications are simply that Britain is an imperial state at war. A referendum called while the occupation of Afghanistan is still ongoing, with the Iraqi and Libyan interventions a recent memory, would be inseparable from the arguments against these wars and the British state's subordinate alliance with the American Empire. Scottish secession would at the very least make it more difficult Britain to play this role, if only by reducing its practical importance for the USA. The Foreign and Commonwealth Office (FCO) has recently been leaking into its favoured urinal, the *Telegraph*, concerns for the international standing of the RUK, post-Scottish independence. The FCO fears that it might be removed as one of the five permanent members of the UN Security Council - with the power of veto which this position confers - as the result of an Argentinean conspiracy backed by other Latin American states, although one imagines that India might also have good reason to see RUK removed. One *Better Together* leaflet, handed to me by a Labour activist on the streets of Dunbar, stated, as a reason to vote no in the referendum: 'The UK means Scots get a seat at the top table at the UN beside Russia, China and America'. Indeed, and the fact that British state managers would find their geopolitical position weakened by the removal of the RUK ('Little Britain') from permanent membership of the UN Security Council seems an excellent reason to vote yes.

There would also be difficulties if the SNP fulfilled its promise to remove nuclear weapons from the Clyde, since there virtually no other deep water bases on the UK coastline where the submarines which carry them can be docked, and to construct them would involve massive expenditure. The Ministry of Defence is currently wringing its hands about the cost of relocating Trident from the Clyde to England, at a likely cost ('to the taxpayer') of £35bn. Although it cannot be said often enough: we cannot rely on the SNP to carry this through the removal of Trident without mass pressure from below. Finally, in this connection, one immediate consequence of Scottish independence would be to place a question mark over the existential viability of Northern Ireland, since the Union has always been with Britain, not England and - as Ulster Unionists of all varieties are perfectly well aware - Sinn Fein would almost certainly begin agitation for an all-Irish referendum on reunification.

Britain has always been an imperialist state, but the overwhelming majority of radicals and socialists previously opposed independence. In my view they were right to do so and both Muir in the 1790s and Maclean in the 1920s were wrong. But devolution has changed the context in which we operate. The British state has already begun to fragment and so to call for its further fragmentation on an anti-war basis, in a situation where a majority opposed the wars in Iraq and Afghanistan, means that independence can be supported as a means to an anti-imperialist end, rather than as the political logic of Scottish nationalism.

That fragmentation brings me to the second set of reasons to vote for independence: the nature of the alternative. The meaning of devolution has changed over the decades. Previously, it was a way of meeting popular aspirations without threatening the economic order; now it also potentially useful to further implanting social neo-liberalism. The more politics is emptied of content, the more social neo-liberal regimes need to prove that democracy is still meaningful - not of course by extending the areas of social life under democratic control, but by multiplying the opportunities for citizen-consumers to take part in elections for local councillors, mayors, Police and Crime Commissioners, members of the Welsh and London Assemblies, and the Scottish, European and British Parliaments. It has not of course reversed the growing public withdrawal from official politics and in that sense has failed as a neo-liberal strategy of *legitimation*. On the other hand, devolution is also part of a neo-liberal strategy of *delegation*, and in this respect has been much more successful.

Here, responsibility for implementing anti-reforms is spread beyond governing parties and central state apparatuses to elected bodies whose policy options are severely restricted both by statute and - as in the case of local councils - reliance on the Treasury for most of their funding. In the case of the devolved nations, the assumption is that the people most likely to participate in local decision-making will be members of the middle-class, who can be expected to behave, *en masse*, in ways which will impose restrictions on local taxation and public spending, and thus maintain the neo-liberal order with a supposedly popular mandate. The distribution of responsibility for decision-making downward to the localities will continue and gather further momentum following the onset of recession and still greater spending restraints. We too easily dismiss the 'Big Society' as a joke, but what it, ultimately, means is atomised citizens voting for which services they want to close. If the essential integrity of the British state was maintained at the military-diplomatic level, devo-max, even to the point of outright federalism, would be an acceptable outcome for the majority of the British ruling class, particularly since it would place the responsibility for raising taxation and cutting expenditure on the Scottish Government. Without fostering any illusions in the ability of individual states to remove themselves from the pressures of the capitalist world economy, the ability to hold elected politicians directly to account is preferable to the current endless displacement of responsibility. In particular, it would make it more difficult (if not impossible) for Salmond to blame Westminster for the decisions of the SNP in relations to cuts, such as the recent onslaught on further education.

Conclusion

What then is Scottish independence for? It opens up a space for struggle, a space that can be filled by either the continuation of neo-liberalism or by the beginning of an alternative; but the only way to ensure that a Scottish successor state is not as committed to the existing capitalist agenda as the British is to build self-confidence and solidarity in unions and working-class communities now. And by emphasising the possibility of change now, the socialist elements of the yes campaign can make a link with those workers who are currently opposed or unsure about independence. There are no guarantees and certainly no possibility of socialism being established within the boundaries of a Scottish state; but independence can be part of a process which, by weakening the neo-liberal imperialist state in Britain, can potentially bring the necessarily international basis of socialism closer.

Chapter 8

Towards a socialist Scotland

Stuart Fairweather

Socialism is about creating different society to the one that we have now: a society that promotes equality, one that celebrates people's diversity, one that shares and sustains the planet's resources.

However strong the forces ranged against socialism, we need to work towards a society of this kind. The present global crisis created by capitalism is causing major pain and uncertainty as well as raising many questions. In Britain, the electoral response to this was the establishment of the Con/Dem Coalition in May 2010. Its policies have added to the pain and to the questions. In Scotland, in different circumstances, May 2011 saw the election of a majority Scottish National Party (SNP) Government to the Scottish Parliament. For many, the scale of the result was a surprise. But the programme of the SNP Government has not addressed the crisis. Alone, its policies never could. But some of the Salmond administration's actions have provided a degree of continued social insulation for Scotland's people.

Traditionally across Britain, the assumed vehicle for socialist advance has been the Labour Party. Expectations have been inflated and depressed many times, but the recent history of war and the embracing of 'casino capitalism' have done major damage to this assumption. Devolution across Britain has allowed for differentiated responses to this. In Scotland, it has led to two consecutive SNP victories at Holyrood, Labour disarray and a 'successful' minority administration contributing greatly to the second of these. It is in this context that we now move towards a referendum on Scottish self-determination, planned for autumn 2014.

None of these circumstances, by themselves, will automatically engender, or even move us towards socialism in Scotland, although one recent historical factor should be borne in mind, namely, the election of socialist MSPs to the Scottish Parliament. In addition to the above, there are three other factors that should be briefly considered: union resistance, civil society and local government ideology, and the cultural construction of understanding.

Union actions have taken place in response to the crisis and the austerity policies of the Coalition government. These actions, included those led by unions with no formal link to Labour, failed to receive anything approaching meaningful support from the leadership of that party. And whilst stoppages have taken place across Britain, there has been a distinct role played by the Scottish Trade Union Congress (STUC). Discussions have taken place in some unions about how to respond to the changing situation. Like the Democratic Left and the Green Party, some unions used the Scottish Government consultation to call for a second referendum question that reflected the concerns and aspirations of their members.

Changes within local government and in the relationship between Labour in office and civil society should not be ignored. For many years, the devolved state was able to sustain the myth that it was contributing to 'social democratic Scotland'. This was in spite of the implementation of privatisation, the Private Finance Initiative (PFI), and the management of inequality and ill health across Scottish society. The referendum result will ask questions of infrastructural organisations and their role in enthusiastically, or not, supporting the implementation and social responses to any new constitutional settlement. This could allow for a rethinking of what actually constitutes 'Scottish social democracy' and what is needed to develop it.

Simultaneously the world continues. Increasingly people build their understandings divorced from both formal politics and the influence of work. Sport, music, media and consumption, for good or bad, inform how people respond to the dominant ideology. The 'local' as well as global dimensions of this process need to be understood if any change to the political situation is to have a parallel impact in wider society. At the very least, cultural figures and events will increasing have an influence on the referendum campaign, but they can also play a major role in determining the direction and health of the outcome. All this constitutes the backdrop against which we need to map out the forward route for socialism in Scotland.

So how do we move forward?

Socialism is about more than the implementation of a range of policies. It is about creating a society where the population and institutions hold values and support actions that benefit the majority. Getting to such a societal situation like this will not be easy. Moving towards a socialist Scotland would challenge those who see our country's future being execrably tied to the entrenched interests that currently benefit from inequality. And, despite the economic and political traumas of recent times, the defence of capital's interests remains strong, domestically and globally. Indeed, this defence represents the current 'common sense' with many people seeing their own interests and indeed identity tied to capitalism. Additionally, the prospects of challenging all of this are hampered by there being, at present, no organisation on the Scottish left that can convincingly provide a believable and implementable project for socialist advance.

For there to be any movement towards a transformed society, or even policies and practices that might lead to this, there will need to be a number of things in place. Including the following: a 'programme' for change; building support; and the creation of a new 'common sense' Taken together, these elements could provide the basis for a project that fosters optimism and which provides the potential for progress.

A 'programme'

Any programme for the future needs to illustrate, in the here and now, how our vision will include and benefit the vast majority of people. It needs to deal with the inequalities of class, but also those relating to gender, race, sexuality, age and disability. Leaving aside for the moment the important question of how we speak to people and how we get them to 'listen', there is a lot to do. The content of any programme would need to be discussed and debated widely but the following could be considered for inclusion:

- Removal of Trident, alongside a plan for just transition where all employed in the associated war economy shift to socially useful production.

- Defending existing universal benefits alongside arguing for a tax regime to support services that meet people's needs, coupled with a broader discussion about work, paid and unpaid, where all can contribute to meeting the agreed needs of all.

- Supporting social owned housing and public space that meets environmental standards, with action on the worst of private ownership that is neither socially nor environmentally just.

- Expanding accessible and affordable transport to an even greater section of the community, with the ownership and manufacture of vehicles and infrastructure included in this.

- Promoting employment, particularly meaningful youth employment alongside ensuring that schooling, further and higher education meet the needs of society and not simply the market. Promoting educational democracy and discussing who educational establishments are actually for and belong to.

- Expanding local democracy to increase participation and to ensure budgets support local needs by increasing the capacity for democratically led local economic development.

The above, alongside policies on manufacturing, health, tourism, fishing, energy, childcare, arts, sport and many other aspects of society are needed. And whilst generating content would not be too difficult, what might prove more so is resisting the temptation to produce a 'shopping list' that attempts to address 'pet causes'. What is much more important and indeed essential is promoting policies that can find support well beyond the ranks of the left but add to promoting social justice and point towards more transformative advance. Of course, seeing these policies adopted and implemented requires addressing issues of power, influence and people's participation in politics.

Building support

In the period running up to the referendum some may wish to argue that 'simply' drawing together the different organisations of the existing 'self-proclaimed' left would be a step forward. Even if this was likely, it would be a fraught process to say the least. Similarly, any organisation that argues that it already has the 'correct' programme - whereby all that is needed is an influx of support for it - is missing the point. This is because the success of the neo-liberal revolution over the last thirty years has been its ability to locate itself within the forward current of mainstream British culture. Scotland has not been immune to this. Indeed, in spite of some countervailing forces, Scotland has been exposed to, and contributed to, an existence dominated by individualism and consumerism. By contrast, over the same period of time, the left has largely stood outside this mainstream, despite occasionally acting as an opposition, e.g. the anti-poll tax and anti-war campaigns. Arguably, the campaign for the Scottish Parliament was the last major victory in which the left was involved.

One reason for this imbalance has been the slowness of some on the left to see the importance of building a living (counter-) culture that can generate ideas, participation and meaningful action. What makes things interesting is whether the dynamics before, during and after the referendum will alter this. There will be those that argue that independence or unionism spell better prospects for socialism, but this is abstract. What is at issue is how those amongst existing left and 'new' advocates of enhanced social justice can act together, before and after the referendum. Increased equality and democracy needs to be fused with either outcome. Those on the left that support the vote No campaign, primarily located within the Labour Party, should not be vilified.

This is not to suggest that the campaign or result are unimportant - far from it. At the time of writing, a Yes vote appears to be likeliest way to increase powers for the Parliament, remove Trident and safeguard existing progressive social policy. But what is of additional importance is that politics is also likely to be different, subject to the outcome. What happens to Labour, to the SNP and to the position of the Green Party are each of importance. Without attempting to predict the outcome, there is the potential for a close result that delivers a big vote but no overall majority for independence. Consideration should be given to how the parties and Scottish society respond to this scenario, as well to a clear cut yes or no outcome. For now, those that advocate more democracy, more devolution and more equality should be talking to each other and acting together. This should provide the basis for an alliance which campaigns for greater social justice in Scotland. This alliance should include advocates of more fundamental transition, arguing for policies and action that moves in the direction of socialism.

A new 'common sense'

In the current world we live in, getting large numbers of people behind a programme for change, in anything but a passive way, will be difficult. But the referendum campaign could be shaped in a way that allows for discussion about the type of Scotland we want to see. In spite of the complex lives that people lead and the multiple influences on their consciousness, there is an opportunity to put forward an alternative that has some purchase. The key question for some is: Can you win people for a different kind of future whilst 'defending' the *status quo*? Labour can offer no guarantee that it can deliver greater capacity for providing 'Scottish solutions to Scottish problems' whilst defending the Union. By definition, the Yes campaign can provide greater momentum for a different kind of future. Connecting this future to a progressive 'programme' and people's real life experiences is the best way to support 'a new common sense', a common sense that questions market solutions to every aspect of people's lives. Care, however, needs to be taken not to tie the future of socialism too tightly to any one constitutional settlement. Our job is to progress our agenda post-2014, irrespective of the referendum outcome. In the here and now, support for progressive policies needs to find a home in workplaces, communities, in - and across - political parties, in civil society and the unions, in popular culture and on the web. Individual self-determination needs to be about people collectively taking action against austerity where they can, in addition to Scottish self-determination being inculcated with progressive demands.

Scotland 'alone' - what about Britain?

The notion of a 'Scottish road' begs a question of whether it can be done. It also means reassessing the prospect for socialism across Britain. At present, the notion of a rapid move to a socialist Scotland, where capitalist relations are relegated to a minor position, seems fanciful. The path is more likely to be a long and difficult one. But equally at present this seems unlikely, or more unlikely, in the British context. Below, both the British and Scottish scenarios are looked at in turn.

In the tradition of 'the British road to socialism', the election to Westminster of a 'Labour Party of a new type' would create policies that benefit the working class and its allies. This would be done with the support of mass extra-parliamentary activity, with the union relationship to the Labour Party being pivotal. Whilst the clearness of this strategy has merit, there are questions about its likelihood. Arguably Ed Miliband wants to move Labour on from Blairism and 'new' Labour but this still leaves his party a long way from one of a 'new type'. Unite and others in the union movement have made great play about winning back the Labour Party, but in spite of their size and strength, other forces with a vested interest in retaining the British state as it is have an influence too. Recent history suggests this influence increases the closer Labour gets to office. 'One Nation Labour' will seek to meet the needs of the City and business much more than the needs of working people. And whilst things can, of course, change, this does not look like a positive route for advancing towards socialism.

Added to this the 2015 post-referendum UK general election will not automatically see a Labour victory. In spite of the Coalition's growing troubles, the peculiarities of the Westminster voting system need to be taken into account. Labour's response to this will be one of promoting policies that will not scare off potential converts that presently vote Conservative or Liberal Democrat. In England, the extremely limited prospects for the smaller parties means that only in a handful of constituencies will there be a realistic alternative. Labour will again shape its message to appeal to the centre ground. It will distance itself from any workplace militancy or any serious campaigning against inequality that could develop a constituency for change.

So can socialism in Scotland be progressed alone? As outlined above the referendum process offers opportunities. The result will have implications for the main parties and the balance of forces across a range of issues. Arguably, space exists to the left of both the SNP and Labour. The electoral system and the electorate have shown this is possible. Who, if anyone, fills this space remains to be seen. There may be the potential for new organisations and alliances. But looking at what we have now, the Greens could possibly make inroads if they continue to highlight their social as well as environmental agenda. The Scottish Socialist Party (SSP) might possibly resurrect itself if its credibility issues can be addressed. The involvement of these parties in the Yes campaign will provide impetus for their members and a place in an unfolding political development that at least has the potential to engage and foster people's political imagination. This will particularly be the case if the campaign embraces more than the constitutional and builds contentions between people's concerns and the country's future. If the removal of Trident can be written into Scotland's constitution, so can the aspiration to reduce the huge differentials in the incomes of rich and poor.

This scenario questions the role of the relationship between the unions and Labour in government as being the established route to change. But if we are to move forwards, we may need to change many of our existing assumptions about how we get there. Labour in Scotland remains significant but its involvement in the No campaign, handing out of Union Jacks on the high streets of our towns and cities, and its confusion over universal benefits locate it within an apparent defence of the *status quo*. For many union members across Scotland this at least raises questions, ones that the STUC and its affiliates are required to respond to. Similarly, organisations across civil society need to assess whether their objectives can be better addressed in an independent Scotland. This is particularly the case in the absence of a second question in the referendum. A more plural approach to change suggests a different relationship between the left and democracy - one that better reflects the nature of contemporary Scotland. And one that sees self-determination as a participatory process, not simply a decision to be made on one day in autumn 2014. This is what socialists in Scotland should be discussing and working for.

Taking forward a socialist agenda would be greatly assisted by establishing a party or alliance that includes people from existing organisations and looks to involve existing members of the Labour Party and the SNP, alongside people not as yet involved in politics. Offering the organisational infrastructure and ability to elect councillors and members of parliament (MSPs), coupled with extra-parliamentary campaigning, would create the basis for promoting left policies and pressurising the mainstream parties. In this regard, it would place the Scottish left in a similar position to that of other Europe countries. Links should be made with European left organisations and parties. This of course would not, and should not, preclude solidarity with the left in England and Wales, with progress in Scotland acting as an example. Indeed, joint action by workers against common employers and global capital would continue. At governmental and other societal levels, joint arrangements should be put in place where appropriate and required.

Taking on power - building the alternative

Attempting to determine a timescale, as well as suggesting that advancing towards socialism could be problem free and without resistance, would be foolhardy. However, discussion and debate, maximum unity, effective organisation and clear objectives will assist, along with establishing a political culture that is a central part of Scottish life. Involving as many people as possible in being part of the vision, and action, for a different kind of Scotland would be the biggest defence against internal and external powers that would wish to curtail or limit policies for peace, redistribution and social and environmental justice. Winning a future 'non-socialist' Scottish government to support these policies would require lobbying, argument in the media and mass action - difficult but not impossible. This would be particularly important because forces outwith the country would attempt to exert influence and the flight of capital, remove investment and impose a variety of sanctions. Legal and fiscal limitations to sovereignty are the reality of today's world. How governmental parties and the left respond to this will in part determine the political make-up of the early years of the 'new' country. But ahead of these possibilities there would appear to be one early test of Scottish democracy, the government and the left, namely, the removal, or otherwise, of Trident.

This general perspective adopted here illustrates of the way that the left can act to influence the agenda that the post-referendum Scottish government will require to address, by adopting positions that reflect the wishes and needs of the Scottish people and, in particular, the working class. Progress on these issues should not be left to the government but it could play a role in creating the conditions to tackle inequality and injustice. Of course, the right can adopt this approach too.

Returning to Trident - working for the maximum involvement of people in the process of it removal will play a big part in establishing a different political culture where people can be involved in social change. To make this relevant, the moral and environmental arguments need to be aligned with material reality. The positive implications for the Scottish budget need to be spelt out ahead of the action. A broad democratic alliance would need to be built that brings young (and new) people into practical political activity. By contrast, the present passive parliament-focussed politics of the UK seem dull and disempowering. Mass involvement would require running with the grain of people's lives by creating creative spaces for people to take part.

By itself this would not address the hard work of responding to vested interests. Major direct effort wil be required amongst the workforce, unions and communities associated with Trident's production and servicing. But this could be done. Moving people out of the war economy and into more useful production would not be simple but would be hugely beneficial to our society. A role for the left would be to illustrate where else this could happen in our economy, and begin a process of fostering an expansion of localised, meaningful production that challenges ideologically and practically our present 'waste driven' production. External vested interests would equally be difficult to address, but Scotland playing a full part in global institutions like the United Nations, whilst also developing solidarity with other unaligned nations, would assist with this. Here, a moral case could be made for our new state positively contributing to the Nuclear Non-proliferation Treaty. The Netherlands, Denmark and Germany would be watching closely.

An alliance, one that extends well beyond what is understood of as 'the left', that contributed to this local and global process of getting rid of Trident would create considerable motivation and political capital for addressing other major issues created by capitalism. In all these matters, a left that contributed to the delivery of major democratic change would be well placed to contribute to further major social, economic and environmental change.

Yes or no, and the future?

In the period running up to the referendum, everyone in Scotland, our institutions and political organisations, will be asked to take a view on the future. This has the potential to awaken people's interest in what is a political question, particularly if the debate is moved onto the relationship between real lives, the economy and the environment. Socialists are not primarily concerned with the constitutional arrangements in and of themselves. But democratic socialists need to be concerned with their impact on society. We cannot be agnostic. The result of the referendum and independence, should it happen, will not by itself determine the potential for Scotland to move in the direction of socialism but, particularly in the absence of a second question, participation in the campaign, and the early days of any new settlement, will go a long way to shaping socialism's future in Scotland. Thought needs to be given to an outcome where there is a substantial, but not majority, Yes vote. In this situation, those that have promised more powers for the existing parliament would require to be pressed to deliver and gains could still be made. But this by itself appears to hold far less potential than a campaign and Yes vote, followed by action on the agenda of the left and the people of Scotland. This outcome, participation in creating it, and the momentum it creates are the best possibility for getting the most out of a 'sovereign' Scottish government, with all the limitations that will be in place, and moving it in the direction of policies and practice that develop the potential for socialism in Scotland and our contribution to progressive internationalism.

Chapter 9

Against dividing and ruling

Neil Findlay and Tommy Kane

Since the first book, *Is there a Scottish road to socialism?*, was published in 2007 the catastrophic, predictable and inherently flawed nature of capitalism has once again been exposed. The extensively peddled myth, that the cyclical character of capitalism had been somehow changed and that boom and bust was a thing of the past, has been brutally revealed. Capitalism in Scotland, the UK, Europe and across the world has reached a genuine crisis point; and the people know it, as demonstrated by the wave of general strikes across Europe in November 2012. As austerity bites and nations compete for finite resources, the need for a planned, progressive alternative to the instability and chaos of the free market is increasingly clear; confirmation that socialism is needed now more than ever. We accept that all of the contributors to this book have a desire to see a socialist Scotland, a socialist UK and a socialist world; internationalism after all is the very essence of our philosophy. The difference, as always, is how we get there. For Scotland, discussions over how we can achieve socialism, or at least how we advance and make some progressive steps towards it, has become inextricably linked to the constitutional debate. In short, progressives are asking what constitutional arrangement offers us the best potential to pursue a socialist agenda. In making our contribution and outlining our view on the best direction of travel, we do not intend to argue about different conceptual frameworks, theoretical approaches and whatever socialist tendency or strain or strand offers the best, or most pure, direction. We will offer no arguments over 'deid Russians', though we may stray into debates over nationhood and class. First and foremost, we will consider the practical possibilities of achieving socialism and/or advancing socialist policies, both in Scotland and throughout the UK.

As noted, scrutinising whether socialism is possible is more necessary now than it has been for some time. The post-war consensus of the welfare state and the mixed economy challenged by Thatcher are now under sustained attack. Thus, current political and economic conditions and developments require a precise and evidenced analysis. In Scotland, we are at a juncture where constitutional change of some sort is a realistic prospect and not just the dream of nationalists. Whether independence would advance or set back the cause of socialism in Scotland is a fundamental question for the progressive forces of the broad left. Answering that question would help clarify whether there is, or can be, a Scottish road to socialism and how we can best advance it.

In examining, this we assert that any analysis must be rooted in the political, economic and social realities of present day Scotland. It is not good enough to present independence as the end in itself; based on romantic notions of Scottish self-determination. Any constitutional settlement has to be the means to a socialist end and the questions always have to be what constitutional arrangement offers the best potential to pursue the interests of working people. In deliberating these questions, we must reflect on whether independence will lead to, or offer the potential for socialist development.

Scotland today

Scotland, like the rest of the UK, has suffered under the adherence - some might say subservience - to neo-liberal orthodoxy. Since 1979, successive UK governments have succumbed to and embraced the Washington consensus and the neo-liberal policy agenda that emerged from it: a worldview that is predicated upon the free market, the breaking down of international boundaries and neo-liberal, economic globalisation. This agenda includes the systematic dismantling of workers' rights, privatisation or corporatisation of public goods and services, regressive taxation policies and the flight of money and dividends to tax free offshore accounts. It has resulted in the hollowing out of the state, a growing democratic deficit, increased inequality, low personal and corporate taxation, de-regulation, health inequalities, growing fuel poverty, disparities in educational attainment, and a range of other regressive outcomes for working people. Today, the destructive manifestations of market failure in Scotland and in the UK are clear: increasing inequality and poverty; the expansion of food banks; rising youth unemployment; declining wages; soaring living costs; attacks on public services and draconian cuts to welfare. These socially damaging consequences are all too obvious in our local communities and across Europe and the wider world. In these circumstances, maybe unsurprisingly, some socialists see solutions in independence. For them, independence appears to be an attractive option, which offers the opportunity to take an alternative route. Their argument is based upon the view that democracy will be enhanced and brought closer to the people, and that an independent Scotland will provide a platform upon which to build a socialist alternative. In doing so left advocates of independence have capitulated to a belief that there will not be, indeed there cannot be, a British road to socialism and only Scots, who they assert are more egalitarian, can build socialism.

Scottish road to socialism

Let us be candid. At this stage, there is little prospect of socialism occurring either within the UK or in any post-independent Scotland. The view that independence will provide the platform for socialist advance is based on naive hope rather than grounded in reality. Nevertheless, it is undoubtedly true that the current political and economic reality in the UK is regressive, with little sign that things are going to fundamentally change soon. However, even with that knowledge we believe the debate has to be framed around what offers the best potential for change in the future. Given the adherence of successive UK Governments to the neo-liberal agenda, it's unsurprising that socialists ask whether we have anything to lose from independence. Yet such a view fails to consider what we have to lose; namely, the ability to organise, on a UK wide basis, as part of a concerted fight back against the power of global capital. We recommend reading the work of Richard Leonard, John Foster and Sandy Baird (see *Scottish Left Review* issue 64, 2011 and issue 24, 2004) to see how global capital will remain in Scotland long after political independence should there be a 'Yes' vote. It is ludicrous to suggest that City power will simply transfer from London to Edinburgh should Independence occur. Semi-political self-determination (remember the sterling zone, Bank of England, Monarchy, EU etc.) will not lead to economic self-determination and by extension, the fairer Scotland that we all would want to achieve.

But socialists arguing for independence say that it is all to play for after independence is achieved. Sovereignty will, so the narrative goes, transfer to the people of Scotland and they will have the power to make change and see, over time, political self-determination translated into economic self-determination - in the process, building a socialist republic of Scotland, which would, in turn, act as beacon and inspiration for the rest of the world including the workers of England. If we thought this were true we would sign up for that in a red heartbeat. Unfortunately, this argument is another unsubstantiated wish which wilfully neglects the current political and economic realities.

Socialist and green elements which form part of the 'Yes' campaign are electorally weak. The SNP is, by some distance, the strongest party in a marriage of convenience that unites right-wing venture capitalists with left-wing groupings such as the Socialist Workers' Party. If Scotland votes for independence, it will be the vision of the SNP that will dominate for some time after a 'Yes' vote; and it will be its fingerprints that will be all over any subsequent written constitution. Therefore, across the broad left, we have to ask whether its version of independence will advance socialism or, even for that matter, social democracy.

The SNP's vision will result in an ugly race to the bottom where they would do whatever is needed to attract inward investors. The social democratic mask is already slipping as they promote a 10 per cent rate of corporate taxation and lower rates of personal tax for high earners. They champion and welcome the likes of Amazon, but ignore their aggressive tax avoidance and evasion, and they peddle the myth that you can provide Scandinavian levels of public services with a Reaganite taxation policy. A clue to some of the thinking within the SNP ranks is evident in the writings of current Education Secretary, Mike Russell, in his co-authored *Grasping the Thistle: how Scotland must react to the three key challenges of the twenty first century* (2006). Russell buys into neo-liberal orthodoxy. He argues that taxes are too high and proposes a cut of a quarter in rates of personal taxation and the implementation of a flat rate across the board. He says the Barnett formula is too generous and is 'killing us with kindness'. He goes on to argue throughout the book for the selloff of the NHS, a voucher system in our schools, a small state, the end of inheritance tax, the expansion of privatisation into the civil service and other public services, and end to universality and increased support for private education.

Another political reality for socialist supporters of independence is Scotland's continuing membership of the EU, a membership which sees half of the legislation passed at Westminster coming from Brussels. It is no surprise for any socialist to hear that, since the Treaty of Rome, the role and purpose of the EU has been to enable capital accumulation. Directives, such as the Services Directive and the Procurement Directive, illustrate how this function has been accelerated in recent times. Moreover, an independent Scotland may have to join the Euro - a currency that has brought Europe to its knees. In short, the EU, as it stands now, is a central barrier to socialism being achieved in an independent Scotland or, indeed, anywhere else on the continent.

Of course, the Westminster Government is also subservient to the EU. However, the UK has the (potential) strength to stand up to the EU, if (as we acknowledge) it has the political willingness to do so. We suggest there is the potential to mobilise a level of political pressure that could be applied at a UK level but that simply could not be replicated at a Scottish level. Most significantly, the education, organisation and agitation for a political system and policies which advance the interests of the working class would be best achieved and applied through the combined labour and union movement across the UK. We ignore class solidarity at our peril. Class solidarity and action is a fundamental component of change.

Supporters of independence say that independence would not create a fissure between Scottish and English workers citing how unions in the UK and the Irish Republic work together seamlessly on a range of issues. This, however, misses the point; Irish and UK workers are involved in different, often localised, struggles and disputes. There may be bureaucratic links but what affects an Irish worker more often than not does not directly impact or resonate in the UK.

Using the recent electricians' BESNA dispute of 2011-2012 as an example, we see can the benefits of workers across the UK fighting together. It was the combined actions of the UNITE rank and file, targeting major infrastructure projects in England such as the Olympic Park and Crossrail and in Scotland the Commonwealth games Velodrome project and the Grangemouth refinery, that secured a UK wide victory for electrical workers. If Scottish and English electricians were governed by different terms and conditions, as is likely under independence (and it's quite likely that terms and conditions here would be worse); then that fracture in union unity could see English workers continue with existing national agreements, whilst Scottish workers are left weakened to fight on their own. Is this in the interest of working people?

So we should think long and hard before severing our common, historic organisational links with our comrades from other areas in the UK. To repeat the often trumpeted mantra, workers across borders have more in common with each other than they do with the bosses in their own town, region or nation who profit from their labour. Workers are stronger together and we would do well to remember old but timeless truths such as 'unity is strength' and 'divide and conquer'.

Left voices say that independence will be a progressive step in the fight against the dark forces of capital, imperialism and a degenerative and racist British nationalism. This ignores the reality of class and politics. Socialist utopia will not be reached the day after the independence referendum. Neither will a 'yes' vote strike fear into those who own and control Scotland's industries. Conversely, it could make it far easier for the real power brokers to remain in control; as an independent Scotland will take away its ability to strike back at the City of London. Indeed, in an independent Scotland there will be no democratic mechanisms to do anything to curtail the activities of the City of London.

As far as xenophobic and nationalistic attitudes in England are concerned, we would do well to avoid complacency, especially in light of a debate over Scottish independence which plays on the politics of national, rather than class, consciousness. Of course we can point to examples of progressive nationalism uniting issues of class and nation to defeat oppression and imperialism, but these are not quite the conditions that prevail in Scotland today.

Socialist policies today

In considering whether socialism in Scotland is possible, we should not merely think, in an abstract, speculative fashion, about accomplishing full-scale socialism at some point in the far and distant future. We must also think about incremental progressive steps in the here and now. Today, both Scotland and the UK are crying out for change, or at least a willingness to adopt and introduce policies with more than a hint of socialist influence. Austerity, poverty, inequality and unfairness are rampant and growing. To state the obvious: the current policy direction needs to be confronted by socialist alternatives. We cannot be, indeed we must not be, fatalistic about what can (or cannot) be done. There are policies and choices that can be promoted now: albeit they require the right political organisation and pressure to help shape and achieve the necessary political will.

So what policies could we pursue and achieve now under the present arrangements? Central to socialist thought is the collective pooling and then sharing of resources based on the ability of each individual to contribute to a pot from which they take in times of need. Currently, this function is performed to some (albeit limited) extent by the UK wide Barnett formula - moving money from the more wealthy south east to poorer areas across the UK. On that basis, we would argue for a progressive taxation system that would substantially re-distribute the huge wealth that already exists in the UK and Scotland today. The *Sunday Times* 'rich list' recently confirmed that the wealth of the richest is at record levels, while, as the old cliché goes, due to wage stagnation and rising inflation, the rest are getting poorer. The wealth exists but it is hoarded by relatively few individuals and corporations.

For us progressive taxation has to become a central cornerstone in the arguments made by all forces on the left - whether you advocate further devolution or independence. Increasing the tax base provides governments with greater ability to intervene directly in the economy and provides governments with the tools to improve the life chances of the British people. For instance, raising more revenue could enable the governments in both Westminster and Scotland to embark on a much needed social house-building programme, creating employment whilst tackling the housing crisis. Huge hikes in energy costs are another critical issue facing working people across the UK. People increasingly have to choose between heating and eating. Yet at the same time the big six private energy companies enjoy soaring profits. This glaring unfairness continues to exercise politicians of all persuasions. But they obstinately ignore the most obvious solution - common ownership. With sufficient political will, the re-nationalisation of energy (and indeed of the railways) could be attained and would enjoy overwhelming public support.

Privatisation has been accompanied by the promotion of the 'public sector bad - private sector good' ethos. So entrenched is this thinking that little thought is given to developing and creating industry which would be publicly or cooperatively owned and where the benefits would be retained by government (local and national) and spent on public services. Take renewables for instance. The present Scottish Government speak of re-industrialising Scotland with a renewables revolution but rather than develop projects which could have seen the government, local authorities or communities owning the schemes, we see instead increasing subsides offered to multi-national corporations and private equity firms to develop speculative private projects with the profits repatriated to the boardrooms of London, Madrid, Paris and Copenhagen. This is a tragic missed opportunity.

The Scottish Government, working alongside local authorities and applying some political imagination and willingness, could have developed its own schemes which would have provided them the opportunity to accrue and spend the surpluses generated here in Scotland. Instead, the mantra of neo-liberalism is applied, despite the overwhelming evidence that privatisation, PFI and PPP schemes are more expensive, often less efficient, bad for workers and the environment and generally not in the best interests of Scotland and our people. Nevertheless, with the right political will, we could still develop community and co-operative ownership and see the benefits remain here and invested in socially productive ways.

Socialism, of course is not simply about redistributing economic power, it's also about redistributing political power. Today, ironically, given that the citizens are asked to vote in more elections than ever before, it seems that people feel more out of touch and detached from politics than at any time since universal suffrage. Scotland and the UK is the land of unelected Non-Departmental Public Bodies, or quangos in everybody else's language. Here, important decisions are often made by 'experts' with little democratic input from the Scottish people and/or their elected representatives.

Public service boards such as police or health, often have few, if any, community or union representation, while those councillors who sit on health and police boards are bound in by collective responsibility once decisions are made - even when they are not in the interest of the communities they represent. While, of course, in opening Scotland up for business, with little regulation, many workers and communities are at the mercy of the business strategies of multi-national corporations. A simple reform, democratising the boards of our public services could be introduced here and now and quickly. Likewise, with the right political will Thatcher's union laws could and should be repealed and companies could and should face regulatory conditions that would make it much more difficult to take government subsidy and then simply get up and go when market conditions change or a better offer comes along just as NEC, Motorola, and just recently Halls have done.

So socialist policies can be advanced; progressive taxation, social house building, common ownership, the development of co-operatives, and the decentralisation and democratisation of Scotland are all areas which can be developed now. Taken by themselves and collectively, they do not mark a transition to socialism but they do represent progress with more than a hint of socialist influence. We can and must fight for such a policy agenda as, with the right political will, these priorities could be advanced now.

Federalism

Arguably, debates over the constitution are a distraction that we could have well done without. The real fight must always be against the policies advocated by the powerful interests of capital. And, currently there are many fights to be fought. However, as the old saying goes, 'we are where we are'. The constitutional debate dominates contemporary Scottish politics and will continue to dominate until 2014. Whatever the outcome, it is our contention that further constitutional change will emerge in one form or another. Now, for all the reasons explained above we hope that this will not result in full independence. But as socialists, we must think about what constitutional arrangement could be promoted and that meet the interests of that big proportion of Scots who want further powers but not full independence. An enhancement of the current devolution settlement is popular amongst Scots. Proposals such as, Devo-max or Devo-plus had been suggested by some commentators including former First Minister, Henry McLeish, and right-wing thinktank, Reform Scotland. These proposals are not a progressive option. If introduced these proposals would end the Barnett concept of pooling and sharing of resources across the UK. What could be developed is an option, which sees Scotland retain and develop social and economic solidarity with our sisters and brothers across the rest of the UK, whilst also having a capability to re-distribute in Scotland. Such a redistributive function is key to pursuing a progressive, political agenda. Pauline Bryan (see this volume and the Red Pepper Collective 2012) has suggested recently that a federalist structure could be developed to achieve these objectives, pointing us at least in some small way down a socialist path. We do not have the space here to discuss this concept adequately, but this is an arrangement that socialists should explore in some detail in order to ascertain whether it could help take us in a progressive direction.

Conclusion

What we need is a Scotland and a UK that builds upon our democratic traditions and values of fairness and justice, and that builds a coalition of progressive social movements creating a narrative that puts compassion, equality and social progress at the heart of policy making and where the elimination of poverty and inequality inform and drive our every decision; where community empowerment rebuilds solidarity as a bulwark against the forces of conservatism and individualism; where we work with the nations and regions of the UK retaining a level of UK wide redistribution based on need; where we work with our union allies across the UK in the interests of all workers and do not allow the forces of capital to divide and rule; where we work internationally for peace, justice and disarmament respecting human rights and international law; where we place sustainable development over the blind pursuit of ever increasing economic growth and reject the notion that increasing GDP is the only way to happiness and wellbeing; and where education and health services serve people and not markets and where public services are recognised and respected as the civilising glue that bind society together. We would contend that this would be a programme that would gain popular support and change our country significantly for the better in Scotland. Here's an idea: we could call it socialism, or at least steps on the road towards it.

Chapter 10

Working class inter-nationalism to win economic democracy (A perspective from the Communist Party of Britain)

John Foster

Communists have for the past eighty years championed the right of the Scottish people to have their own parliament (1). Communists first made this demand in the 1930s. In the 1970s, they won the Scottish union and labour movement for this demand and played a central role in developing the movement that ultimately secured the Scottish parliament as established in 1999. Since 1999, Communists have called for a further strengthening of its powers. In this, they have remained true to their position as argued since the 1930s: that such constitutional forms are only of value in so far as they enhance the ability of working people to contest the power of big business, that is, to challenge the state power of monopoly capitalism. This is the ultimate test for any constitutional change under capitalism, namely, how far it advances democracy in the true sense of enhancing the class power and organisation of working people and their allies.

Communists do not believe that the proposals of the SNP government will serve this purpose. On the contrary, they would limit the ability of working people to contest state monopoly capitalist power at British-level and, thereby, weaken Scotland's democracy. Power over monetary policy would be held at British-level and, hence, drastically curtail the ability of the Scottish parliament to borrow and fund development as determined by the Scottish people. EU law would continue to prohibit any interference with the market power of big business and prevent most forms of public ownership. Article 42 of the EU Treaty and the conditions of NATO membership would together require proportionate contributions to military expenditure and a commitment to the strategic objectives of NATO as determined by EU and NATO policy.

The chapter outlines the Communist perspective on how the democratic and national rights of working people in Scotland can best be strengthened. To do so, it will outline its understanding of:

- The Marxist approach to nationality and the relationship between nationality and the class-determined development of society

- The character of the Scottish nation and its relationship to the British state

- The current crisis of state monopoly capitalism in Britain and its implications for Scottish democracy

Marx on the nation

As with any other aspect of society, Marx saw nations as being profoundly moulded and determined by the processes of class struggle and the transition of human society from one mode of production to another. Marx traced the emergence of ethnic social formations from the tribe and clan to the first slave-based societies to feudalism and the revolutionary creation of the capitalist nation. In this process, he presents nationalities and nations as being transformed as each new ruling class puts in place the state power requirements for the new mode of production. To overthrow the state power of the old order, each new ruling class has to create wider mass alliances mobilised around the emancipatory potential of the new order. In doing so the class identity of nations and nationalities will be transformed and in some cases new nations created. At the same time, the dominant identity and culture of the transformed nation will be that of the new ruling class and serve to sustain its specific form of exploitation.

In Scotland's case, a national entity first emerged ten centuries ago as pre-existing ethnic groupings, Pictish, British, Saxon and Irish-Scot, came together in struggle against Viking slavery. But the new kingdom was formed under the rule of a feudal aristocracy. Five centuries later that rule was in turn challenged and overturned by a new class seeking to introduce mercantile capitalism. To do so, it had to mobilise mass popular support. Yet the resulting Scottish state was no less defined in class terms -in this case those of legal institutions and a Presbyterian religious order that gave unlimited power to the owners of land and capital. This new order continued to be challenged throughout the seventeenth and eighteenth centuries by a democratic and plebeian opposition as well as by supporters of the old order. But it was the culture of the new ruling class which was the dominant one and which defined the Scottish nation for the following four centuries.

As Lenin argued, although within any national identity there will be two and sometimes three conflicting class-based cultural trends, it will be that of the ruling class which will be the dominant one. And the ruling class will always seek to exploit people's general and uncritical identity with 'their nation'. They will do so to mobilise them for external 'national' expansion, imperialism and war and also internally to divide working people on the basis of national origin. This is the danger of any approach to nationality that does not understand its fundamental inter-relationship with the class nature of society. Marx summed up the implications of this understanding of the nation in the *Communist Manifesto* where he argued that in advancing to socialism:

> *Since the proletariat must first of all acquire political supremacy, must rise to be the leading class of the nation, must constitute itself the nation, it is, so far, itself national, though not in the bourgeois sense of the word ... though not in substance, yet in form, the struggle of the proletariat with the bourgeoisie is at first a national struggle.*

By this, Marx did not mean that workers should become nationalists. What he sought to stress was that Communists had to engage with the substance of nationality. To carry out a socialist revolution, the working class must itself redefine the nation in progressive terms in order to create the broader alliance needed to overthrow the capitalist order - and in doing so it had to draw on all the democratic and emancipatory elements in a nation's past culture. To do otherwise will, as Dimitrov later argued, surrender national identity to the ruling class and allow it to be used in the most extreme and reactionary way as the struggle develops. Internationalism is not an abstract aspiration but depends on hard, difficult work by socialists in redefining 'their' nation in anti-imperialist terms which can unite all working people against the power of capital.

The Scottish nation and the British state

This approach, therefore, demands a specific historical analysis of the class forces involved in every nation's development and also in its relations with other nations whether as oppressor or oppressed. No nation is the same. Scotland's development as a nation started in the early feudal period and then witnessed a protracted and never quite conclusive struggle to stabilise a capitalist social order in the sixteenth and seventeenth centuries. Its pro-capitalist forces had to turn repeatedly to those in England to consolidate their rule against the return of pro-feudal elements. In the seventeenth century, they successfully established a Scottish controlled enclave in the north of Ireland and unsuccessfully attempted to develop a colonial base in the Americas. The Act of Union of 1707 gave them access to all parts of England's colonial empire in return for support for the pro-capitalist Hanoverian succession - while enabling them to retain control of internal state institutions in Scotland. These distinctively 'Scottish' institutions, legal, religious and educational, provided Scottish property owners with an even more detailed control of working people than their competitors in England. In addition Scotland's capitalist ruling class was directly represented in the British parliament and used their position to consolidate their grip on colonial assets in India and the Americas. This relationship with England was, therefore, quite different from that between Ireland and Britain. Ireland became the world's first capitalist colony. Its resources of land and labour were conquered, sold and subordinated to an external ruling class. Scotland's were not.

The subsequent development of Scotland's working class movement has been profoundly marked by its complex relationship to a Scottish ruling class and a British capitalist state. Early trade unionists were confronted by the comprehensive control of local life by Scotland's employer-dominated presbyteries and magistrates who regulated family relations, access to poor relief and education and enforced particularly oppressive employment contracts. At the same time, effective union organisation in the dominant industries of cotton and coal demanded unity with fellow trade unionists in England and Wales. In consequence, the creation of a British capitalist (and imperialist) state resulted in the converse development of a working class movement organised at British level which saw the struggle for democracy at British level as part and parcel of the struggle for democracy at local and Scottish level - a struggle that was seen as particularly necessary in Scotland given the nature of its own 'internal' national institutions of class oppression. In Scotland, working class organisation itself faced great obstacles and until the early twentieth century remained less developed than that in England and Wales. Keir Hardie had go to London to secure election and, still in 1918, there were only two Labour MPs in Scotland as against over fifty in England. Union membership was also lower.

This should remind us that there is nothing inherently left-wing or radical about people in Scotland. Such left-wing commitments have to be won and sustained in class struggle - and historically the development of class conscious, anti-capitalist politics in Scotland has occurred only when union struggle became fused with a wider political challenge to capitalist state power. Such challenges have of necessity depended on the forging of class unity at British level against British capitalist state institutions. And such periods have been relatively rare - though critical for political advance. The first was in the earlier nineteenth century around the first great struggle for democracy culminating in the 1830s and 1840s. The second was that in the early twentieth century, culminating in the 1910s and 1920s, which finally secured formal democracy. The third was in the 1970s when the defence of union rights against a Conservative government was transformed into a battle for economic democracy - and where one outcome was the demand for a Scottish parliament that would have powers to own and control productive resources on behalf of the Scottish people.

During these periods, the class identity of the Scottish nation did shift in a progressive direction and the reactionary values of the old order were challenged. But these moments were never fully sustained. As the wider struggle subsided, as the generations that fought it passed away, so the values of the capitalist order, reinforced and in new forms, again became dominant. This, therefore, is one of the special features of Scottish identity and a critical one. Its radical and progressive elements, in terms of working class values of solidarity and class power, have always been very closely interlinked with the development of class unity, and to some extent the forging of a new progressive working class national identity, at British level. The progressive elements in Scottish and British national identity rise and fall together.

This is why the programme of the Communist Party emphasises 'the need to maintain and enhance unity between the labour and progressive movements across the three nations of Britain. The Communist Party does not advocate separation because it would fracture working class and progressive unity in face of a united ruling capitalist class'. Instead, the programme argues for parliaments in Scotland and Wales to have 'the full economic, legislative and financial powers necessary to protect and develop the economic, social and cultural interests of their peoples' but opposes the type of separation that enables big business 'to use threats and promises on jobs and investment to exert pressure on Scottish, Welsh and English governments to outbid each other in 'business friendly' and 'pro-market' policies'.

Unfortunately, this is precisely the type of separation which the SNP proposes. It would involve subordination to the power of big business, very largely external, and would entrench neo-liberal assumptions and policies. Such separation would not necessarily prevent the eventual emergence of a new working class consciousness. But it would make it much more difficult. Capitalist state power would be held elsewhere: in Brussels and the City of London. Its representatives in Edinburgh would for a considerable time be able to divert popular disenchantment against the 'English'. And, as always when the working class movement is weakened, Scottish national values and identity will shift further in a pro-market, neo-liberal direction.

These objections apply no less to the arguments of those on the left who support a Yes vote in the referendum. Essentially, their argument is that once Scotland has an independent parliament it will be up to the Scottish people to decide their future and that, on past performance, they will opt for socialist or at least social democratic alternatives. In addition, they argue, Scottish independence would of itself destroy the British state and therefore be a major blow against imperialism. These expectations ignore key realities.

First, the way the new Scottish state will be established. The terms of independence as set out in the referendum will form the basis for the subsequent Treaty of Separation and, thereby, determine the provisions of the new Scottish constitution. Constitutions are not easily changed. The straight jacket of the EU treaties and of externally controlled monetary policy would remain and could only be removed by a lengthy and difficult process of treaty revision and constitutional amendment.

Second, the subsequent political influence of the SNP as 'national' party. The SNP is highly likely to emerge as the ruling party subsequent to a Yes vote in a referendum. Attitudes will have been further polarised on nationalist terms in the course of the referendum and the subsequent process of treaty negotiation. The apparatus of the post-independence Scottish state will be committed to establishing the 'new' nation on the terms set by the SNP. The same terms will be backed by the external owners of Scotland's economy and media and by the EU whose membership Scotland would seek. These attitudes would be difficult to shift.

Third, the state power of 'British' finance capital would remain and be strengthened. The belief that Scottish independence would somehow 'break' capitalist state power at British level is based on a confusion between a territorial state and capitalist state power. The removal of Scotland's territory and 8.5 per cent of Britain's current population would mean a redrawing of maps. But it would in no way alter the fusion between state institutions at British level and finance capital in the City of London - in turn integrated with finance in Edinburgh, Glasgow and Aberdeen and controlling the great bulk of the Scottish economy. Worse still, 'independence', as currently set out, will divert and disrupt working class unity at British level and hence strengthen the state power of finance capital during a crucial period of change.

The next few years will be critical in determining a new balance of class forces. Our (joint) ruling class is set on destroying key democratic gains from the past. The working class movement equally has the opportunity to build a much broader anti-monopoly alliance that can defeat it.

The crisis of state monopoly capitalism in Britain and Scotland's democracy

Today, as in the 1970s, big business in Britain is in the grip of a massive economic crisis. Also, as in the 1970s, it is seeking to pass on the costs to working people. Unless stopped, it will over the next three or four years seek to reverse the historic gains of the welfare state, decimate pensions and benefits, privatise what remains of the public sector and use mass unemployment to drive down wages. The 'independence' debate as currently conducted will divert people from this struggle. The SNP will argue that a separate Scotland would somehow provide shelter from this assault.

The 'Better Together' campaign will be conducted on largely negative terms against the SNP, will ignore the ruling class assault and have no wider demands. Indeed, the nature of the cross-party alliance on which it is based makes this inevitable.

This is why Communists argue that, as in the 1970s, the union and labour movement must itself take up the issue, make it part of the wider struggle and call for a strengthening of Scotland's democracy against big business and neo-liberal economic management. It must make the demand for economic democracy in Scotland central to the overall fight-back against the ConDem government –and thereby ensure that the national identity of the Scottish people is once more transformed in a progressive direction.

The nature of crisis facing big business in Britain is both general and specific. It is general in so far as all capitalist world economies face a crisis of over-accumulation of capital and unused capacity resulting from the massive growth in inequality and consequent levels of impoverishment, debt and piratical speculative lending. This is the general crisis. It is specific - in so far as Britain was the key world centre for such speculative lending. The level of private and commercial debt held by British (including Scottish-based) banks is four times GDP, by far the highest of any major economy. For decades governments in Britain have, in subservience to British big business (and also the US banking interests that now dominate the City of London), boosted finance at the expense of the productive economy. In particular, in order to secure control over financial services in the EU, British governments have sought rigid adherence to the neo-liberal market rules of the EU which prohibit any form of public democratic ownership - now virtually the only way of ensuring developmental investment in industry.

It is because of the magnitude of this private debt crisis faced by the British banks that the ConDem government is enforcing cuts in public spending only matched by those in Greece, Spain and Ireland - together with privatisation programmes designed to suck still more income out of the state to sustain the profits of the investments banks and hedge funds that control the economy.

A separate Scotland, as envisaged by the SNP, would in no way be immune from this crisis. The Scottish economy is controlled by the same hedge funds and investment banks. Its industrial sector is proportionately even smaller. Those who previously owned its economy a generation ago are now among the super-rich who direct the investment houses in the City of London and its subsidiary centres in Edinburgh and Aberdeen. The array of millionaires backing the SNP, Souter, Grossart, Matthewson, Gilbert, McColl, Farmer, all ultimately operate for, and on the terms set by, finance capital at British level and look to the same solutions in terms of privatisation and further cuts in the public sector. For them, a separate Scotland as promised by the SNP would provide the additional bonus of lower taxes on corporate profits and 'high net worth' individuals. But such a Scotland would also be part of the sterling area with public sector finance controlled by the City of London - and, as part of the EU, bound hand and foot by neo-liberal regulations banning public sector intervention in the economy.

Unfortunately, all the constitutional variants on offer today, with one exception, have basically the same character and depend upon the same neo-liberal assumptions. 'Devo-Max', as defined by the SNP, would provide powers over taxation - but within existing neo-liberal limits. 'Devo-Plus' is, if anything, worse. It provides power over income tax but not VAT or national insurance. The Reform Scotland group of business people who back it see the consequences of a lower tax take as beneficial and producing a leaner, less dependent Scotland with a smaller public sector.

The same largely applies to the *Scotland Act 2012*. This gives greater controls over income tax, provides some borrowing powers and retains the principle of a limited geographical distribution of income within Britain based on social need. But this grant itself is being drastically cut as the current ConDem coalition government slashes public expenditure - and all the neo-liberal prohibitions on public ownership and industrial intervention would remain in place.

The one exception is provided by the proposals in the Red Paper Collective's (2012) *People Power: The Labour Movement Alternative for Radical Constitutional Change* and which are elaborated elsewhere in this volume. These proposals do challenge neo-liberal assumptions and engage with the fight-back against the ConDem assault. They do so by returning to the two basic principles adopted by the union movement in the 1970s. One is that the Scottish Parliament should have powers to develop public democratic control over the economy, namely, to own and control public utilities and to have a developmental role in regenerating the productive economy. This demand is for economic democracy (or 'Democracy-Max'). The other is the principle of redistribution of income across Britain. This would retain the Block Grant but ensure that it fully responds to social need for all parts of Britain in terms of poverty, unemployment, health needs and population dispersal. It would, therefore, need to be supplemented by a radical redistribution of income from the rich to the poor to reverse the current cuts. This is the demand is for social justice: 'Redistribution-Max'.

These proposals have important constitutional implications. They require a fully federal structure for the nations of Britain - with each nation having a parliament with powers of economic democracy, in other words, the power to own, control and develop a nation's productive resources. They also require a federal parliament with power over currency, money supply and elements of taxation in order to re-distribute income and to undertake wider aspects of infrastructural ownership - within a new relationship to the EU. In essence, however, these proposals are not constitutional. They are about mobilising the forces that can change the class orientation of our parliamentary institutions by shifting the balance of class forces in Britain against monopoly capital and changing Britain's institutional relationship to the European Union. This will require both joint struggle with working people across the EU and a direct engagement against the policies of the ConDem government - with the objective of embedding the resulting gains in institutional change. The result would not be socialism. But it would provide the working class and its allies with important levers by which to begin to prise apart the structures of state monopoly capitalism - above all in terms of the power to develop forms of public and social ownership at national level in Scotland, Wales and England.

So, to address the question posed by the title of this volume, Communists would argue that there is there is a Scottish road to socialism. But, they would also qualify that answer. Socialism in Scotland has to be won on an inter-national basis, where its essential requirement is the dismantling of state monopoly capitalist power at British level - and which requires not just dismantling but, critically, its replacement by the mobilised power of the working class movement and its allies. One key instrument in this process is the democratically elected parliament at British level - won by the labour movement over two centuries. Political separation would remove it. Within this wider process, the achievement of economic democracy for Scotland, England and Wales is, however, crucial. The democratic power to socially own and develop productive resources would directly challenge the logic of state monopoly capitalism. The working class movement, in leading this struggle, would indeed, in Marx's words, become the 'leading class' of each nation, the defender of its productive economy, and in doing so ensure that national consciousness was transformed in a progressive and inter-national direction.

Notes

The title of this volume makes implicit reference to the Communist Party programme, *The British Road to Socialism*. In the 2007 edition of *Is there a Scottish Road to Socialism?* the contribution from the Communist Party of Britain outlined some of the basic assumptions of this programme. There is no space here to repeat this material but the definitions of socialism, state monopoly capitalism and the anti-monopoly alliance remain integral to present arguments and can be referenced there.

This theoretical approach, quite different to the Weberian approach of Breuilly, J. and Gellner, E. is developed in Hoffman, J. and Mzala, N. (1990-1) 'Non-Historic Nations and the National Question' *Science and Society*, 54/4:408-26. A Scottish application can be found in Foster, J. (1989) 'Nationality, social change and class' in McCrone, D., McKendrick, S. and Straw, P. (eds.) *The Making of Scotland*, Edinburgh; and Foster, J. (2004) 'Marxists, Weberians and Nationality: a Reply to Neil Davidson' *Historical Materialism*, 12/1:155-179.

Chapter 11

Yes: there is a Scottish road to socialism

Colin Fox

I must begin this chapter on the case for socialism in Scotland by apologising to the book's editor, Professor Gregor Gall, for missing his initial deadline. I am sure he must have thought I had taken a leaf out of the late Douglas Adams's book, *The Hitchhikers Guide to the Galaxy*, who famously declared: 'I love deadlines. I particularly like the noise they make when they whiz past'. But I delayed submitting these remarks in order to reflect on the Radical Independence Conference (RIC) held in Glasgow on 24 November 2012. And I am grateful to Professor Gall for granting me some 'extra time'.

The RIC said much about the left in Scotland and, it seems to me, the questions posed by this book. Self-trailed as 'a major one day conference to discuss independence and the way forward for Scotland', the event brought together 800 pro-Independence activists and academics on the left of Scottish society to discuss a variety of progressive causes and how they might be advanced. It was an enjoyable day and a successful display of the left's ability, when it put its collective mind to it, to attract a wide range of activists and thinkers to debate important political questions.

Ahead of its opening, I was struck by two particular thoughts. First, how broad, imprecise and, therefore, of questionable merit the term 'radical' is. And if the turnout at the Radisson Blu Hotel that day was anything to go by, its ambiguity was liberally interpreted to include; socialists, greens, left nationalists, peaceniks, feminists, social democrats, LGBT activists, disability rights campaigners, militant trade unionists, cultural dissidents, republicans, anti-racists and many more shades of opinion. It goes without saying that there could just as easily have been a Radical anti-Independence conference including Labour radicals, the Communist Party, those from the Liberal Democrats and even the Tories. Whatever the vagueness of the term 'radical', we can at least agree that it does not have the same meaning as 'socialist'.

The second feature of the RIC that struck me was how academic the whole thing felt. This was no gathering of representatives from industry, workplaces or communities but rather a self-conscious conference of - and for - 'intellectuals' and the academy. Set out in the usual educational sector style with an eclectic list of speakers and presentations delivered, on this occasion at least, with restricting brevity, it therefore had a tendency to shallowness. The disconnected workshops, for example, posed important questions but were, for the most part, left unanswered. In the end, it was an occasion lacking a sense of direction and dominated by a rather narrow milieu of 'radicals' from Scotland's 'elite' universities. A pity. Then again, it might be the start of a wider process of reflection, engagement and action. Let's hope so. I came away with the wise words of Marx ringing in my ears, and I paraphrase him here: 'Philosophers earn a nice living interpreting the world, reading books and delivering academic papers, the point however is to change it!'

So what, if anything, does the RIC tell us about the socialist cause in Scotland today? What traction do socialist ideas have among the mass of the population? And, how are we to achieve this socialist society we strive for? These then are the questions I wish to pose in this chapter.

To the editor's central question, my instinctive answer is to say 'yes, there is a Scottish road to socialism' but like any other road, it needs conscious and careful construction. Above all, we need to develop a clear and popularly backed programme for changing Scotland from a neo-liberal capitalist society into a modern democratic socialist one, with people prepared to confront the existing neo-liberal corporate hegemony, argue for a socialist alternative, persuade the population at large of its merits and insist they help us in its construction.

There has been a surprising degree of criticism of the left from some quarters following the worldwide financial collapse of 2008. Those who believe socialists should automatically have gained from it and who are, therefore, despairing of our collective failure in that regard seem particularly vocal. And yet whilst the collapse was indeed profound and widely felt, those who thought neo-liberalism would be automatically displaced display a failure to understand both how capitalism maintains its control and how socialist successes are achieved. Finance capital - without doubt the main political player in the global economy today - saw vast amounts of its capital written off, but these 'masters of the universe' as they refer to themselves, continue nonetheless with their reckless neo-liberal strategy with its iron grip on world trade and its brutal exploitation of the earth's peoples and resources. And, the term 'neo-liberal' seems to me singularly inappropriate to describe the process involved given that there is nothing either new or liberal about it.

Despite being bailed out by huge amounts of public money, the bankers show little sign they have mended their ways. Indeed, the major banks and finance companies seem only to regard the events of 2008 as an occupational hazard where the weakest fall by the wayside as their unregulated free market activities continue largely unchallenged and unchanged. And - if it is fundamental change we are after - surely the main conclusion to be drawn is, as Marx famously insisted in the 1860s, only the active intervention of the masses themselves will defeat finance capital's stranglehold and usher in the progressive economic, social and political reforms needed.

The Occupy movement, with its admirable spirit of resistance in 2010/11, appeared to believe it could appeal to morality to beat rampant capitalist greed. It clearly did not understand the basic nature of the beast it was trying to slay nor the tasks involved in constructing a force capable of defeating it by arguing along such lines. Moreover, there will be nothing automatic about the replacement of capitalism with socialism. Capitalism will have to be defeated by a popularly backed alternative with a profoundly socialist programme as well as an uncompromising, organised and disciplined political leadership. Otherwise you can forget it. As socialists, our job remains to painstakingly develop such a programme and party as others have rightly emphasised throughout the ages.

The orthodox view of the path to socialism in Scotland has it that an acute economic, social and political crisis will develop and precipitate resistance to the attacks on working class living standards by capital the likes of which we have never seen before. The existing social divisions will become much more starkly posed and the most conscious layers of the working class will provide a leadership that is both anti-capitalist in its programme and an organisation able to inspire the broad masses in word and deed.

Lenin highlighted four prerequisites for the 1917 socialist transformation in Russia and his writings on this subject remain a valuable source of study today. He wrote that an acute economic and social crisis where the ruling classes could not rule in the manner to which they - and everyone else - had become accustomed was the central catalyst for change. And the state's inability to provide the basic necessities of life became the main driver for socialist revolution amid a deeply unpopular war. The inevitable vacillation of the middle classes was clear as they flitted between support for the working masses, who they suspected were about to take over, and the rich elite still in nominal control, depending on where they felt their own interests were best served. The working class with a long and bloody history of struggle, having learned that there are no easy routes to success, finally realised political struggle was essential if victory was to be achieved. And, the existence of a well-organised party with a clear programme and orientation to the most politically conscious layers of the working class with leaders prepared to fight to the end was vital. Such a party with mass popular support and an acute understanding of the political situation and an iron will to replace the decrepit state institutions that hold the working classes in check had been years in the making.

The present 'crisis of capitalism' in Scotland - with the worst recession in 80 years - will again be 'survived' by the ruling elite, if it has its way, by driving down the living standards of millions of working class people, poor and disorganised just as they have done in previous occasions. That 'survival' is likely because for the moment there is no force organised, conscious and powerful enough to replace them and their system with a lasting alternative.

Scotland is a country let's not forget where a handful of people control our economy and its political levers. They are, nonetheless, backed up by international capital and the state. The recession has proceeded to a 'double-dip' and many predict it may well develop into a 'triple-dip' downturn in due course as the economy stumbles along in a stagnating condition for the rest of this decade. Large sections of Scotland's working class have already seen a considerable fall in its living standards as household budgets come under even greater pressure. Space constraints do not allow me to outline the full extent of the expected economic and social crisis here but two or three examples of its worsening impact should suffice to paint an accurate picture.

One remarkable feature of this recession is that unemployment figures have not markedly increased as they have in all previous downturns. Official figures, undoubtedly 'massaged' by the government, nonetheless show the number of people in work has actually risen year on year since 2008. And the main reason for this unusual phenomenon is the dramatic rise in what is now termed 'under-employment', where workers looking for a full time job must settle for a part-time one. It is now common to find employers at the Royal Mail, the NHS, civil service, local authorities and in retail, for example, taking on staff on short term, part time contracts and keeping them in that position for several years. These casual contracts are simply extended and extended rather than being made up into full-time work as they wished. 'The number of people in Scotland classed as under-employed has soared by 37 per cent since the start of the economic downturn in 2008, official figures have revealed' announced the *Scotsman* (29 November 2012). Employees wishing to work more hours jumped from 178,000 in 2008 to 244,000 now with the average number of workers as a whole [part-time and full-time] up from 2,452,000 to 2,474,000 during the same period. The impact on wages, union membership and militancy is clear. Workers feel exploited, isolated and yet cowed. And this 'flexible' feature of the labour market has serious consequences both for their standard of living and their inclination to protest.

Perhaps, the most visible expression of the widespread deterioration in living standards has been seen in the huge rise in households now living in fuel poverty. With gas and electricity prices having doubled in the last six years, the number of families in crisis has quadrupled. Since wages, pensions and benefits have lagged behind the rise in energy bills, figures from Energy Action Scotland show that the number of people paying more than 10 per cent of their disposable income on heating and lighting has risen from 292,000 in 2002 to almost one million now. There has also been a staggering rise in the number of households in what's termed 'extreme fuel poverty', i.e. paying more than 20 per cent of their entire income on gas and electricity. Professor John Hills, the eminent health economist at the London School of Economics estimates that some 27,000 people will die this winter across Britain from 'cold related deaths' or exposure to persistent and chronic fuel poverty.

In some local authority areas of Scotland, the senior citizen not shivering in the winter is the exception with 86 per cent of pensioners living in fuel poverty. As the Scottish Socialist Party pamphlet (*End fuel poverty and power company profiteering*) made clear, the human wretchedness behind these stark figures paint a scandalous picture of misery in our society. The SSP has presented a comprehensive programme to eradicate fuel poverty which includes freezing the bills for a prolonged period, investigating claims of energy company 'profiteering, doubling the winter fuel allowance and extending it to other 'at risk' groups, doubling investment in renewables to diversify away from expensive fossil fuels, building 100,000 new, energy efficient houses for the socially rented sector annually and - last but not least - returning the energy industry to public ownership. This is precisely the kind of transitional programme the left must popularise and champion in dealing with all the social ills Scotland faces today.

Another appalling feature of working class life in Scotland is our social housing crisis that shows no signs of abating either. The *Scotsman* (29 November 2012) reported: 'The number of council houses in Scotland has hit a record low according to Scottish Government figures. There are now just 319,384 homes in this sector.' Despite a manifesto pledge to address the chronic shortage of affordable, quality, social housing, the SNP Government built just 866 council houses last year. There are 187,935 people on the waiting list. Shelter has demanded 100,000 new social housing units are built annually as much of the country's existing housing stock is unfit for human habitation.

And yet as millions of us continue to take a hammering on wages, fuel bills and poor housing conditions the rich continue to prosper. Inequality and class divisions have widened considerably over the past decade according to the *Sunday Times* 'Rich List'. It shows there are now 619,000 millionaires in Britain. Among them, predictably, are David Cameron, Nick Clegg, Ed Miliband and George Osborne with their six figure salaries augmented by inherited wealth and income from their many interests outside Parliament. 'The richest 10 per cent of households are 850 times wealthier than the bottom 10 per cent' reported the *Guardian* (4 December 2012) commenting on the latest Office for National Statistics (ONS) figures. And, the impact of the unprecedented austerity/cuts being implemented by the Con-Dem Government adds insult to injury.

So what has the socialist movement to offer working people in Scotland as a way out of this morass?

The promise of full employment, a guaranteed full-time, permanent, secure job for everyone who wants one that would be a very good starting point for the left to argue in the face of the recession's injustices and inequality. A national minimum wage set at 2/3rds of the average to ensure an end to the 'employed poor' and a maximum set at ten times the average would also help narrow inequalities significantly. Pensions also need to be significantly increased and linked to average earnings to ensure everyone obtains dignity in retirement. The same rights are owed to those living on wholly inadequate state benefits.

And to pay for all these reforms, we need a truly progressive and fair tax system similar to Scandinavia where the higher the income the higher the tax paid on it - and with stiff penalties for those individuals and corporations who seek to avoid their responsibilities to the rest of society. Public ownership of industry is another popular left policy which sees need as our primary objective not profit, and where surpluses are re-invested in service delivery improvement programmes.

These then are just some of the economic and social programmes the left needs to champion in order to eradicate poverty in Scotland and enhance the life opportunities of working class people. Whilst these proposals enjoy widespread public support, the question on everyone's lips is how are they to be achieved? In other words, who is going to break down the resistance of the rich, their politicians and media to secure this programme of reforms? The answer to this question is crucial and it lies with the organised working class itself conscious of its own strength and the brutal class nature of our society. Where then is that class-consciousness today?

The morale of the organised working class has certainly taken a battering in recent years. Political and industrial defeats have been suffered. Indeed, the very term 'working class' has been bastardised as it faced a neo-liberal ideological onslaught. Let me highlight one example of many to show how the public debate on the concept has been corrupted. Commenting on the challenges facing the new Chinese Communist Party leadership, Labour's David Milliband told the 'Today' programme on Radio 4 on 30 November 2012 that there were 300m 'middle class' people in China now. To back up his absurd claim, he referred to the UN definition of 'middle class' as being 'anyone earning more than $6,000 per annum [£80 per week]'. These comments are intended to obscure the real identity of those who must sell their labour every day simply to survive. It is hardly surprising then that the Scottish working class are confused about their political place in society. However, 'working class' consciousness and identity remains the key to social change. And, as socialists we need to rebuild that class-consciousness, collectivist thinking and to challenge feelings of political impotence and isolation.

To whom then have the working people in Scotland been turning in recent years for political solutions? The answer unfortunately is to Labour and the SNP, but in truth they have not turned to them with much confidence or expectation of improvement. Still reeling from the battering it took at the hands of the Tories at Westminster and the SNP at Holyrood, Labour has responded by moving even further to the right. They are now a thoroughly pro-capitalist, neo-liberal, warmongering party. Its economic and social policies, like scrapping universal benefits, are to all intents and purposes indistinguishable from the Tories. Its historic attachment to the union movement - still worth many millions of pounds to the party annually - is clearly an embarrassment it would dearly like to end. And, in truth, it is only a matter of time before they do. In the SNP, Scotland has yet another pro-capitalist, neo-liberal party moving to the right. Their U-turn on keeping an independent Scotland in NATO, abandoning a 30-year political commitment to do otherwise, was significant as yet another sign of its desire to appease right wing supporters of Independence.

Whatever else might be said about the Scottish Socialist Party in recent years, it has not lost its ideological ballast. And it is surely now indisputable that neither Labour nor the SNP offers a credible home for those wishing to build a socialist Scotland. If there is one issue, however, where working class people can be mobilised for progressive advance it is on independence. Whilst the polls suggest only 35 per cent support self-determination, the figure is higher among the working class majority. There is a sense in working class areas of Scotland that we could be better off if we were freed from the grip of Tory Governments and better able to implement our own social democratic goals. The Scottish Socialist Party offers a vision of independence which would not only free us from the shackles of British imperialism, but could also ensure Scotland's working class majority are economically, socially, politically and culturally better off. If all Scotland's wealth remained here rather than be siphoned off by the UK Treasury or boardrooms across the world, it stands to reason our country would be better off.

The case for independence is that it is a step forward and would represent a significant defeat for the British state and its stranglehold over our economy, society, culture and politics. There are those who mistakenly draw the conclusion that big business wants independence because they see mavericks like Sir George Matthewson, Brian Souter and Tom Farmer backing it. The fact is big business in general is the fiercest opponent of independence there is. These mavericks are non-socialist supporters of independence who back the SNP currently in the majority at Holyrood. I have no illusions in the SNP. They are a pro-capitalist party who favour neo-liberal corporate control as much as anyone. But the key question is can the socialist cause be advanced in Scotland through independence or not? And the answer is yes it can, but only provided it involves a complete repudiation of neo-liberalism, corporatism, the financialisation of our economy and existing class relations. And that's the essence of the debate inside the 'Yes Scotland' movement. The referendum can be won if it offers independence as change, not dressing up the political *status quo* as radical.

I fully expect the 2014 independence referendum to be won. I am increasingly confident a majority of Scots will realise they can be better off and I see them swinging behind the burgeoning independence movement over the next two years. I believe the referendum can be won by persuading our fellow Scots of independence's transformational potential. The prospect of an SNP government employing the same economic and political levers as any other Western European state to exploit the working class majority will clearly do nothing to ensure success in 2014. But if socialist ideals are raised clearly and unequivocally in the independence debate, there is every chance real change can take hold and our cause will be considerably strengthened both in the short term and longer term.

Socialism in Scotland may often look like a distant dream in today's circumstances but change can come quickly as latent class-consciousness crystallises particularly during periods of acute political crisis. Working class people face the worst economic recession since the 1930s and reductions in their living standards worse than any it is has seen in decades. I am confident we will see resistance to these attacks and yet the fight back needs to be both encouraged and influenced by the left as it grows and succeeds.

And of the questions posed at the beginning of this chapter? What traction do socialist ideas have among the mass of the population? There are grounds for optimism as the evidence shows there is widespread support for public ownership, for full employment, redistribution of wealth, union rights, equal opportunity and peace. These are all issues closely associated with the left. However, it is also clear the left lacks credibility as many question our ability to deliver on promises made. So the left's own fight back must involve far better presentation of our case, greater degrees of activism and ensuring our transitional demands are secured in the short term. We need to get organised in workplaces and in the wider community. There is no shortage of issues for us to campaign on and no shortage of persuasive arguments to use in taking our case to working people. We need, in due course, to grow our forces in Scotland into a mass base, organised around an uncompromising socialist programme, led by those forged in the fierce battles of yesteryear.

Chapter 12

Don't crowd the map

Lynn Henderson

An interesting conversation recently with my 16 year old daughter on the referendum revealed that for her, the autumn of 2014 is a first opportunity to exercise her democratic right to vote, and her passage to adult citizenship. Too young to remember a time before the Scottish Parliament, my offspring was exercised to learn that before 1999, there was no Scottish Parliament because we merely had a Secretary of State for Scotland. The Secretary of State was accountable to the UK Cabinet, with a Scottish Office corps of civil servants in Edinburgh to administer and implement the legislative will of Whitehall, as embodied by the Secretary of State. Those young people participating in the referendum, 16 or older will be the first Holyrood generation. Scottish devolution is coming of age.

For my own generation, the real debate cannot be characterised by the Yes Scotland or Better Together camps. Some notable exceptions aside, both are populated with the hacks, harbingers and even has-beens of the Scottish political establishment who have long since ceased to recognise that they are merely exchanging insults with the mirror, addicted as they are to the same neo-liberal market prescription. The reality for the left and progressive forces is that, however, Scotland votes, our future is tied in to monetary, fiscal, policy, services and structural transfers with the rest of the UK. Capital is concentrated in the City of London, the European super-market and the international global forces of capitalism, militarism and repression remain intact. In that context, therefore, the real debate for the labour and union movement is not if or how we may achieve a Scottish road to socialism through Independence, Devo Max or defending the collective social solidarity of the *status quo*, but how we tackle class inequalities, poverty and exclusion within Scotland and how we deliver our society and services to a more socialistic model and in doing so, protect public services from the dominance of the market.

The twenty-fifth September 2012 will be remembered as a milestone in Scottish politics. It was the day that Johann Lamont, Scottish Labour leader, abandoned support for universal provision and instead pinned her support to means testing. Ironically, this gave focus to Labour's withdrawal from a fundamental principle of universalism, and drew light away from the fundamental issue of the low tax agenda of the SNP. The day of dialectal debate being led by Scottish political parties, however, had long since gone - indeed, if it was ever there. In Scotland today, there is no left –right division between the two main parties. Scottish Labour and the SNP at a leadership level are firmly embedded in centrist social democrat politic that market capitalist economics can co-exist with socially just objectives. As the STUC puts in its *A Just Scotland* series of papers: Scandinavian style social justice with US style low taxation. But Scandinavian style social justice with US style low taxation just doesn't add up.

The tribal warriors within the Scottish political parties remain reduced to thin pickings in their yah-boo point scoring. Only the constitutional question provides them with any real difference. It is for that reason that in the main, the people of Scotland remain disengaged. What is required is for real class warriors to engage in the debate through proper community organising and by fully utilising the existing democratic structures of the organised labour movement. From the shop floor upwards, unions are collectivised, organised, have democratic and communication networks in action and are in touch with the members in real on-going, everyday relations.

So let's leave the Saturday flag waving, balloons, neighbourhood 'blitzing' and door chapping to party zealots and let's also leave the public meeting floor contributions and paper selling to those who prefer to exchange pre-determined solutions back and forward across half empty rooms, and let our movement look outwards. The real debate - if it is to take off - must come from inside the workplaces and gathering places of Scotland, organised amongst those who are already organised and trusted - our own representative structures. The real debate must be open, inclusive and engaging to seek the genuine participation and contributions of members and non-members of our movement, and it must be educational and challenging against the austerity defeatists, the narrow 'something for nothing' welfare apologists and the flawed left analysis that calls on the class to wait until after independence before any improvements to our conditions can be possible. The real alternative must be routed in a strong belief that Scotland can become a better collective, socialised society regardless of the constitution and that must be presented through a clear class analysis and a popular economic alternative.

The Scottish union movement is, therefore, once again charged to take up its historic lead to make the demands for Home Rule in the interest of the workers, their communities, in support of those in need and in solidarity with those in struggle here and globally. For my Union, the Public and Commercial Services' (PCS) Union, engagement and education on the future of Scotland is part of our ongoing messages themed under 'Austerity Isn't Working: Tax Justice, the Economic Alternative, and the Welfare Alternative.'

Rather than starting with the determinist propositions of 'yes', 'no' or 'three bags full', PCS wishes to engage our members in a discussion on what kind of Scotland we wish to live in: powers over how and where we live; how as civil and public servants the work that we do contributes to that society and how it is valued and how we can receive a living wage and fair pay, terms and conditions in exchange for our labour; whether the services we deliver can be more publicly accountable, less market-driven and that internal industrial democracy can be developed in the workplace and throughout the structures of the services we provide; union freedoms, employment rights, health and safety regulation and equalities and human rights regulation, protection and enforcement; how we seek to participate economically, as citizens and in our communities; how our children are educated as future citizens and how our dependents are cared for by society; what kind of social security and assistance we expect in return for our national insurance contributions when we are ill, out of work, vulnerable or elderly; how justice can be accessible and fair and restorative; how our natural and carbon environment is protected and secured for future generations; how our transport and technology can be improved; how we rid these waters of nuclear weapons; and on retirement from work; what sort of pensions and dignity we require to sustain us into old age.

PCS is preparing for widespread debate on the future of Scotland throughout our structures. Of the 30,000 members of our union in Scotland, almost a third are civil and public servants within the Scottish government, its agencies and non-departmental public bodies including Scottish Courts Service, Registers of Scotland, Scottish Prison Service, Scottish Natural Heritage, the enterprise agencies, national galleries, museums etc. A small, but growing number of our members also deliver public services on privatised contracts mostly through large multinational corporations. The majority, however of civil servants in Scotland, representing almost two thirds of PCS members currently, work for UK departments, delivering services from within Scotland to the public throughout the UK on welfare, taxation, defence, borders, immigration, passports, transport, tribunals, equalities, health and safety regulation.

Therefore, in addition to the civic, social and economic interest that PCS have in common with the whole population of Scotland, there is also a massive industrial interest on how central government services are to be organised, transferred and delivered under the different models for Scotland's future.

Of course, PCS has experience of restructuring and upheaval in machinery of government changes that occur under every Government in which departments are merged, reformed, broken up and dispersed, only to restructured again under the next administration.

The debate on Scottish public service delivery has been doing the rounds since the Home Rule campaign of 1978-1979, resurfaced in the Scottish Constitutional Convention in the 1990s and, of course, the future status and structure of the civil service has been the subject of much discussion and speculation since the establishment of the Scottish Parliament in 1999 and more prominently since the election of the SNP as a minority (in 2007) and then majority government (in 2011).

If we are to look at a more socialistic Scotland, what role must the civil service have? Her Majesty's Home Civil Service is the permanent bureaucracy of Crown employees that serve Her Majesty's Government and the three devolved administrations - the Scottish Government, the Welsh Assembly Government and the Northern Ireland Executive. As employees of the Crown, civil servants are not accountable to the UK or Scottish Parliaments, but retain statutory responsibilities and protections to ensure their political neutrality - unlike the US system in which the bureaucracy is cleared out at the end of every administration and the governing party appoints from amongst their own.

In spite of the antiquated and outdated notion of these public sector workers being 'servants' to the Crown, the British civil service over the two centuries of its existence has been regarded around the world as the 'gold standard' for public administration, comprising independence, probity and professional. The political classes often hold civil servants in contempt, characterised as all powerful and manipulative by the 1970s comedy of *Yes, Minister* and as ineffectual and irrelevant in the current viewing, *The Thick of It*.

Since Chancellor Gordon Brown stood up in the House of Commons in 2005 and announced to cross bench cheers that 100,000 civil service posts would be slashed, the civil service has seem the haemorrhaging of hundreds of thousands of jobs, taxes going uncollected, benefits delays, IT failures and long queues at airports and ports. Devolved areas are not immune - although PCS negotiated and won a no compulsory redundancy guarantee with the SNP administration in 2008 - over 2,000 jobs have been lost to the sector over that period, with many more to go.

Academics Roger Seifert and Mike Ironside undertook a study in 2005 for PCS called *The Case for Civil and Public Services* which considered an alternative vision of the civil service as an essential part of democratic society and tackles the economic orthodoxy that privatisation and marketisation of public services and cost cutting means greater efficiency. Whilst not addressing the national question that we face in Scotland today, this work is essential reading for anyone interested in how the civil service and public services must be placed in a more socialised democratic society.

But our union has also played a significant role in the shaping of the civil service we have today in devolved Scotland. Under the leadership of Pat Kelly, my predecessor as PCS Scottish Secretary, our union was fully engaged in the Constitutional Convention on the Scottish Parliament would be run, but also how Home Civil Service would serve the Scottish Government. At that time, it was carefully considered whether under Scottish devolution, there should be a separate Scottish civil service - distinct from the UK Home civil service - directly accountable to Scottish Ministers, with senior appointments such as the Permanent Secretary made by the First Minister, and for all aspects of civil service employment, pay, redundancy protection and pensions be brought to Edinburgh. That model was rejected. It would have been costly and cumbersome, difficult to administer and transfer pensions, rights under the Civil Service Compensation Scheme, the writing of a separate Scottish civil service code, tackling the mobility clause and transferability of civil servants which is held dearly particularly at senior grades. In the event, it was agreed that 'if it ain't broken, why fix it'.

Civil servants working for the Scottish Government, its agencies and NDPBs were retained as Home Civil Servants by agreement in the Constitutional Convention. Therefore, even they are subject to UK civil service pensions, redundancy compensation schemes and transferability. Pay however, is devolved to Scottish Ministers in the 40 bargaining areas covered by Scottish public sector pay policy. However, successive devolved administrations, including the current SNP administration, have adopted the UK Treasury guidance on civil service pay, and PCS members have received the same two year pay freeze imposed by John Swinney as their UK counterparts had imposed by George Osborne. Going forward Swinney will introduce a one per cent pay cap on civil servants - the same as Osborne in the year running up to the referendum in 2014.

Following years of attack by the UK government on the Civil Service Compensation Scheme, and the Principal Civil Service Pension Scheme, and the slavish adherence by Scottish Ministers to UK Cabinet Office pay freeze policies, many PCS members in the Scottish Government must now not just be asking whether the advantages of retaining that Home Civil Service status was worth it, but also whether a Scottish civil service controlled by Scottish Ministers of whatever political colour, would actually see any improvements on these fundamentals.

The appointment of the Permanent Secretary to the Scottish Government is under control of Whitehall. Far from 'going native', as reported in the Scottish media, Sir Peter Housden remains in close check with that very tight network of departmental permanent secretary mandarins. His background and experience before coming to Scotland cannot lead anyone to suggest that this appointment is at the behest of the First Minister. Like all senior civil servants, his role is to serve his political masters and deliver their policies and priorities. For the current administration in St Andrews House that means preparation for a referendum on independence. Of course, there have been debates raised on the public sector landscape in Scotland. The parting shot of Sir John Elvidge, the previous Permanent Secretary, was to suggest that local and central government in Scotland could be centralised under one service. Report after report point to joined-up governance, the most latest being the findings of the Christie Commission, chaired by the late Campbell Christie, a former leader of civil service unions and STUC.

What has proved impossible is to put any of this into action in any coherent and meaningful way across the silos of Scottish public sector delivery. Co-location, shared services, IT networks, workforce development, pay coherence and HR functions all remain cumbersomely out of step. Unions have consistently raised the need to take a long-term view on these matters, but our cries have fallen on deaf ears and closed minds, especially because to seriously address the parity issues would involve a project scale beyond the one year budget round or even the five year Scottish Government administrative term. Networks of senior civil servants, chief executives, human resource heads and leaders in health, local government and Scottish public services may come together to endlessly discuss these concepts, but it always come down to the same barrier 'subject to affordability'.

The Scottish Government staff complement today is, therefore, populated by Home civil servants, who are subject to all the UK civil service codes, protocols, pensions and benefits - although their employment and pay are devolved to Scottish Ministers. Decisions on senior civil service pay are retained with the Treasury, and the Permanent Secretary is appointed by the UK Prime Minister. This latter move was an attempt to retain the role as a non-political accounting officer. It is interesting to consider whether some of the media coverage on the views of Sir Peter Housden and his predecessor Sir John Elvidge may put that to the test.

It is worth noting that for different historical reasons, there is a separate civil service for Northern Ireland. The Northern Ireland Civil Services (NICS) while remaining Crown employees is distinct from the UK civil service and there is also a distinct Northern Ireland Civil Service Commissioners body. This is relevant because the 2007 SNP manifesto sought to create a Scottish civil service on the Northern Ireland model. PCS undertook a comparative study with our sister union in Northern Ireland, NIPSA, as to what this model might mean. Of course, it is impossible to discount the historical context in which the Northern Ireland civil service has formed over time and most importantly geo-political location, but our primary concern was what the Northern Ireland model would mean if applied to Scotland.

PCS findings were that it certainly meant lower pay - NICS pay is lower than elsewhere in the UK civil service. The Northern Ireland model would also mean a contractual relationship with UK departments such as the

Department for Work and Pensions, whose functions are carried out by NICS staff, whilst the policies and decisions over benefits level are retained by the UK government. Civil service pensions and transferability are retained in line with the Home Civil Service.

I wrote a piece for the *Guardian* (14 August 2012) public sector leaders' network blog in response to some whopping inaccuracies and assumptions about the nature and function of the civil service in Scotland. To be fair to the author, David Walker, to whom I was responding, his view is one held by many outside of the corridors of St Andrews House or Victoria Quay - that it would be simple and straight forward to create a Scottish civil service. Indeed, further devolved, delegated or post-independence transitional powers to Scotland will be subject to scrutiny, negotiation and may take years, if not decades in some cases to transfer. What is clear though is that in the post-referendum period between 2014 and the 2016 Scottish Parliament elections, it would be the current SNP administration that would be laying down the terms of that engagement. Post-election, SNP or Labour are likeliest to be running Scotland. Concerns over Labour's withdrawal from the principal of universal provision, and the SNP's obsession with low taxation, reducing corporation tax must be a concern for us all.

Our members, whether in UK or Scottish civil service departments, are struggling to manage pay cuts, jobs culls and the resultant service reduction. So what hope is there for a secure future for public services in Scotland? It is, therefore, essential that unions, not the political parties, lay down some firm principles on key industrial structures for workers not only in the civil service but across the public sector in Scotland that are non-negotiable. I have already listed civil service impartiality, professionalism and probity. Such notions of a civil service are being tested against not only the US politicised model. The current UK government's civil service reform agenda is seeking further inroads for the private sector at leadership role. Francis Maude's clever commissioning of the left-of-centre IPPR to study 'how to make the civil service more efficient and accountable' needs to be carefully watched. The awarding of the contract to an outside private body is in itself the first step in outsourcing core policy work of the civil service. Watch this space for the heralding of the French *pantouflange* system where senior civil servants step in and out of private sector industry roles over their career. I suspect, however, closer to home the Northern Ireland model is of greater appeal to Alex Salmond and John Swinney's vision of a future Scotland negotiating the transfer of powers from Whitehall.

At the forefront of the PCS agenda in the debate over the future of Scottish public services will be the protection of our members, the dedicated civil and public servants who have gone through more restructuring in the last 12 years in Scotland than in the entire history of the UK civil service. For those Scottish civil servants working in the Department for Work and Pensions - who have faced years of jobs cull within the department, jobcentre closures and the transferring of employability work to profit-driven companies - they will be looking to see what kind of welfare system a Scottish government - independent or further devolved would provide, and what their roles would be within it.

Tax workers, once again seeing their numbers depleted by job reductions and their expertise and skills replaced by lean management, are wondering why John Swinney had to announce - on the creation of Revenue Scotland to administer the new revenue powers brought in by the Scotland Act - that it would be cheaper to administer than HMRC. Scotland has been over many years a haven for tax dodging - our hillsides are still scarred with tax plantations, our land ownership is still in the hands of feudal lairds. Scotland needs to raise revenue, not cut it, and those powers need to be enforced.

Our members that work in the Home Office - Borders Agency, Passport Office and Immigration services want to know that their services will receive proper investment, but will also be backed up by policies that secure our country and are fair and humane and welcoming to peoples from other parts of the world. PCS national policy is to get rid of Trident. However, Ministry of Defence civilians need certainty that their jobs are secure and for those working in Trident-related activities that Scottish policies on defence diversification and alternative work is fit for all of those that have served and administered - not just engineers and serving personnel. Many staff of the Equalities and Human Rights Commission, Health and Safety Executive, Tribunals Services and other UK bodies working here in Scotland also want to know that a future Scotland will invest in their expertise but will also be strong on enforcement. And, for the many professionals working for the Department for International Development in East Kilbride - what vision of Scottish international relations and development policies will develop to match their global role in supporting the poor throughout the World.

So for PCS, what is essential is that there is proper consideration and detailed open discussions with those who carry out essential public services every day. My union has started a process to ensure that whatever Scotland decides, the people who work every day delivering key public services are at the forefront of developing a model for modern Scottish public services accountable to the people of Scotland. Crucial to the debate on Scotland's constitutional future will be how welfare, revenue, customs and defence work in Scotland might come under control of a future Scottish Government, and what will happen to the work carried out by thousands of civil servants located in Scotland but providing services for other parts of the UK. Whilst it will be natural that civil and public servants have a more direct industrial interest, perhaps more so than many other workers, in the future constitutional powers and governance of Scotland, this is not merely the only way that PCS is seeking to engage our members in this debate. We are focused on:

- fair and progressive taxation collected and enforced

- jobs and employment - public and private

- universal services and adequate social security when we need it and dignity for recipients

- decent pensions when we retire and state support and care for the elderly

- union freedoms, employment, equality and health and safety improvements and enforcements

Let's not crowd the map with too many different routes to the Scottish road to socialism, many of which lead nowhere, off cliff edges or are circular. Let's plan and build that routeway by securing and investing in the sort of Scotland that we want to live in and making sure that we provide the services and structures to deliver that.

Chapter 13

To make common cause

Bill Kidd

If there isn't a Scottish road to socialism, then there isn't one anywhere. The usual motivation behind this question is that for Scotland to go along the road to constitutional change people of a left-wing bent will demand that it will have to be a socialist independent Scotland or not independent at all. This tends to suggest that there really is a British road to socialism, though if there is it must be just beyond thon there sunlit pasture, around the next bend and over the next hill. It's a peculiar form of far-seeing insularity that infects the British left in Scotland which insists on harking back to great figures of the late nineteenth and early twentieth centuries such as Keir Hardie, John Wheatley and Jimmy Maxton, though not John Maclean, to talk of a particular species of internationalism which includes only the nations of these islands in the north west European Archipelago. This is to infer that only through the medium of the British state can Scots contribute to the class struggle, because it would seem capital is uniquely concentrated in London and that to separate the working class of this country from its brethren in England would be to abdicate responsibility from the fight to achieve a fairer society for all. After all a labourer in Bridgeton has more in common with a seamstress in Brick Lane than he has with the Duke of Buccleuch! Aye well such a revelatory analysis in stating the bleedin' obvious regarding the human condition obviously ranks alongside the, also early-twentieth century, scientific analysis of the universe in Einstein's $e = mc^2$.

Is that really to be the measure of success in the socialist movements' hopes and aspirations for the working class of Scotland? That we should aim to be the storm troopers of the British labour movement and that after almost sixty years since we started the steady slide of the Conservative and Unionist Party, and all it stands for, into its present state of near oblivion in our country, we should continue to know our place and allow the Eton/Winchester Oxbridge brigade to rule over us until the glorious day when the walls of the City of London are breached and capitalism is overthrown on the steps of the Bank of England?

Capitalism is global and its effects are such also but I have rarely heard a British socialist say that he/she wants to work hand in glove with the working class of say France. Why is that? Could it be that chauvinism is not simply a peculiarly nationalist trait? Or, is it that Britain itself is seen as a nation worth proselytising over by some on the left and that the workers of other nations are first and foremost economic rivals and not the potential allies they may be in advancing wages and conditions if only the imperialist mind-set was at last shrugged off?

Of course, there should, and indeed must, be continuing cooperation between unions in Scotland and the other nations of the present U.K. when global capital visits its predations on any of our communities. No question. However, this must be done on the basis of equity and the present devolved political situation in Scotland, Wales and Northern Ireland means that particularly those involved in working in the public sector have varying changes occurring in their wages and conditions, such as the introduction of the 'living wage', which can leave those who are not in receipt of such benefits discontented. With the potential for greater devolvement of powers, even if such may be unlikely under the present legislation at Westminster, this discontent could potentially grow. There seems no likelihood on the horizon that any government in London has the intention of emulating the changes in social conditions which all three devolved legislatures have made moves toward even within their limited powers. Could it be that an end of the self-satisfied former colonial power in Whitehall may see a change in the societal make up of England also? I believe that could be so.

The devolved settlement which set up the Scottish Parliament has seen the possibility of Tam Dayell's nightmare scenario of the slippery slope to independence developing into a potential cascade of nationalist sentiment, which should be seen as an opportunity for socialists to create new converts and develop new compacts with both local and national governments - and not as an impediment to the advancement towards a society of greater equalities.

The majority SNP Scottish Government (2011-) was not elected by many thousands of extra votes coming from the right for they stood fast in voting for the Union. It was through the votes of working class and poorer people, very many of them trade unionists who see their and their families best hopes for the future in being as far from the Toff culture as they can manage to be. People who see the 'social wage' as a human right and who do not want to be at the behest of a Westminster government which has as its aim an intention to eliminate the Common Weal - and which they not only did not vote for but have actively campaigned and voted against for years. It may be that not all of those are now thrilled to the SNP as a political party but they like the cut of its jib well enough as the country sails into the stormy economic seas ahead. Likewise, the SNP Scottish Government must acknowledge where that vote has come from historically.

Socialism in whatever guise, certainly in that of social democracy, has to be achieved through education and persuasion but it also has to be reached through taking forward those opportunities which present themselves at propitious moments in history and national independence has more than once been the vehicle for such social change when it has presented itself around the world. For those who profess the socialist cause to actively campaign against the working class of their own country having the opportunity to come closer to a state of society where equality of the mass of the people can exercise real political power is to condemn themselves to the status of political tourists and long-distance revolutionaries, where it's alright to cheer on Chavez in Venezuela but the brown stuff oozes when the issue is on your own doorstep.

The City of London is not the only repository of investment banking in these islands let alone Europe or certainly across the world. However, when a onetime academic of some repute, who followed a political route in order to emulate the proud past of his socialist hero, Jimmy Maxton, became a stooge of that Square Mile of economic mayhem and stood for all the world in white-tie and tails, looking like the corpulent ghost of Fred Astaire, to tell the 2005 Mansion House audience that under his Chancellorship there would be, 'not a light touch but a limited touch on the economy', then we saw the true scale of the Westminster cul-de-sac up which many a socialist commitment has disappeared. Gordon Brown was willing to play the patsy for Tony Blair, up to and including bank-rolling the illegal Iraq War, in order to have his turn at grinding the organ in which so many ordinary citizens hopes and dreams were turned to dust along with the delusions of socialists past and present.

Never more is this seen than in the desperation to sit at the big boy's table with greasy fingers wrapped about nuclear phallic symbols as 60 years on Britain's 'independent' nuclear deterrent is primed for upgrading. Like toilet roll salesman beaming in delight at his new Mondeo, a succession of British Labour Prime Ministers have posed proudly alongside this weapon of mass murder. Only this upgrade costs billions we do not have and if ever used would bring death and environmental destruction on a scale impossible to imagine. Introduced by a Labour Government and updated by them in the Sixties through the Chevelane, what socialist would contemplate such an abomination? A present to Bonnie Scotland.

Scotland is, of course, intrinsically no more a socialist country than any other. However, it does have a long history of educating all classes of the population and also a history which includes such as the eighteenth century Friends of the People; the 1820 Martyrs from the weavers uprising of that year; the Chartists; the Crofters League; the women-led Rent Strikes against profiteers during the First World War; Red Clydeside; and from the UCS work-in to the anti-poll tax campaigns. So, there is a history of which the people of Scotland are justifiably proud and which is neither inward looking nor Kailyard and it's on the shoulders of these honourable campaigns on behalf of the workers of this country that socialists should hoist themselves in order to see beyond the waters of the English Channel and the North Sea.

Socialism cannot for long survive in one country alone and certainly municipal socialism is a flash-in-the-pan. Therefore, is it not time for the fates to fall in line and for Scotland and the working classes of Scotland to see a future where they have the tools in their own hands to shape a Scotland in their own image and, thereby, make a break from an imperfect past and build common cause with others in England, Ireland, Wales, and France, South Africa, Japan, Australia and Bangladesh? Is there a Scottish road to socialism? No more and no less than there is a road to socialism in any other country in this world of ours and to get there we need to take responsibility for our own past, our own present and our own future.

Chapter 14

More than 15 hours of sovereignty

Richard Leonard

Fraternal greetings from the workers in the Old Home Land to their comrades in the new. The aim of our worldwide movement is the same - the Economic Emancipation of earth's toiling millions. (J Keir Hardie's postcard to Andrew Fisher, 14 December 1907)

There is a wonderful postcard archived in the National Library of Australia from Labour's first MP and leader, James Keir Hardie to Australia's first Labour Prime Minister, Andrew Fisher. Written in 1907 from one former Scottish miners' union organiser to another, it is a sharp reminder that at its heart the labour movement is - and always has been - part of a worldwide movement in a way that the movement for an independent Scotland simply is not and never will be. But it also draws our attention to the inescapable truth that our principal aim was - and is - above all else to secure economic liberation from the domination of a ruling capitalist class, not political emancipation from an imaginary colonial yoke to England.

Politics remains at its core a choice between left and right: tackling inequality, injustice and poverty and a redistribution of power, on the one hand, or relying on trickle-down and the free market, on the other.

The shift in power we strive for is not and has never been a shift in power from one Parliament or one set of politicians to another. It is the shift in power from those who own the wealth to those who through their hard work and endeavour actually create it. That's the decisive struggle, sometimes waged industrially but one which will ultimately be won politically. And, that's the real divide. Not one between England and Scotland, but the fundamental division between exploiter and exploited, rich and poor, earners and owners, and between ideas of left and right. There is a very real danger that the pursuit of an independent Scottish state is blurring these issues of class and inequality at the very time they should be in sharp focus.

The current attempts by the Tory-led government at a UK level to destroy the National Health Service in England and dismantle the welfare state right across the UK are nothing to do with their Englishness and everything to do with their Tory ideology. Similarly their raids on public sector pensions, their attacks on the weakest in our society, the removal of protection against unfair dismissal, and their pledge in David Cameron's own words to 'kill off the health and safety culture for good' are not anti-Scottish, but anti-working class. That's precisely why we need a unity of purpose from the labour and union movement in every part of these islands.

Founded to liberate people inside the workplace, unions increasingly have a critical role in people's self-realisation outside the workplace. The union movement unites the weak with the strong not merely to create a protest movement, still less to be a pure and simple wages movement or a narrow sectional interest but rather to forge the best organised force for social justice and change. It is critically also the democratic voice of workers in and against the current economic order and so at its best when not simply getting the most advantageous deal for union members in the current economic and social system but educating, agitating and organising for its radical and irrevocable change.

Unions need at all times to be agents of change and providers of the vitality and vision needed to bring the great change about. And because inequality and injustice is not simply about wealth but power, much of it extra-parliamentary, unions need to organise as part of a wider democratic and citizens' movement, as well as a workers movement.

How do we move forward to a socialist Scotland?

Economic relations determine power relations. The essence of capitalism is that property is power and its defining characteristic is the private ownership of the means of production, distribution and exchange. In Scotland, it can also be characterised as a highly centralised, concentrated and patriarchal pattern of private ownership at that. This is not a force of nature but a wilful act which is the ultimate source of the injustice, exploitation and growing inequality which we see all around us. It is an economic system which generates its own logic. So instead of an economy run for need it is one run for over-consumption, profits before people, and the over-accumulation of capital wealth in too few hands.

By contrast, a democratic socialist society is one where these power relations are changed, where there is economic as well as political democracy, most obviously socialised, common ownership and control in the economy and so a co-operative and ultimately a classless society. It must be a society where fear, privilege, injustice and monopoly cease to exist and one where money, materialism and economic power are neither the dominating values nor the sole measure of success. And so it must be sustainable and carry ambition beyond simply a different distribution of the same fruits of growth. Such a society will not emerge overnight and those who give the impression that a Yes vote in the 2014 referendum will give birth to an immaculate conception of socialism in Scotland are offering a false prospectus.

Whilst there is no doubt that an independent Scottish state is viable. The more relevant question is whether an independent Scottish state is preferable, would we be better or worse off and not just materially at that? For the Left the overarching question is whether it would make our underlying purpose and our historic goal - which is not merely to get the best deal for working people from the current economic and social system but to fundamentally change it - more or less achievable?

As the co-founder of the *Scottish Left Review,* Jimmy Reid (1984, p12), once put it:

> *My perception of the progression to socialism in Britain is a process towards a fuller democracy where government of the people, by the people, for the people applies in the economic as in the political sphere. It's ridiculous when decisions affecting entire communities, or the nation, can be taken in a democracy and not be subject to any form of democratic control or accountability. Yet it happens.*

So a humanisation of the economy and an end to the tyranny of the few over the many, that is, a redistribution of not just wealth but power is critical. Note too that this must not be confused with a simple transfer of wealth and power from private ownership to an unaccountable state machine. It must mean a transfer of power and ownership from capital to organised labour through new forms of common and co-operative ownership, self-management as well as municipal and national public ownership. And so, a co-operative - not a command - economy. At its very root, this challenges a narrow definition of democracy and calls for popular power not merely representative democracy, and so a new relationship between people and government. In so doing, it also challenges patriarchy and unequal access to power. Our history shows us that suffrage may confer the right to govern but not always the power to do so. Positive action is needed so that women in particular so long excluded from economic decision making will be included in the new economic democracy.

Of course, vested interests will not readily cede power and there remains a compelling need for state intervention, but with the emphasis on state intervention to secure popular control and accountability rather than popular intervention to secure state control. And this is precisely why I believe that Scottish political independence whilst perfectly possible would move us further away from bringing about socialist change not closer to it.

It may allow us to nibble at change but not make the breakthrough we need. Thus, the insufficiency of nationalism is that not only does it not concern itself with the transformation of those property and economic relations, but that it will also remove from the people of Scotland the best opportunity to change them.

The changing anatomy of the Scottish economy

The ownership of the Scottish economy has undergone a profound and fundamental change over the last century. From being owned by regional business dynasties drawing on local sources of investment funding, including local banks, today most of the commanding heights of the Scottish economy are quoted on the London Stock Exchange and are mediated and owned by institutions and corporations based either in the South East of England or increasingly, overseas.

By January 2012, the *Scottish Business Insider's* 'Top 500 companies in Scotland', ranked according to annualised turnover and pre-tax profit, revealed a Top 20 dominated by energy particularly oil and gas multinationals and financial services corporations. With the exception of the drinks giant, William Grant & Sons which is family owned, and Scottish Water which is publicly owned, all the rest are either public limited companies listed on the London Stock Exchange or wholly owned subsidiaries of big multinational corporations. The Scottish Government publishes its own annual figures on the ultimate ownership of Scottish registered companies. This also shows that more and more of the commanding heights of the Scottish economy are owned outside Scotland. The most recent figures reveal that amongst larger enterprises (defined as those employing 250 people or more) 64 per cent of employment and 78 per cent of turnover is in enterprises with ultimate ownership outside Scotland. This compares to 54 per cent of employment and 69 per cent of turnover ten years ago.

Amongst larger enterprises in the manufacturing sector the results are even starker with 72 per cent of employment and as much as 87 per cent of turnover in companies owned outside of Scotland. This compares to 60 per cent of employment and 71 per cent of turnover a decade ago. And, these figures are based on Scottish registered companies only. They do not include big supermarket chains like Tesco and Asda, or military industrial corporations like Rolls Royce and BAE Systems which have a huge turnover in Scotland, and are major employers but do not separately register here.

One major accelerator of this trend of rising external and concentrated ownership has been privatisation. Take the old South of Scotland Electricity Board as an example. Initially broken up into Scottish Power and Scottish Nuclear (later British Energy), its constituent parts are now owned by the Spanish trans-national corporation, Iberdrola, and the French public corporation EDF. The other significant catalyst has been the 'Big Bang' deregulation of the City of London in 1986 which created the most open and ferocious predator style economy in the world. It was built on the Thatcherite nightmare of an economy devoid of ethics but geared to short-term gain and greed. It gorged on the transfer of existing assets not the creation of new ones and the remorseless pursuit of capital gains overseas was put before support for our indigenous productive base. It was - and remains - even after the global financial meltdown one of the worst examples of power without accountability.

There is no longer a coherent Scottish business network (see Baird *et al.*, 2007). External institutional investors are dominant and the lines of accountability run outside Scotland, invariably via the London Stock Exchange, increasingly on their way to overseas boardrooms. This is not to talk Scotland down but to talk the hard facts of the Scottish economy today. For with ownership comes domination and Scotland's recent economic history tells of deindustrialisation going hand-in-hand with a denuding of ownership on a grand scale. A branch plant economy is a vulnerable place for working people to be especially in an era where classic free trade economics and laissez faire industrial policy are in the ascendancy.

The democratic road to socialism

The importance of this pattern of ownership to any democratic socialist is that it first illuminates and then determines the level we need to intervene at. Economic power does not lie in Scotland. It still predominantly lies at a UK level. That is why if socialism is defined as the ownership or control of the means of production by the people, it cannot be secured in Scotland on its own. And so in this sense alone nationalism is not a liberating ideology but an inhibiting one.

This is not a call for a British or a Scottish road to socialism but for a democratic road to socialism. At its centre will be the ballot box, but it requires a participatory democracy especially in the economy through organised labour. And it is not exclusively a parliamentary road in the sense that change can come from below including through local as well as central government. Indeed, decentralisation and localism are important. Strong self-sufficient local government with significant powers devolved to it can help bring about real change from below. And as pioneers like John Wheatley showed local practical socialism can sow the seeds for change on a national scale.

There are other economic considerations too when weighing up calls for an independent Scottish state. According to the most recent Global Connections Survey, published by the Scottish Government, in 2010 the annual value of the export of goods and services from Scotland to the rest of the United Kingdom was estimated at £44.9bn. The value of exports from Scotland to the rest of the world was estimated at £22bn. In other words, Scotland is not only in a highly advanced state of industrial integration with the rest of the UK, it is also economically interdependent too. Scotland exports more than twice as much to England, Wales and Northern Ireland as we do to the whole of the rest of the world put together. The fiscal relationship is also well charted, if a little contentious, depending on the counting of oil and gas revenues and the apportionment of burdens like the banks bail out: £497bn of toxic assets from the Legacy Lending Books of RBS and HBOS alone were protected by public money.

But Treasury estimates in 2011/12 show that because of the redistributive Barnett Formula, identifiable public expenditure per capita in Scotland was £10,088 compared to £8,491 in England: that's an additional 18.8 per cent of public spending per head of population.

Scotland is part of a unique sterling single currency zone too: a position favoured by the SNP post-independence. Indeed, the SNP's vision of the Scottish state looks remarkably similar to the British state with the same head of state, the same currency and monetary governance, defence alliance and European Union membership. Questions, therefore, arise about what precisely 'independence' would mean economically: monetary wise, fiscally and, of course, industrially. Where lies the benefit in Scotland's elected representatives giving up a direct vote on the fiscal and monetary policy framework of Scotland's largest market, its biggest economic area, its currency control including exchange and interest rates and the level where corporate power rests? Of course, it can be done, but what would be the advantage?

It was Aneurin Bevan who wrote in the opening to his seminal work, *In Place of Fear*, that the fundamental question for socialists was simple: 'Where was power and which the road to it?' If we want to build a democratic socialist future for Scotland we need to act at the level where power lies. And so, the Scottish economy is not autonomous but integrated, not self-sufficient but essentially a branch plant. Whilst political separation can be contemplated, economic separation is virtually impossible. One without the other renders the promise of socialism in Scotland rather hollow.

A politically independent Scottish state may mean the end of Britain as a politically defined entity but it would have little impact on British state power which would continue to dominate the economy of Scotland whether the people of Scotland and our representatives were withdrawn from it or not. Scottish independence would also mean abandoning the very democratic road along which working people in Scotland, jointly with those in the rest of these islands could hold to account and even control corporate and economic decision makers. If we are to have any semblance of economic and industrial democracy that is the level at which we need to intervene.

To take another example the economic power owned by working people but not controlled by working people in our pension and insurance funds. This too is predominantly organised at the UK level, with the largest UK pension funds. According to the *Pensions Pocket Book 2011*, the BT Pension Scheme (£31bn), Universities Superannuation Scheme Ltd (£22bn); Railways Pension Scheme (£20bn); Royal Mail Pension Plan (£20bn) and Electricity Supply Pension Scheme (£19bn) are all British wide in their membership and organisation. So if democratic reform of pension and insurance funds is, as I believe it should be, a significant element of new left strategy to re-direct investment and to provide for both popular socialised ownership and control in the economy it is at the UK level that reform will be at its most effective.

The union movement, of course, is also predominantly organised at a British level, and since the industrial revolution it is at this level that working class unity has found expression. Which is not to say that a union could not cope with the creation of a separate Scottish state for, of course, it could. But the litmus test remains: does it strengthen or weaken organisation and does it bring the power shift that we really need closer or does it push it further away? Does it change the structures of domination and exploitation in society and bring about a fundamental redistribution of power, property and provision? In my view it does not.

Is socialism a real prospect in contemporary Britain?

I remain optimistic that change can be brought about at a broader British level. This is not driven by a faith in one state or one flag over another, but because I genuinely believe that co-operating, campaigning and organising at that level still remains by virtue of size, solidarity and therefore popular power our best hope of bringing about socialism in our time. We need to counter the cynicism sown that change is not possible at all or, indeed, only possible by turning inward not outward. And we need to challenge any hint of chauvinism that being Scottish provides any greater or lesser claims on radical traditions or democratic socialist advance compared to other parts of these islands. Nationality should have less not more meaning in a socialist civilisation.

Of course, there have been setbacks and defeats and it will require sustained, strenuous and intelligent effort but we should have the confidence not just to carry on but to press on. Every battle for social and economic justice is one more step on the march for social and economic equality. Working people combining and taking the initiative can bring about a shift in power: the Chartist radicals who won the vote, the campaigners for women's suffrage and emancipation, the pioneers who built the union movement and the great co-operators from Robert Owen onwards, the generation which gave us the welfare state from the cradle to grave including the National Health Service, campaigners for the right to work, for women's rights and equal pay and treatment, as well as international struggles like the Anti-Apartheid Movement all worked according to higher ideals and so captured the mood of a rising class. That same idealism and combination can bring about democratic socialist advance today.

To reflect on this our shared history is not to wistfully look backwards but to draw inspiration for the future. Just as the challenge at the start of the last century was winning and extending political democracy, so the great challenge for our age is winning and extending, both industrial and a wider economic democracy. There are those who say this is not 'realistic' but as Raymond Williams (1988, p257) with insight remarked: "Let's be realistic' probably more often means, 'let us accept the limits of the situation' (limits meaning hard facts, often of power or money in their existing and established forms) than 'let us look at the whole truth of this situation' (which can allow that an existing reality is changeable or changing).'

There is much that remains to be done in a devolved Scotland. Land ownership is still the narrowest in Western Europe with 343 landlords owning 50 per cent of all private land in Scotland, and nearly all of them the old aristocracy. This relic of feudalism is unfinished business which can be tackled by a devolved home rule Parliament. In a country of 5.25m people with a land mass of over 19m acres it is a matter of shame that we have homelessness, a shortage of decent affordable housing, poverty and mass unemployment. Land reform is critical to Scotland's democratic and economic renewal and provides the means of redistributing not only wealth, but power.

The opportunity to create a democratically run investment and reconstruction bank and a vibrant workers co-operative sector along continental European lines has so far been missed. In Italy, the Marcora Law gives workers the statutory right to bid for their place of work if it is facing closure. In Scotland, the Land Reform Act gives communities the right to bid for land when it is put up for sale. Why not give workers and communities the chance to convert an enterprise to democratic ownership when it is put up for sale, facing a takeover bid, threatened with closure or asset stripping? As many as 50,000 people work in a network of workers co-operatives in the Mondragon Region of northern Spain. Why shouldn't we have the bold vision of Scotland in European terms becoming a 'Mondragon of the North'? This may require additional powers for the Scottish Parliament but could be implemented by a re-invigorated Co-operative Development Scotland with powers and resources for change, together with state support for the development of worker and community alternative plans.

There is also ample scope under the present devolution of power to strengthen the powers of Scottish local government and introduce progressive local tax reform and so help support a municipal contribution to travelling down the road to socialism with popular support from below. There is room too to harness the powers of public sector pension funds to aid in the regeneration of local economies, including the provision of alternatives to private finance in the public realm including housing and infrastructure. And following the winding up of the UK Defence Diversification Agency in 2007, there has existed the opportunity to set up a Scottish Defence Conversion Agency working to social and industrial not defence goals. In turn, this may provide a template for a wider Just Transition Agency aimed at moving us from a toxic economy to a sustainable society, where every job is a green job and the whole economy is guided by social usefulness and human need rather than naked profiteering.

For us the political option should not be between independence or the union but about taking back power from the elites who run the country without accountability at the moment. That is the most important self-determination we should seek. Not bestowing sovereignty in the people for 15 hours in a one day referendum but permanently shifting power back to the people. A once and for all shift so that democracy can be properly exercised and power held to account. If we want to pursue the goal of a more equal, socially, economically and environmentally just Scotland, and so realise the vision of the pioneers of the labour movement who believed that the salvation of the community lay in the collective ownership of industrial capital and land and an end to monopoly and unaccountable corporate power, then it is not to nationalism or patriotism but to democratic socialism that we will find the alternatives and the solutions.

Chapter 15

It's not about day one

John McAllion

After a series of early set-backs during the American Civil War, and on hearing one of his generals boast about the licking he intended to give the Confederate Army, Union President, Abraham Lincoln commented: 'The hen is the wisest of all animal creation because she never cackles until the egg is laid.'

All socialists would do well to heed Abe's wise advice when individually or collectively plotting the way forward to the building of a workers' paradise. History is littered with socialist projects that failed to deliver the change their creators had dreamed of. Again, and again, different worlds were imagined that never came to pass. A typical example can be found in the declaration of the founding congress of the Second International in Paris in 1889: 'Our aim is the emancipation of the workers, the abolition of wage-labour and the creation of a society in which all women and men … will enjoy the wealth produced by the work of all workers.' Exactly one hundred years later, the Berlin Wall fell and with it the last hope of the twentieth century's 'really existing socialism'. In truth, the realities of workers lives in the Soviet Union and its satellites in Eastern Europe bore little relation to the different world dreamed of by the likes of Engels, Hardie and Plekhanov, all of whom were among the delegates attending the Paris congress one hundred years earlier.

The history of the nineteenth and twentieth centuries is haunted by disappointed socialists confounded by the chasm between their revolutionary predictions of what would happen and the terrible capitalist realities of what actually did happen. In my own time, I have witnessed the collapse of soviet communism, the embrace of capitalism by an authoritarian Chinese Communist Party and the dead-end of a British parliamentary road to socialism. There are many other examples that could be added to that already depressing list. There is more than a hint of truth in one modern commentator's detection of similarities between much modern communist and socialist ideology and the thinking of various religious millenarians from our distant past. Self-styled eighteenth century prophets such as Richard Brothers read the *Book of Revelation* and foretold the coming of a time when god would ensure there '... shall be no more war, no more want, no more wickedness, but all be peace, plenty and virtue.'

Twentieth century communists and socialists rejected all religion, but they too believed themselves to be close to an end-time when landed and industrial wealth would come under worker and peasant control, thus, abolishing poverty; a time when world peace would bring an end to global killing and when all inequalities based on class, sex, nationality or religion would be abolished. Richard Brothers ended his days in an eighteenth century mad-house, his millenarian dreams unrealised. Many twentieth century Bolsheviks and Chinese communists ended their days in the Gulag or facing a firing squad, their hopes of socialism crushed beneath the tyranny of their respective one-party states. Today's few remaining British road socialists cling on desperately to the wreckage of a party re-modelled along one-nation bourgeois lines and purged of any trace of socialist or class content.

Past failures, of course, need not mean continuing failure in the future. Mick McGahey was surely correct when he predicted that the working class would go from defeat to defeat to final victory. But that final victory will only become possible if we learn the bitter lessons of all of the defeats inflicted along the way. Above all, it will only be possible if we apply those lessons realistically to a clear analysis of our ever-changing twenty first century. What then is to be done? Firstly, let me be clear about what I mean by socialism. The old Clause Four of the Labour party is as good a place to begin as any:

> *To secure for the workers by hand or by brain the full fruits of their industry and the most equitable distribution thereof that may be possible upon the basis of the common ownership of the means of production, distribution and exchange, and the best obtainable system of popular administration and control of each industry or service.*

It is no detailed manifesto. It is silent on how to achieve its aim. It was coined in an age very different from our own. It had an anti-revolutionary purpose. It has nothing to say on a range of modern challenges such as climate change, racism, imperialism or the threat of nuclear annihilation. Yet it represents a fundamental re-ordering of our capitalist economic system in favour of working men and women. It also opens up the possibility that our future can be determined democratically. Of course, stated in these simple terms, it might also be dismissed as just another manifestation of millenarian aspiration on the left, doomed never to be realised. It survived less than eighty years as part of the British Labour project. Yet, while it survived, it provided a direction of travel for British Labour that generated progressive change including the NHS, the welfare state, progressive taxation, public ownership and much more.

The value of Clause Four as a kind of lodestar towards which the Labour project was proceeding should not be underestimated. Labour governments, dominated by the centre-right, never seriously considered its full implementation. But while it was there, it served to pull the policies of Labour governments in a progressive direction. Even a right-wing Chancellor like Dennis Healey felt obliged to threaten to 'squeeze property speculators until the pips squeak' and to tax the rich until there were 'howls of anguish'. No-one should underestimate the importance to the New Labour project of eradicating any surviving links the party might have had with Clause Four socialism. New Labour laid the blame for four successive election defeats on the 'old left'. It rejected the left-right divide in politics. It embraced the free market and the private sector. Public ownership was ruled out. The unions would get no favours from them. Low taxes and means testing were public imperatives. Blair's scrapping of Clause Four did not modernise 'old' Labour. It murdered it.

The original instigators of New Labour have now moved on to reap their financial rewards in the private sector. But their legacy remains firmly in place. 'Red Ed' Miliband currently invokes the one nation politics of a nineteenth century Tory Prime Minister, while refusing to reverse Tory cuts and threatening more cuts by a future Labour government. Scottish Labour leader, Johann Lamont, has firmly nailed her political colours to the mast of economic austerity and means-testing. The British parliamentary road to socialism, comrades, is at an end.

But as one road closes, others open up. The potential for progressive change on this island is no longer locked into the mechanism of the British state. That state itself has been in economic and political decline since the 1970s. The existence of the Scottish Parliament and the Welsh and Northern Ireland assemblies is testament not to Britain's continuing strength but to its gathering weakness. Labour's devolved parliament in Edinburgh was supposed to 'kill nationalism stone dead'. Instead, it has created a unionist nightmare - a majority nationalist government that will usher in an independence referendum. A Scottish road to socialism is no longer a pipe dream. There will be a referendum on Scottish independence. The break-up of Britain could be one Scotland-wide poll away. Scotland could be standing on the threshold of a new political era for itself and for all of the other nations on these islands. Like the lion in William McIlvanney's poem, Scotland's voters can now smell 'the terrible distances of freedom' Of course, like that lion, they may yet opt to play safe and stick with the British state they know.

Scotland's socialists, however, now have to choose between two alternative nation states. They should not make that choice on the basis of one form of national identity being preferable or superior to another. Nor should they hide behind the lazy assumption that in class terms Britain's multinational character trumps Scotland's small nation status. Banging on about solidarity with the victims of capitalism, north and south of the Scotland/England border, begins to ring hollow when that same spirit of solidarity suddenly stops at the English Channel and the Irish Sea.

Workers in Athens, Barcelona, Turin and Dublin are as much in need of our solidarity as workers in the rest of Britain. As the working class in Greece is put to the economic sword and elected government is sabotaged in the birthplace of democracy; as Spain and Portugal teeter on the brink of economic collapse; as Eurozone unemployment levels hit record highs, many on the British Left continue to argue in support of a Britain that outlaws solidarity action between workers within and across national boundaries. They advocate withdrawal from a multinational EU on the basis of its neo-liberalism and centralisation while supporting a multinational UK that is equally neo-liberal and centralist.

The question of Scottish independence demands a much higher and more consistent level of debate on the left than that. Socialists cannot allow themselves to be diverted into a constitutional cul-de-sac where the sole focus is the threat to our 300 year-old union with England. For example, the 'Better Together' campaign's attempt to exploit Team GB's success in the Olympics and Paralympics borders on the banal. What Sir Chris Hoy MBE thinks about Scotland's constitutional future matters only to the extent that he, like everyone else, will have one vote in the referendum.

Nor should we respond to other 'Better Together' scaremongering such as Scots being denied access to BBC English based programmes like 'Eastenders' or 'Match of the Day' . Pathetic attempts to distract public attention away from serious issues of public policy deserve only our contempt. Our unfailing focus should be on the central question of whether Scottish independence will help or hinder the struggle for socialist and progressive change on these islands. Unfortunately, the major stakeholder in the 'Yes Scotland' campaign thinks otherwise. There are undoubtedly socialists in the SNP. The SNP itself, however, is not and never has been socialist. Its only objective is independence. Every other consideration is secondary to that overriding goal. This explains its current strategy of trying to secure a yes majority in 2014 by stealth.

Fearful of opinion polls showing continuing support for the union, the SNP leadership has set out to reassure worried voters that independence will not change anything much. The SNP's independent Scotland will retain the monarchy, the pound sterling, military bases along with membership of nuclear-armed NATO and the European Union. It will be fiscally responsible. It will be pro-business. People's everyday lives will go on as usual. The only real difference will be that we choose to embrace neo-liberalism ourselves rather than having it imposed upon us from the outside.

Scottish socialists cannot be fellow travellers on such an SNP road to independence. If the 'Yes Scotland' campaign is to be genuinely a big tent within which socialists, greens, social democrats and nationalists can work together for a yes majority, then 'Yes Scotland' will not only have to distance itself from the SNP strategy but will also need to allow space for socialists and greens to articulate very different visions of what independence will mean. In articulating that different vision, socialists now need to come up with specifics of what an independent Scottish socialist republic will look like. For the foreseeable future, it will continue as a parliamentary democracy. Since the arrival of universal suffrage in 1928, representative democracy has become part of our political DNA. There is no realistic alternative to an elected Parliament in an independent Scotland.

What matters is the nature of that Parliament. If it is to be truly representative, it will be elected by proportional representation. In a socialist Scotland, the people and only the people are sovereign. Political parties will continue to exist but not necessarily as they are now constituted. Recent SNP electoral success owes more to the party's left-of-centre policies than it does to support for their core policy of independence.

George Galloway's comment that every country needs a Labour Party registers with many people. The problem for George and other unionists is that Britain currently has no such party. A mass democratic party rooted in the Scottish union movement could yet be the biggest winner in an independent Scotland. Such a party could learn from the mistakes of New Labour and 'old' Labour alike. A revised version of the old Clause Four could guarantee its socialist direction of travel. Embracing popular sovereignty and political pluralism could safeguard it from the monolithic one party city states of recent memory in the West of Scotland.

Politics, of course, can never be the preserve of parliamentarians. Politics is too important to be left in the hands of those who see it as a paid profession. There should be a written constitution, incorporating a Bill of Rights, and guaranteeing popular sovereignty, the liberty of the individual, freedom of speech and association, the role of civil society and the limits to parliamentary and executive power. The Parliament itself should be open and accessible to all with every citizen able to lobby it through a powerful petitioning system.

Given historic voting patterns, there will be a powerful left of centre bloc in such an independent Parliament. This Scottish left, in whatever party form it assumes, can then begin the agitation for socialist and progressive policies to be implemented. It will require to be supported outside Parliament by an organised labour movement prepared to use its industrial and economic muscle in defence of its members' wider economic, social and political interests. Environmentalist, anti-poverty, civil liberty and other civil society campaigns will also need to be brought on board if the old social and economic order is to be seriously challenged. A parliamentary majority on its own can never hope to take on and defeat a deep-rooted conservative establishment that will undoubtedly survive the shock of political independence. Only a movement with genuine grassroots popular support will be able to withstand the assaults of privilege.

Murdoch's *Sun* and other privately owned press and media outlets will rage against progressive change. The corporate and business sector will unite in opposition to anything that threatens their profits. Legal, civil service and military elites will seek to impose limits to what can or cannot be done. The political right will rally behind a reactionary vision of another Scotland open to business and integrated into the neo-liberal world order.

Independence alone is no guarantee of socialist advance. However, it does open up the terrain for such advance. There is currently a British all party consensus around the model of a low-tax, deregulated economy as a means of attracting foreign inward investment and promoting economic growth. It is a model supported in the past by an SNP leadership keen to cut corporation tax in pursuit of what they believe would be a Celtic lion economy. Yet there is an alternative social democratic model that involves higher levels of taxation and substantial public investment in infrastructure and a welfare state universally available to all. The best example of this model is Norway, the country currently rated number one in the United Nation's Human Development Index. Norway has a higher level of life expectancy, better literacy and educational standards and enjoys a standard of living among the highest in the world. It has low unemployment and almost a third of its workers are employed by the state. It is not a member of the European Union but maintains close relations through its membership of the European Economic Area, the WTO and the OECD. Norway has its own currency.

It does not follow that independence will transform Scotland into another Norway. What is certain, however, is that sticking with Britain will guarantee that Scotland can never become another Norway. British 'big power' status ties Scotland into weapons of mass destruction and third highest military spending in the world after the US and China. It locks us into what is effectively a warfare state. Britain has been involved in 22 different wars or conflicts since 1945. It saddles us with the toughest anti-union laws in Europe. It guarantees that our economic interests will always be secondary to those of the powerful financial services sector in the city of London.

History teaches us that you cannot dream socialism into existence. You need a plan of action that starts from we are in the present. We find ourselves in a unitary, multi-national British state that is politically locked into a neo-liberal world order. In 2014, we have the opportunity to break free from that state and to start again in a newly independent country. The first step is to win a yes majority in the referendum. That will only be possible if in the year or so we can convince our fellow citizens that the risks involved in breaking free from Britain are worth a candle. Promising socialism the day after independence will convince no-one. Offering a vision of a modern parliamentary democracy based on popular sovereignty and human rights and with the potential to follow the social democratic model of economic development is more realistic and more likely to win the necessary support. It may not be socialism as such. It will at least get us back on the road to socialism.

Chapter 16
A nail in the coffin of the British State

Mhairi McAlpine

The struggle for Scottish independence is, at its heart, an anti-colonial struggle. It is worth stating that upfront, for although it is implicit in a lot of the analyses that socialists bring to bear on the independence movement, many shy away from using the term. The nation state is a problematic entity for socialists. All but the most committed Stalinist would recognise that socialism in one country is impossible. There is no Scottish road to socialism. However, Scottish independence is a blow at the heart of imperialism, a fracture in the hegemony of the Western powers and their dominance. And as such it is a step towards genuine socialism, a socialism which can be nothing but global. The referendum in 2014 is an opportunity to throw off the shackles of empire, not only for the good of the people who live in Scotland, but for peoples across the world.

The 1707 Act of Union was a declaration of civil war on the people of Scotland from its ruling class. Right at the start of the shift from feudalism to capitalism, people were burned from their homes and left to die of exposure on hillsides, because the land on which they lived and toiled could make more money if they did not live on it. The financial appeasement given in the form of industrial investment saw the desire for Scottish independence diminish as the security of being part of an imperial power bought off the rebellious Scots - locating the investment within a proximal land with close links between the capital invested there and the political domination needed to secure it.

The referendum in 2014, will determine how Scotland takes its place in the world, and the terms of our engagement on the international stage as well as being able to take full fiscal control of our resources and determining ourselves where our priorities lie. We will gain full control over our social security spending, tax raising powers and borders, while being able to determine our own defence and foreign affairs strategies - all of which have thus far been denied to us. But, as the example of Cuba shows us, no country is an island entire unto itself. We will still be subject to the whims of international capital which no matter how much we struggle will always try to co-opt us to its purposes.

The ability to raise and spend our own revenue raises critical questions about what the priorities are for our future nation. The UK government's spending on lavish extravaganzas and bigger and better toys for the military belies its belief in circuses to distract the masses from its war-mongering agenda. With full fiscal control, greater transparency over where our income and spending are going will enable the Scottish people to determine its own priorities. For tempting although it may be to celebrate our independence once we get it, we should never forget Guevara's words that although national liberation is a blow to the world imperial system, it is only when the economic domination over a people is ended that true liberation is achieved.

The recent fiasco over the golf course in Aberdeenshire - where approval was given to Donald Trump to build a playground for the rich, destroying the homes and livelihoods of those living there, by Alex Salmond in the face of massive local opposition is testimony that independence alone cannot save us from the power of international capitalism and those within our nation who would capitulate to it. Instead, we must look to developing our own resources, capacities and capabilities with an eye on its effects on the rest of the world.

Nationalism is a tempting ideology, the plucky little nation up against the world, and it is easy to slip into nationalist rhetoric when advocating for independence, but that is a dangerous route to go down and one which we should challenge wherever and whenever it appears, not only from self-identified nationalists, but also from those who seek to use it to garner popular support.

Nationalism is on the rise in Europe. Conflicts within Europe, through the European Central Bank's interference in the financial affairs of members of the Eurozone and the construction of Fortress Europe, have seen a rise in nationalist sentiment and the far right. Its most worrying manifestation is in Greece, where an openly fascist party commands up to 10 per cent of the popular support, while its members beat, maim and kill third world migrants on its streets. But Greece is only part of a wave of neo-nazi resurgence across the continent. Scotland is one of the few places in Europe which has no history of fascist ideology gaining a grip, but it would not be the first nation to find its struggle for national liberation hijacked by those with sinister ends. In contrast, there are some nasty right-wing types hanging onto the coat-tails of the unionist bandwagon, promoting a Brit-nationalist ideology all wrapped up in a Union Jack.

Our movement must be internationalist for there can be no freedom for any wo/man while another is enslaved. Socialists in the West have long supported struggles of national liberation all across the world, from the decolonisation of Africa to the ongoing struggle in occupied Palestine. In most of these cases, the relationship between the coloniser and the colonised is obvious. Within the West, and particularly in the context of Scottish Independence, that relationship is far more complex. For we should never forget that Scotland was - and still is - a constituent part of the British Empire. Investment flowed into Scotland in the nineteenth century from the enslavement, murder and theft from peoples all across the globe. We cannot escape our history, but we can change our future. We can reject the British state and all that it stands for, refuse to remain a part of a diminished empire which holds the world to ransom with weapons of mass destruction, which holds a military alliance with the current imperial superpower and uses its economic power to force others to bend to its will.

As we take our place in the world, we should not only look at how our independence can benefit those suffering from the ongoing effects of colonisation, but also what they can teach us about the process of liberation. Franz Fanon has explained how one of the first steps in achieving liberation is to develop the national culture that the colonial power has upsurped and suppressed. This is not the stultified 'tartan and shortbread' so beloved of the ruling class any more than any other appropriated national culture sold back to the natives, but the living breathing culture that the people create of their own accord. The upsurge in a distinct Scottish cultural identity from the 1980s onwards is one which has carried the independence movement forward and it is a momentum that we should be careful not to lose. At the same time, Fanon gave warning that once national liberation had been achieved and the coloniser gone, the bourgeoisie would seize their chance to nab the reins of power, whose interests in time become allied with that of the former coloniser - the maximal exploitation of the natural and human resources of the country. It is a warning we should heed. While in Africa the national bourgeoisie rose from nowhere, within Scotland there is a ruling class fully formed, currently it aligns itself with the British state, but in its absence would sell us out just easily.

It is also worth looking to Africa for examples of states which have liberated themselves from more powerful neighbours - notionally considered equals, where one geographic area exploited the other for its own benefit. Both Eritrea and South Sudan have liberated themselves from a more powerful neighbour. The initial hopes of both states - that the women's liberation and intellectual freedom the Eritrean liberation movement activated and the hopes of a respectful peace in South Sudan have not materialised, as Eritrean women have been pushed back into traditional roles now that the independence movement is over and its only university has been closed, while South Sudan, bumps along in an uneasy state of tension with its northern neighbour. These situations highlight the need for the independence movement not only to fight for liberation, but to encapsulate and articulate a vision of the society that we wish to see, and to view independence not as an end goal, but as a milestone on the road.

We need to build a vision of Scotland which is not only oppositional to the current UK state, but which embodies our hopes for the new society. At the moment we have London rule, and we must be wary of that turning into Edinburgh rule, where a concentration of capital makes decisions on behalf of the rest of Scotland in the interests of the domestic ruling class. We have impoverished inner city areas with some of the lowest life expectancies in Europe, and at the same time rural communities heavily dependent on subsistence farming. We have new citizens from all over the world enriching our culture and national life, as well as a diversity of indigenous ethnic groups, such as the Gaels, the Scots-Irish and the travellers. We must ensure that our new society takes into account the needs of all of our citizens. A haughty Edinburgh rule may bring our master closers, but does nothing to eliminate our subjugation.

At this time, when the crisis in global capitalism is hitting Europe's shores, and austerity measures are touted as the only game in town we should be mindful of what we consider is essential. The health and education of the populace is an investment far greater than any capital project; meaningful work, which allows people to contribute to our new nation is critical, and the people's safety to go about their business is an important element of the state. In prioritising these issues, we should be remember that commerce and industry should work in the interests of the people and that the safety and security of our population is best guarenteed when people lack fear of a state and its actions, rather than because it has bigger weapons - be those weapons nuclear or hand held.

In a world which is facing ecological crisis, with global warming and climate change we must take our newly gained national responsibilities seriously, committing ourselves to reducing the hoovering of resources from the planet that the British Empire has been so good at and critically examine the resources - both natural and human - that we have on these shores and look at how best we can utilise these resources for the benefit our people without damaging the resources of others.

In a world where religious tensions are utilised to isolate, marginalise and cause conflict between peoples, we must respect the rights those with faith, yet be wary of those who seek to use that faith to justify breaching the rights of others. Valuing the faith groups of Scotland and accepting the right of individuals to practice their faith in a manner of their choosing does not preclude intervention to prevent organised faith groups seeking to impose their values on those who do not share their belief.

The situation of women in our new society must be carefully considered. Moving from a position of domestic servitude, where our resources are collected and doled back out to us under the Barnett formula, we are reminded of the position that many women, particularly young mothers are placed in - dependent upon male providers to see to the needs of themselves and their children. Liberating women not only means strengthening policies of violence against women, allowing a base level of security for half our population, but also ensuring that women have a level of economic independence which enables them to fulfil their potential.

That violence against women must take into account the sexualised violence which is tolerated throughout our society in the form of prostitution and pornography, where the objectification and sexual servitude of women is sold. Creating a society which values women means eradicating the abuse they face, not only for those directly involved in the sex industry, but for other women who live with the consequences of those who freely abuse women through prostitution and pornography living among us.

The cuts currently being imposed by the UK government are exacerbating the situation of women. Not only are women finding themselves laid off in higher numbers as the public sector where women workers - particularly higher paid women workers - congregate, but the majority of benefit cuts come directly out of women's pockets. Beyond the direct cuts that women face, they are also expected to shoulder the burden of secondary cuts, in their traditional roles as carers. The cuts to housing benefit will see young people in particular unable to establish or maintain an independent lifestyle making them reliant on family support - both practical and financial for longer periods of time, while the cuts to disability benefit will reduce the ability of disabled people to pay for essential equipment to cater for their needs, not only reducing their own autonomy, but also imposing a duty on others to support them, and that carer support more heavily falls upon women.

Provision for when women cannot provide for themselves and their families - during confinement and post-childbirth - must be protected, but moreover the state must provide security to women in their employment roles, ensuring that carers - both of children and of adults - have their needs taken into account and their rights protected. For it is only when the situation of being a carer becomes a viable choice rather than a sacrificial obligation that women will be freed to genuinely allocate their time according to their desires rather than be bound by a biological and social destiny.

Disability within our new society must be rethought. Many of the challenges that disabled people face come less from their own bodily limitations than through the social set up that surrounds them. Consideration of how best disabled people can contribute to society and be valued within it means not a top down demand that disabilities are miraculously overcome and wished away through a bureaucratic dismissal of people's limitations, declaring them 'fit for work' as a money saving exercise, but a matching of the abilities of people to the needs of the society. Few people 'cannot work' in the sense that they have nothing to contribute, but many have limitations on the work that they can perform and the type of contribution that they can make. Ensuring that the contributions made are valued and appreciated and that time is taken to remove barriers to any participation can ensure that the human resources of our society can be maximised for the benefit of all, including the self-actualisation of those who have limited abilities.

The care of our population must be at the top of our agenda. Not only care in the traditional medical sense, but also in the interactions between the state and its populace. The bullying and harassment which is currently being experienced by many, most notably through the benefits system, where sanctions threaten vulnerable people with destitution should they not obey orders, must end. These orders which are frequently contradictory and for many ultimately harmful must be replaced by a recognition that the state is there to support its people, not as a coercive entity but as an enabling one.

Nowhere is that more apparent than within the justice system, which sees vulnerable and damaged young people confined and restricted as punishment for illegal acts with little consideration of the social conditions which led to their transgressions. The addiction issues that are faced by the vast majority of the population of Corton Vale women's prison - a concentrated village of abused women who self-medicate from the streets with imports from a country where we bomb its citizens to hell - must be tackled at its root. The provision of hope and opportunities would do far more to reduce offending than any level of incarceration could ever do. While across the land, troubled men are locked up for long periods of time with few opportunities to overcome the issues that led them into that situation, then released back into the community to reoffend all over again.

None of the above will achieve socialism. We cannot achieve a socialist Scotland. We can only make our own little corner of the world a place where socialism can be possible by eradicating the racism and sexism which perpetuates divisions between people; remove the state as a coercive force of control and attempt to utilise it to encourage those within to liberate themselves; and bolster the state as a protector of our people against international capitalism which seeks to syphon off our resources for the good of the rich. We can develop a transitional society, one which enables the emergence of socialism in conjunction with the rest of the world.

If we want to see socialism in land that we call Scotland, we must recognise that it is bound with the struggles of others, for as long as one wo/man is not free, none of us are. We can be a beacon to the rest of the world - most notably to the rest of UK, demonstrating that another future is possible, that misery and poverty are not part of the human condition, but a deliberate strategy that capitalism uses to keep us working in their interests and that there is a better way. Moreover, we can be a force of liberation, not through invasion of other countries in the name of 'freedom', but by removing ourselves from the oppressive Western hegemony - both economic and military - that keeps the majority of the world enslaved.

The first step of that is extracting ourselves from the UK state - from its militarised global interventions which sees millions murdered to protect its interests; from its economic coercion which leaves families all across the globe impoverished for the benefit of the UK ruling class; from its kyriarchial vision, which perpetuates sexism and racism as a means of upholding capitalist values and maximising human exploitation. And in extracting ourselves from it, we send a clear message that will no longer tolerate our people and our natural resources be used for the domination of others.

But there can be no socialist Scotland on its own, for socialism is global or it is not socialism. There is no left-wing nationalist case for independence, only an internationalist approach will see us achieve our aims. There is no extracting ourselves from global capitalism - there is only the greater protection that we can achieve from its ravages through a commitment to re-engineering our society for the benefit of people not profit, and through putting a nail in the coffin of the British state and its appropriation of our resources for its murderous and exploitative agenda.

Chapter 17

We have to stop complaining and up our game

Robin McAlpine

I used to spend a lot of time thinking about how to transform Scotland into a 'socialist' country. I am now lucky enough to get to do this as a day job, and it has been instructive. For more than a decade, I have edited the *Scottish Left Review* (SLR) and in 2004 set up the Scottish Left Review Press. Both of these initiatives were rooted in one great hope - that ideas change things. I kept the SLR going in evenings and at weekends but each morning went to my day job as a political strategist and lobbyist. I left to set up the Jimmy Reid Foundation for a simple reason; time and again we published articles with a really good idea at their core or a brilliant analysis of why things weren't working. But they very rarely came to anything. Why? Because ideas are never enough. If a client seeking public affairs advice came to me and asked if they would be able to change Scottish Government policy simply by having a good idea, I would have smiled politely and sat them down for a long talk. That is not how it works - if achieving policy outcomes had anything to do with good ideas the CBI would be in trouble.

So why is it different for the left? It isn't. That's why we created the Foundation, to do the things that actually work. It has meant a subtle shift in my perceptions. Where before the question, once every two months, was 'what ideas can we publish this issue?', now I wake up every morning and ask 'what can we do today to make a difference?'. The answer to this, as often as not, is a practical answer. Today, we can help sympathetic politicians with a briefing on a subject they are about to debate. Today, we can set up a media story to create some momentum around an issue we want on the agenda. Today, we can quickly assemble a coalition of support for this initiative. I still get to be involved in 'big ideas' - we're a think tank after all and produce reports that are of a high quality filled with strong thinking. But now, I don't get to let myself off the hook when big ideas get lost and come to nothing; that becomes my responsibility as well.

By the time this book is published I will have turned 40. When I was 20 I was happy to argue with people for hours inventing whole new political systems in our heads. When I was 30 I wanted a big national debate. Now

I just want something done, something real. I am losing patience. This is a simple explanation of what I think, how I came to think it and what I think needs to be done. But above all, it is a plea for the left to stop letting itself off the hook. Marches that change nothing, public meetings only we go to, sharing articles among ourselves on Facebook so we feel better. Meanwhile, outside the window the powers of neo-liberal capitalism control our country. We need a message of hope; they can be beat. But not if we keep doing what we've been doing up until now.

So let's go back to Marx for a second, from his afterword to *Capital*. He complains that he is criticised because: '[I] confine myself to the mere critical analysis of actual facts, instead of writing recipes for the cook-shops of the future.' Yet he spawned a century and a half of cook-shop recipes and stimulated lots of critical analysis somewhat divorced from actual facts. So let's deal with some actual facts about Scotland in 2012. First of all, there is no revolution around the corner. The idea that the financial crash of 2007 has pushed the Scottish population into a level of dissatisfaction with their society great enough to motivate them to participate in an active overthrow of capitalism is fantasy. Even the argument that the conditions are right for such a shift in public sentiment is almost impossible to sustain. People are annoyed; they are nowhere near a revolution. The problem with wishing otherwise is that people prepare for a revolution that isn't going to happen. Put away your Molotov cocktails and lay down your book of military tactics; they are just anarcho-porn and irrelevant as tools in contemporary Scotland.

Should that bother us? Not really. In the debates about reformation or revolution there is an important point that needs to be made; you can have a revolution and then a reformation, you can have a reformation and then a revolution, or you can have just a reformation. But any way you look at it, you need a reformation. Since that is the only option which seems to be on the table, let's get on with it.

Next, what does socialism mean? Continuing our critical analysis of actual facts, we can answer that question roughly but not exactly. Should that bother us? No, but it does. This is the point at which the left has encountered its biggest problems. If we think of socialism in percentage terms we have developed a habit of agreeing on 90 per cent of it and arguing endlessly (and often unproductively) over the other 10 per cent. Increasingly, I have come to believe that we need to assemble an actually-working starting point, a programme of things that have worked in other places. Nordic welfare, elements of mixed-economy strategies from across Europe, industrial democracy structures from southern European cooperatives, Cuban overseas aid policies, democratised institutions along the Nordic lines and so on. This will not provide all of us with a programme for government that goes far enough for our liking, but if we accept it as a starting point we can pull together the biggest possible coalition and greatly increase our chances of success.

What is stopping this from happening right now? The way our society is structured. The conditions that would allow for the social shift suggested above are blocked - and intentionally so. It would require a free and balanced media, the regulation of power and money to reduce its excessive influence on public policy, the restructuring and democratisation of institutions that define society and so on. These will be considered in a little more detail below. But returning once more to a critical analysis of actual facts, the primary incarnation of all these disabling conditions is the British State. The merest hint of a little modest media regulation brings it out in a fit of apoplexy; no principle is to be held higher than the rights of rich people to own all the means of communication and to do with them as they see fit for whatever ends they may desire. The military and security services are not about to let their stranglehold on our foreign policy slip any more than the City of London is going to let anyone reform the economy. London won't even take seriously basic voting reform to make governments proportionate to the public will. I find it simply impossible to look at Britain and conceive of any strategy at all that might even nearly bring a hint of socialism to London. The British state is not beyond reformation, but it isn't going to happen for a generation. Wishing otherwise is futile.

Scotland is not a done deal for the left, but it is reformable. It is quite easy to imagine a basic re-regulation of media ownership taking place in Scotland. Not certain, but imaginable. That is a giant step forward. If we want change in our lifetimes, we're going to need independence. I can arrive at no other conclusion.

But why is being able to imagine reform such a giant step forwards? Because even more than the British state, the ideological despair of the population is our biggest barrier. As I have written at length elsewhere, the real trick of neo-liberal doctrine was not to defeat the labour movement but to defeat the idea that a labour movement is even possible. Apathy and resignation have been the most powerful tools of neo-liberalism. It is instructive to watch the neo-liberal critique of independence which is a case study of the sort - absolutely nothing which does not already exist can ever work, all change is not only undesirable but impossible. There is only one real antidote to this: we need to be able to talk about change in a way that people can imagine. If people can close their eyes and envisage an alternative idea in practice, you're half way to winning the case. If people close their eyes and see only confusion, they will not embrace change. We need a truthful, compelling story about alternatives; critiques, no matter how convincing, are insufficient. Complex theoretical alternatives are even worse if they are hard to understand. Simplicity and clarity are the keys, along with a very clear expectation that we are taking one step at a time;

before we jump to advocating a Citizen's Income, let's deliver a Danish 'flexicurity' approach or something similar.

We then need to resist the temptation to find fault with all of our first steps. No, they will not overturn every wrong in society in one go. Yes, there is always a chance that we get 'stuck' at step one and fail to move to a more fundamental redefinition of society. But shall we wait another decade in the hope that if we keep marching, someone somewhere will come up with a fail-safe plan for revolution? Again, I have grown too impatient to wait and too cynical to believe in the *Deus ex machina* philosophy of futurology.

Finally, we then need to be more self-critical on why it is that we've not had more success. We tend to assume that everything is stacked against us and, therefore, we have no chance of playing the game by 'their' rules. This I find particularly interesting since most of the people I hear advocating this position haven't really tried to play by 'their' rules. I worked for many years for an important part of the Scottish establishment. We had a high media profile, a key political role and some serious budget. I was in charge of lobbying and media relations. Do you imagine we won every fight, even with money and connections? Do you think we just phoned up newspapers and dictated stories down the line to them? No, we worked really hard to create stories that got our message across in a way that was of interest to the media. If you want to influence the media there are things you have to do - make sure there is a point of contact that can always be reached and make sure everyone knows, provide copy that people want to read and journalists want to write, only pitch stories if they are really stories and so on. There are a tiny, tiny number of people who can just 'magic' news out of the air either by being incredibly rich and famous or by having extremely close connections with newspaper editors and owners. For everyone else, you need to work. It is no different for the left.

Now is not the time for another burst of soul-searching or for us to congregate once more in rooms where no-one can see us. We have two options; we can keep marching and complaining it isn't working or we can come together, set identifiable targets and work hard to deliver them. And we need to stop finding reasons not to try. 'An independent Scotland will just be run by RBS anyway...' goes the refrain from some. Fine. We will just give up. We won't try. Pick our best battle, choose the best place to fight it, fight it well. Then start again. This is how the other side won. This is how everyone whoever won won. Do we want to win?

If so, let me offer three lists. The first list is a list of three 'big ticket' policy agendas we could assemble and congregate round quickly. The second list is a list of reforms it seems to me will be necessary to embed social change in the fabric of Scotland. The third is a straightforward list of ways in which we need to improve our leadership of the movement.

First, a very short three-part policy programme:

- The first and most important battle is to set out a clearer and simpler alternative to the British tax-and-spend model. Supporters of independence have rightly been criticised for apparently advocating a 'Scandimerican' model of low tax and high public spending. This is a fallacy that has got into people's minds because of poor SNP policy-making. This needs to be refocussed in order to explain how almost any alternative to the British fiscal model would make 75 per cent of the population better off and increase the tax take. A seriously reformed tax system would rapidly increase revenue without having to tax most people any more than now simply by closing avoidance opportunities. If we can show that a flatter society and fairer tax system can increase spending power of individuals and the government and use this to expand the provision of high-quality social services, we signpost a way forward. This is the fundamental reform - changing the general perception of the relationship between tax and spend.

- We also need to challenge the perception about 'economic value' to move away from 'profit motive' to 'productivity'. Simply by encouraging an economic model on the basis of return to society and economy rather than return to owners will mean a significant shift in opinion. This does mean different ownership models including nationalisation of key industries (including retail banking), more cooperative ownership and so on. But it also means a cultural shift in private ownership, pushing towards the long-term ideology of the German *Mittelstand* rather than the short-term 'Dragon's Den' obsession of company ownership in Britain. Simply by knocking down the fatuous idea that a small class in society are 'wealth creators' and the rest of us 'leaches' would significantly change public policy in everything from tax and immigration strategies to economic development practices and economic regulation.

- We should be taking big steps forward on the idea of social ownership and provision. This must start with strong defence of the universal welfare state. We must then look for other areas of 'social failure' where society leaves large groups with anxieties about the capacity to secure necessary social support. For example, the extent to which childcare is left to 'the market' is experienced by very large proportions of society either as an unaffordable luxury or as very heavy financial burden - communal provision would be massively more efficient and much, much fairer. If we also think about non-market strategies for providing what people need and want in their lives we can make remarkable steps in reforming the nature of society. As a small example, if a twenty first century library really means a large intranet with lots of resources we buy collectively and people can access free at home (ebooks, music, films and so on), we reduce the power of corporations to order society and enable people and communities to do it instead.

Now, the conditions we need to reset:

- There needs to be a major overhaul of media ownership rules. The principle held by the media above all others is that first and foremost democracy demands the main means of communication with the public must be owned by rich people alone and that they must face no barrier to the free abuse of that ownership for any personal purpose they see fit. This conflates freedom of the press with freedom of ownership. The criteria for media ownership should include not only a 'market share' test by owner but a 'market share' test for political balance. Indeed, a radical 'franchising' model where all daily newspapers franchises were granted to independent trusts by an independent franchising body with a duty to promote political diversity in the media is perfectly achievable. This would be a press free from financial abuse, and would change the terms of political debate almost overnight.

- Education needs to be taken out of the realm of 'functionality' and back into the correct realm of 'existential necessity'. It is so widely agreed that the first function of education is to create informed, balanced citizens that it is hard to understand why education policy still puts 'employability' above all other issues. Approaches such as 'entrepreneurialism' should be consigned to history in favour of essential elements of our understanding of the democracies in which we live. Until people understand the choices they won't choose well.

- Politics needs substantial change. Scotland is stuck with a giant political Berlin Wall. It divides people not on the basis of political affiliation but tribal affiliation. Almost everyone in Labour and the SNP can point to at least as many people in the other party that share their politics as they can point to in their own party. They are both coalitions too wide for democracy and, therefore, simply too unaccountable to their members and far too easy for corporate lobbyists to pick off. There will eventually have to be some political realignment in Scotland. It would be foolish to predict or plan it, but we need a party system which means the public can express their political views at the ballot box without the need for yet another clever-clever commentator telling us what they *actually* meant. And we need a means of limiting undue financial influence over parties.

- Parliamentary reform is much easier to ask for than to invent. We all wish there was a system with greater independence of politicians from their leaderships, where there is open-minded debate on all sides and whipping and narrow party advantage wasn't the primary order of the day. It is unlikely we will entirely achieve it, but there are certain things we can do. One is to follow a strict programme of action to reduce elite access to, and influence over, parliament. We need many more forms of truly participative democracy in Scotland - if members of the public can decide the guilt or innocence of murderers as part of a jury, why can't they decide if we need to merge police forces or privatise Scottish Water? Why is this only for a small elite class? Parliamentary reform isn't just about letting parties get on with it but about making parties answerable and letting in new voices.

- The British civil service is, in my experience, one of the most contrary organisations in existence. It simultaneously boasts of its neutrality and its capacity to 'stop politicians making mistakes'. Which is it? It claims a very high degree of quality and yet is typified by caution, conservatism and a marked lack of any real quality of thinking or output. And it believes itself to be largely beyond reproach and yet it is utterly, utterly unaccountable (how many senior civil servants can you ever remember resigning as a result of their mistakes?). The civil service has become an unaccountable mini-state with a network of links into the financial sector which is at the same time highly effective in pursuing some agendas and utterly ineffective at doing any good whatsoever in others. A major overhaul of the civil service would be one of the great possible outcomes from Scottish independence.

- We need to take governance out of the hands of people who define 'the public good' in purely neo-liberal terms. There needs to be a strong and coordinated programme of 'democratisation'. The findings in a research project recently published by the Reid Foundation suggest that the 70 per cent of the population that gets by on the average salary of £24,000 or less make up only about three per cent of those parliament and government invite to shape their policies. This means that a tiny minority of the population make all the decisions according to their own world view, with much of the rest of the decision-making being outsourced to legal and accountancy firms which are part of the financial service sector and its highly neo-liberal ideology. Through a sequence of policies (including outsourcing, privatisation and managerialism), a small elite now controls political ideology with little or no reference to the public. Big institutions like universities are controlled by small management teams answering to weak governance models. Until we have a governance arrangement that reflects society and not just the top ten per cent of society there will be an in-built control system which will seek to prevent reform.

- 'Recreation' is a word that should be rehabilitated as a way of understanding a missing strand of public policy. To 're-create' ourselves through activities is an on-going and important aspect of social policy which is not seen as crucial to democracy but is. Neo-liberal dogma assumes that after full-time education there is absolutely no role for public policy to say anything about what we do (other than campaigns to discourage damaging behaviour). This is wrong. Dumping people out of school and from that point on leaving the commercial sector as the only sector that influences human activity means people have been continually pushed and coerced into behaviours which benefit corporations and often harm themselves. Everything from poor health and obesity to low voter turnout, unsustainable private debt and the financial crash have roots in an ideology that states that only corporations have anything important to say about our leisure time. It is 'our decision to make', with a multi-billion pound advertising industry only there to 'help'. Advertising must be rapidly constrained and much better social provision of valuable but non-commercial options for how we 'recreate' ourselves being promoted. A society dominated not by passive retail but by a diverse range of socially organised activities designed to encourage us to extend our horizons (book clubs, art classes, discussion groups, classes in car mechanics - whatever) would look very different. The assumption that our private lives are a place to be protected from society for the convenience of the commercial sector needs to change.

Finally, aspects of our leadership capacity we need to consider:

- In my view, the left has suffered more than anything from poor political strategy. We have become trapped in a cycle of protest/demonstration/ failure/narcissism. We say what we don't like, we jump up and down about it, nothing happens so we start an interminable debate with ourselves about whose fault it is. Far too much left politics has been one long feedback loop of us pleasing ourselves. A good initiative is often seen as one which keeps all our factions happy, not one that has real wider impact. We have to develop the skills to create and follow more effective political strategies. Surely we've noticed by now that marching, on its own, changes little and forming endless groups and parties, on its own, influences nothing? We need to stop letting ourselves off the hook every time we do something and it doesn't work, blaming instead a media conspiracy or state corruption. I've seen many of these initiatives and put simply they wouldn't work for the CBI either.

- We organise inwards, not outwards. We expend our energy managing our internal conflicts not reaching out and organising with a large and sympathetic group of the wider public. Mostly, we don't have the skills of an on-the-ground political campaign, able to do the things necessary to convert sympathy into action. That has to change.

- Too often we assume that the skills one needs for politics are all learned by doing politics. This isn't true - most other people in politics are in a constant process of development. Thatcher was taught how to soften her voice to stop alienating people, Blair was heavily trained on media, activists on how to use social media effectively and so on. We need the same level of development in the left. We don't have many people with a media profile in part because we don't push people to the media and in part because not many people on the left have much experience of effective media presentation. We have a habit of barking everything as if we are perpetually talking to a half-empty room of activists. That just sounds absolutely awful on the TV. I have been surprised at how few people on the left know how to put out and then chase up a press release. Generally we seem to have very little understanding of important political concepts like targeting, segmentation and messaging. We need much better support and training.

- Narrative is not an idea we are strong at. Slogans yes, fitting them into a concise, simple story which can be properly understood by the public in language the public finds intuitive? No. We are anti-everything, we put our concerns first, we are aggressive and angry a lot of the time. We talk about 'illegal wars' as if it was still ten years ago. We talk about poverty in a way that makes people feel it isn't about them. We don't have a really positive story to enthuse. We need to start focussing upon which parts of our story connect to the wider public. Then we need to rephrase. We can go on and on about the need to 'scrap anti-trade union laws' and still we fail to make anyone out there realise we're trying to protect their interests in the face of abuse by employers. 'Anti-trade union laws' is our interest, protecting the interests of workers is the public interest. We have to stop believing that being right and shouting it loud enough is all it takes. We need to admit that we have been poor communicators on many issues.

- Journalists - scumbags each and every one. I never cease to be amazed just how many people are set in this view without ever having spoken to one. We have justified our lack of success in grabbing the media agenda purely by blaming the media. This is the case even when we haven't tried to get an agenda running. 'Waste of time' we say. Well, that's not what it looks like to me. From where I sit, it looks like we scream loudly in the open air and wonder why no-one reports it. We don't pick up the phone, we don't ever invite a journalist out for a pint and a blether, and above all, we don't really put the effort into manufacturing stories that are worth printing. This last point is crucial - an enormous amount of effort goes in to creating and delivering most good media stories. Everyone I know in all sectors of public affairs and public relations expect to have to work for media space. All of them. We think it just happens and then when it doesn't we think it was someone else's fault. It really is time to start being more honest; grabbing an agenda is hard work. You can't just hold a protest rally, pat yourself on the back and go home.

- Politics is also about the grinding business of making things happen. When you push an idea you need to engage with people to build up momentum, give them reasons to support you, tackle the arguments against. You need to pick achievable objectives, be opportunistic when the occasion arises. You need to plan long-term and react quickly. That's politics. Do we really do these things well? Yes, sometimes, but mostly not really.

For too long the left has spent much of its time asking if there is a road to socialism. We take our seats, put on the radio and start looking out the window to see if there are enemy roadblocks. Sometimes, we see people passing us and we open the window to wave our fists in anger. What we don't do enough is look inwards. If we did we might notice that we're sitting in a garden shed and the reason everyone is passing us on the road is because we're sitting in a garden shed. 'Damn road!' we curse, 'completely biased against us!' Now would be a good time to give ourselves a bit of a shake.

Chapter 18

A strategy without currency

Conor McCabe

Monetary policy is about class power. The intended objective of the Scottish National Party, to secede from the UK while remaining under the remit of the Bank of England, will hand over that policy to those engaged in banking, finance and asset price speculation. There will be no democratic accountability regarding interest rate and credit objectives. The cost of maintaining Sterling as the national currency of an independent Scotland will be internal devaluation as a periodic norm - the burden of which will fall on the workforce via lower wages, higher unemployment and cuts in the social economy. However, for those with asset wealth a strong currency in a devalued economy is a win-win situation. This is the nature of the class power that surrounds monetary policy. Remarkably, this is also what the SNP wants for Scotland.

The case of the Irish Republic, so lauded by Alex Salmond in the past as an economic role model, has salutary lessons regarding central bank and monetary policy. In 1927, the Irish Free State decided to link its national currency to Sterling at a 1:1 ratio –one Irish pound for one pound Sterling. The government had the option to link the Irish pound to sterling in a way that would have allowed the currency to rise or fall in value in accordance with the realities of the economy, but it did not take that decision. The maintenance of the parity link with sterling was kept in place regardless of the cost to the wider economy. Ireland did not break with Sterling until 1979, when the country joined the European Monetary System (EMS) some fifty-seven years after the foundation of the state. It lost monetary independence in 1999 when it adopted the Euro.

The link with Sterling played no small part in the decades of poverty and stagnation post-independence. The current link with the Euro sees Ireland once again engaged in internal devaluation as monetary policy. What follows is an examination of Ireland's membership of the Sterling and Eurozone areas, in the hope that it may add to the debate on what the future might hold for a politically-independent but fiscally-subservient Scotland.

[T]he innocent luxury of a distinctively Irish currency (*Irish Times* 22 January 1927)

On 3 February 1926, the Irish Minister for Finance, Ernest Blythe, announced to the Dáil (the Irish parliament) the establishment of a commission to study the situation of banking in the Irish Free State. Political independence had not led to monetary independence from Britain, and although Irish banks issued their own notes, they were treated and accepted as sterling by both businesses and the public. The value of money in the Free State was dependent on the strengths and weaknesses of what was now a foreign currency. Not only that - the majority of deposits in Irish banks was held in Britain, as had been the case prior to independence. This gave rise to serious issues regarding the issuing of credit and the financial tools the state had at its disposal in order to develop the economy. The government also needed to regulate the supply of legal tender within its jurisdiction. The commission was top-heavy with bankers and financiers - six out of a total of nine members. It held its first meeting in March 1926 and in January 1927 the main findings were released. The commissioners were quick to outline what they saw as the main strength of the Free State's currency - namely the parity link with sterling:

In every newly organised state the fundamental problem of exchange which must be dealt with is that of a monetary or currency standard. The Saorstát [Irish Free State] has encountered no difficulties on this score ... as its monetary basis has been identical with that of Great Britain [which] has been since the close of the war by far the most sound and stable nation, speaking in a financial and monetary sense, in the European world. (*Irish Times* 22 January 1927. All quotes relating to the report from this source.)

The commissioners recommended the installation of a new currency in the Free State, but one which 'shall be stated in terms of sterling, thus accepting the British standard of value for Saorstát Éireann, and that it shall be convertible at par into British sterling'. It made the argument that parity was essential 'in order that there may be no interruption to the comparatively free interchange of money and notes between the two countries, and no shock to the present system of inter-communication between the two, upon a uniform currency basis or standard'.

The commissioners neglected to mention that the free interchange of money between the Irish State and the UK was a one-way street. Irish credit was put on deposit in the UK, bolstering Sterling in the process, but with independence the Irish state lost the fiscal transfers which are a necessary part of any political and currency union. The Bank of England and Sterling benefited from Irish savings and government deposits, but had no responsibilities to the Irish State or to its economic development. Instead, those with Irish paper assets were protected from the necessary currency devaluation which an independent monetary policy would have bestowed.

The commissioners said that the reasons to maintain parity with sterling 'need but little exposition'. There is little, if anything, in this world, however, which does not need explanation. All too often, appeals to 'common sense' or the 'self-evident' nature of an argument are simply covers for the *status quo*. The commissioners were reluctant to explain that, while it suited Irish banks to have an expensive currency, it did not suit the needs of a newly formed state, one that was trying to change its focus from a regional to a national economy.

In 1931, less than four years after the Banking Commission had tied the Irish pound to 'the most sound and stable nation' in Europe, Great Britain broke from the gold standard and devalued its currency. It was not the only country to undertake such a measure during this period - Sweden, Norway, Denmark and India all abandoned the gold standard around this time. However, because of the parity link, the Free State was forced to follow sterling to its new value, regardless of the financial realities in Ireland at the time.

The leader of the Irish government, William Cosgrave, responded to the financial crisis not by disentangling the Irish pound from sterling, but by appealing to patriotism and calling on the Irish people to purchase Irish goods. 'Let us see to it that our courage and our energy are not wanting in the time of national necessity,' he told a civic carnival banquet in Limerick in October 1931, 'to keep the name of our country in the forefront for being able to meet whatever demands may be made on us in difficult times' *(Irish Times* 3 October 1931) The increase in tariffs undertaken by the government at this time was in direct response to similar moves by Britain. In order to avoid the Free State becoming a dumping ground for British goods, it needed to put a marker on imports. In 1933, the World Monetary and Economic Conference in London passed a resolution which called for the establishment of independent central banks with powers to carry out currency and credit policy in developed countries where they did not already exist. It was becoming clear that the Free State's avoidance of a central bank was out of step with the rest of the developed world.

On 26 October 1934, the Minister for Finance, Sean McEntee, announced the appointment of a commission to inquire into banking, currency, and related matters in the Irish Free State. Its personnel represented a wide range of Irish society. It held over 200 meetings and took four years to produce its report. It was finally released in October 1938 and found that while a central bank should be established, parity with sterling should also be maintained, and government borrowing should be curtailed. It also rejected the suggestion that a nationalised bank should be established to provide credit for the expansion of the economy. The commission took four years to conclude that the *status quo* offered the best solution to the problems facing the Irish economy.

The commission also produced a minority report, which was signed by Professor O'Rahilly of University College Cork, and the two union representatives, William O'Brien and Sean Campbell. They stated that they could not:

> ... *acquiesce in the extraordinary view that this country, alone amongst the responsible entities of the world, should not ever have the power to make decisions, and that no apparatus or mechanism for controlling the volume and direction of credit should ever be brought into existence ... We need an organ for the issue and control of developmental credit ... That is our fundamental conclusion, and the only thing startling about it is that it was not accepted sixteen years ago.* (*Irish Times* 9 August 1938)

It was testimony to the power of financial interests in the Free State that after sixteen years, two commissions, and one international financial crisis, their ability to dictate the pace and direction of Irish economic growth to suit their own business agenda to the detriment of almost all other aspects of Irish economic and social life, remained undaunted.

One of the main recommendations of the Second Banking Commission - the establishment of a central bank - was not implemented until 1943. A central bank, the commissioners said, 'has to ensure the maintenance of external stability, to take care of the monetary reserves of gold and foreign exchange, and have certain means of influencing the currency and credit position within the country' (*Irish Times* 8 August 1938). It undertakes these responsibilities in order to assist the development of the economy, and to act as a stabiliser between the right of banks to sell credit, and the right of businesses to trade. As far as the developed world was concerned, a central bank was not seen as a luxury but as an essential element of monetary policy. The failure of the Irish State to establish a central bank led to accusations that the banks, rather than the government, were setting economic policy. 'It is all nonsense to say that we are merely creatures of the banks' said the Prime Minister Eamon De Valera in 1939, continuing: 'We can pass a law at any time to control the banks or to sever parity with sterling. We can do all these things. It is merely a question of whether it is wise or unwise to do them' (*Dáil Report*, 7 July 1939, volume 76, paragraph 2,164). Three years and the outbreak of a world war later, the Central Bank Bill was brought before the Dáil.

The board of the Central Bank of Ireland met for the first time on 1 February 1943. The chairman was Joseph Brennan, who was the chairman of the Currency Commission prior to its disbandment. The board was given the responsibility of protecting the purchasing power of the Irish pound and regulating the issue of credit in the interests of the nation. They made it clear that there would be no change in monetary policy. On 18 September 1949, sterling was devalued by 30 per cent. The Irish Republic, naturally, followed suit. In 1951 the American economic consultancy firm, Ibec (1952), was commissioned by the Irish government to write a report on the status of the Irish economy. It produced a strong critique of agricultural, industrial and monetary policy. 'The fact that the Central Bank has made no use of its statutory power to invest its legal tender reserves in Irish government securities has handicapped the development of an active domestic capital market in Ireland which is one of the country's primary needs' it said, adding 'The commercial banking system of Ireland, as well, has shown a similar tendency to operate in a fashion that channels Irish deposit funds into the British market rather than retaining them in Ireland for domestic use'.

Ireland needed to boost its means of increasing its volume of physical capital formation for internal investment. 'Unless this is done,' wrote Ibec (1952), 'it is difficult to see how any development of Irish industry and agriculture sufficiently vigorous to keep pace with outside competition can take place.' The role of private banks in the creation and distribution of credit in Ireland was quite limited, '[This] cannot be explained in terms of a comparative dearth of personal savings,' wrote Ibec (1952), 'since Ireland's 1949 personal savings represent about twice as large a proportion of gross capital formation as in the United Kingdom'. Instead, it concluded that 'the disparity is clearly chargeable to the fact that an active capital market for domestic issues has never been developed in Ireland' and that 'this failure is immediately influenced by the example of government and private commercial banking agencies which consistently have channelled a very large proportion of their assets into British securities rather than securities of the home market'. Irish commercial banks were seen as directly responsible, along with government, with stymieing Irish economic growth. Here, the Irish Republic was faced with a clash between financial class interests and the state itself: it could keep the heavy currency beloved by banks, or it could introduce a devalued currency backed up with credit movement controls which would aid economic growth but puncture asset values. The solution was to keep Sterling but to import industry in lieu of indigenous development. This policy began in the 1950s and has been a mainstay of Irish economic policy ever since.

Although it was billed as a way of developing the Irish economy, it was the provision of services to foreign companies, mainly around finance and construction, rather than Irish-sourced exports that saw the bulk of indigenous growth. The actual exports remained foreign-owned and foreign-sourced. By the 1980s, Ireland had a declining industrial base but a growing financial sector, and was encouraged to establish the International Financial Services Centre (IFSC) in Dublin as an off-shoot of the City of London (Shaxson 2011). The calls for a single European currency as the next great saviour of the Irish state soon drowned out all opposition.

> *The ugly truth is that countries have to cut their standard of living.*
> (Klaus Regling, European Financial Stability Facility, 7 September 2011)

On 31 May 2004, the then president of the European Central Bank (ECB), Jean-Claude Trichet, gave a lecture in Dublin where he talked about the Euro currency and his vision for its future direction. 'Let me stress' he said, 'that we Europeans have been very bold in creating a single currency in the absence of a political federation, a federal government and a federal budget at the euro area level.' Trichet noted that some observers had argued: 'that without a federal budget of some significance the policy mix would be very erratic [and that] it would be impossible to weather, with the help of the fiscal channel, asymmetric shocks hitting one particular member economy' (*Irish Times* 1 June 2004).

Trichet dismissed these criticisms, and said that there were structures in place to address such concerns, among them mutual surveillance by the Eurozone members of national fiscal policies and the requirement to adhere to a three per cent ceiling on national deficits. However, it was within the private sector - in particular the deregulated financial sector - that problems around credit were starting to form themselves. In the absence of actual productive growth, credit was being used to speculate on asset price. It was something that Trichet, and his colleagues at the ECB were well aware of, and something that they chose to ignore.

One year after his Dublin appearance, Trichet gave a lecture to the Monetary Authority of Singapore on 8 June 2005 where he addressed the issue of asset price bubbles. The Bank for International Settlements had recently argued that due to the keen watch that central banks kept on consumer inflation, the first signs of an inflationary bubble would show up in asset prices, which would have a destabilizing effect on financial markets - the main course of credit for asset price speculation. Once again Trichet highlighted concerns, only to dismiss them. 'I would argue that, yes, bubbles do exist' he said, 'but that it is very hard to identify them with certainty and almost impossible to reach a consensus about whether a particular asset price boom period should be considered a bubble or not.' In his view, 'not all boom or bubble episodes threaten financial stability' and that 'policy-makers should not fall into the trap of attempting to eliminate all risk from the financial system.' For Trichet, such a course of action 'would either be unsuccessful (due to moral hazard) or... would likely hamper the appropriate functioning of a market economy where risk-taking is of the essence' (Trichet 2005)

No matter what the evidence pointed towards, Trichet simply did not want to believe that the Eurozone was in an asset price bubble. It was not in his interests to do so, nor was it in the interests of the class that financed its wealth through such speculation. The collapse of Lehman Brothers in September 2008 brought to the fore the systemic crisis in this interplay between asset price speculation and financial 'innovation'. It also saw the wholesale conversion of these now worthless credit claims into guaranteed payment streams via tax revenue. The purpose of quantitative easing in the US and the UK, the LTOR scheme in the Eurozone, and the bailouts in Ireland, Greece and Portugal, has been to stabilize asset price without causing inflation. This has been achieved at massive social cost. But that is the nature of class power and monetary policy - of a class war that only one side knows it is fighting: in the words of Warren Buffet, the side that is winning.

On 21 November 2010, Alex Salmond appeared on the Andrew Marr show to talk about Scottish independence and its future economy. 'Rather than Westminster handing down cuts in Scotland' he said, 'wouldn't it be better to allow Scots to have the responsibility to grow our economy?' The policy of the SNP to have Sterling as the national currency of an independent Scotland will ensure that it will be the governor of the Bank of England, not Westminster, who will be handing down cuts. And as with the present crisis, there will be winners. For those in Scotland who work within the world of paper assets and financial instruments – the bankers, accountants, lawyers and stockbrokers who handle the documentation - a Sterling-enveloped Scotland will be a boon for business. For everyone else, a litany of cliché-dripping excuses for periodical cuts to the social economy awaits.

Chapter 19

The green road to socialism

Peter McColl

Both Scotland and the world have changed substantially in the wake of the global economic crisis. The Scottish characteristic of this change is marked by the rise of the SNP and the debate about the Scottish constitution, ahead of the 2014 poll on independence. What follows is an assessment of where Greens are at this juncture. The aim is to assess the progressive nature of the Green Party in Scotland (and its close connections to the Green Party of England and Wales) and to map where change is needed. Today's Green movement has its roots in the radical dissent and new left of the 1960s. The German Green Party (Die Grünen) was the first organised political manifestation of this movement. Many of the leaders of the party had been leading activists in the new left, most notably Danny Cohen-Bendit and Joschka Fischer. While for some periods there has been deviation from these origins (notably into middle-class environmentalism), it is clear that the Green movement is beginning to move back to its radical roots in Scotland. Greens have, however, underperformed in the past two Holyrood elections, despite our English counterparts making the hugely significant breakthrough to Westminster. Where Caroline Lucas was able to defeat all of the major parties in Brighton Pavilion, Scottish Greens suffered a major setback in 2007 and failed to make any progress in 2011.

This demands a serious rethink of the core vote strategy pursued between 2003 and 2010. Too often Greens have retreated to comfortable middle class environmentalism at the expense of serious social and environmental issues. While the focus of the 2011 election campaign on defending public services was right, it came on the back of seven years of narrow environmentalism, divorced from a critique of the economic structure of environmental destruction. Often this approach contained implicit blame for those who cannot choose green consumerism or other middle class lifestyles. It has become clearer that it is the moneyed interests of the capitalist class that is the enemy of the environment rather than working class people who fail to recycle. This has allowed Greens to start tackling the economic causes of the environmental crisis. The ability of the plutocratic rich to stymie action on climate change has become apparent to even the least political greens. When combined with aggressive austerity politics to which Greens have led opposition, this places Green politics firmly in on the left. As the demands of equality and environment have aligned, so the Green Party is slowly coming to align its campaigns on this crucial strategic territory.

The independence debate has offered Greens the opportunity to head up the campaign for a radical Scotland. The SNP has, at the current time, taken a position of safety first. Its commitment to keeping the pound sterling, to remaining in NATO and to retaining a member of the British royal family as head of state do not fulfil the promise many want of an independent Scotland. Greens have led with a wide range of policies for a Scottish republic, for Scottish control of our currency and for an anti-militarist Scotland. All of these will be principles held across the left. Greens will use our voice to push for a radical independence.

Green economics - the end of post materialist politics and after the Green New Deal

The world economy and political context has changed profoundly since the credit crunch and collapse of the banking system. These changes have had equally profound impact on Scottish politics. The challenge for Greens has been to maintain relevance in this new context. Greens have had to adapt to a crisis of capitalism for the first time. This has required a fundamental reassessment of Green politics and its focus. Historically, Green politics has focused on post-materialist policies. Green parties have been most successful and green policies most influential where basic material needs have been met. This means that a welfare state, high levels of employment and an expectation of improved quality of life have been a prerequisite for Green success. This means Greens have tended to seek policies that improve already high standards of life by reducing pollution, encouraging wildlife, making cities more liveable and other characteristic concerns of bourgeois bohemians. The thinking of right-wing Greens is highlighted by Jonathan Porritt in his *Capitalism as if the World Mattered* (2005, revised edition 2007). He suggests capitalism is a given, and that Greens should embrace it accordingly. The only thing worse than his argument was his timing, bringing out a revised edition coming only months before events that triggered the biggest recession since the nineteenth century.

The crisis of capitalism has meant Greens can make a much more foundational economic critique of the capitalist system. Indeed, this is a critique that has led to the incorporation of much of the Green analysis into broader left programmes. This is important because it comes at a time where the shortcomings of the reformist and regulatory green politics of the 1990s are becoming clear. Greens have championed environmental regulation, acts of Parliament enshrining targets for climate change emissions and other reforms to late capitalism successfully in Scotland and elsewhere. But it has now become clear that these initiatives are, in themselves, incapable of delivering effective reform. The likelihood of the system of corporate dominated capitalism, focused upon the exploitation of material resources, being changed to deliver environmental or social outcomes other than profit has vanished. Instead of helping to deliver positive social and environmental change, our big corporations have spent money on promoting austerity and denying the reality of climate change. The corporate capitalism that we are offered is entirely inimical to Green politics. And this has driven a change in the focus of Green campaigns. For the first time, Greens in Scotland have begun to reject regulatory and reformist environmentalism. This requires the development of a politics with an economic analysis at its heart. No longer are Greens the party that agrees to the hegemonic economic settlement, but with more environmentalism.

This has required a serious reassessment of what Greens actually stand for economically. This was first articulated in the Green New Deal, a post-Keynesian response to the crisis that emphasised the removal of corporate entitlements, massive investment in public transport, renewable energy and an increase in taxes for the wealthy, such as a Financial Transaction Tax (popularly known as the Robin Hood Tax). This defined, for the first time, a Green economic policy that rejected the defeatism of right-wing Greens like Porritt. This programme has had partial success, prompting Greens in Scotland to stand in the 2009 European elections on an aggressively anti-austerity and pro-worker platform. The 2010 Westminster election continued this theme, although with less conviction. It focused upon the theme, 'Fair is Worth Fighting For', and promised a living wage, renationalisation of rail and state intervention to create a fairer society.

There are significant elements of the Green analysis that have been very broadly accepted by the left. This is part of a culture war where Green politics has become an integral part of the progressive movement. The foundational green principles of equality, environmentalism, radical democracy and social justice are now almost wholly accepted across the left. While some of this is because the Green movement shares its origins in the new left of the 1960s with much of the left, much of it is because of popular front work with other elements of the left, much of it is because of work by Greens to identify equality, environmental and democratic reform issues with the left.

I deal below with many of the ways in which there has been cross fertilisation between Greens and the rest of the left, including participatory democracy, anti-austerity, feminist and generational campaigns. This is part of a contribution played by many on the new left, but Greens have spearheaded campaigns on LGBT rights, union representation and devolution of power.

The 2010 election saw Caroline Lucas elected to the Westminster Parliament, an event that may be a defining event even for Scottish Greens. Lucas aside, most prominent Green Party representatives still come from the old regulatory, reformist right of the party. With Lucas' leadership, they have been forced into advocating progressive policy positions, even in Scotland. Quite simply, it has become clear to everyone in the Green Party that to implement a Green politics we must first create a Green economy. That Green economy cannot be based on the extraction of surplus value and the profit motive. There has been a great deal of work amongst Greens on what this Green economy will look like. It will severely curtail the rights of corporations and instead focus on worker self-organisation and management through co-operatives and mutuals. It will invest in social infrastructure, caring and education rather than extractive industries. There will be a focus on community ownership and control of assets and local and regional currencies. There will be a strong role for unions and worker representation.

The Green economic analysis is still very much a work in progress. But the foundations for a fundamentally different way of working are there. The old Green approach of seeking more recycling and less pollution in a fundamentally capitalist extractive economy has gone. In its place is a nascent economics based on the needs of people not profit.

Response to austerity

Greens have been in the vanguard of resistance to austerity. Through community organising and groups like UK Uncut, Greens have been at the heart of the anti-austerity movement. This reflects the grounding of Green politics in building a collective resistance to the corporate capitalist attack on welfare states and defence of the concessions won by the left through the twentieth century. Green campaigners have focused upon curbing the excesses of corporate power and on tax evasion and avoidance. By placing emphasis on the accumulation of wealth and avoidance of tax, it has been possible to provide a countervailing narrative to austerity. The £13 trillion of unpaid tax hidden in offshore havens is more than enough to pay for a welfare state for everyone, not just in Scotland. One way in which the change in Green politics is evident is in the approach to austerity. Greens have firmly rejected the Westminster government's approach to austerity. Campaigns have included boycotting forced labour schemes, supporting a living wage for all and opposing cuts to social care. Given the tendency amongst some

Greens to see cuts and austerity as a way to deliver 'degrowth', this is a significant victory for progressives in the Green party.

Generational politics

Greens have also harnessed the new generational politics. Where other parties have focused on benefits for older people, like preserving universal bus passes, winter fuel payments and pension levels at the expense of provision for lower people like Education Maintenance Allowance (EMA) and £9,000 a year university fees, Greens have stood firm on these issues. This is part of the broader anti-austerity movement. Howker and Malik's *Jilted Generation* (2010) outlines how those born after the 1979 general election have had their lives systematically structured through market relationships. This generational position has been crystallised by the stand taken by Greens against university fees. The betrayal of students by Labour and the Liberal Democrats in supporting a doubling or trebling of fees for students has reinforced Greens' position as a generational party.

The neo-liberal strategy is to avoid resistance from those who have enjoyed welfare through their lives by retaining their benefits. Government should instead withdraw support one generation at a time. So pensioners living in southern Europe get winter fuel payments and high earning workers in their 60s get bus passes. Meanwhile, today's students have to pay for their education after they leave school and have a discriminatory lower level of minimum wage until they reach the age of twenty one. Few significant benefits have been withdrawn from older people, while those born after the election of Thatcher are forced into a market relationship at every stage of life.

Greens, of course, do not think that older people don't deserve these continuing benefits. We believe we have the common wealth to pay for benefits for all, a common wealth being secreted overseas by tax avoidance and evasion. We are stronger together, and these benefits are very effective at eliminating poverty and ensuring social solidarity. What Greens demand is that we level up the solidarity available to those under thirty, not level down those enjoyed by other generations.

Greens reject the spurious argument put by Conservatives, like David Willetts, that inter-generational justice requires the destruction of the welfare state and social infrastructure. This argument is based on a simplistic understanding of public debt - that it is always a bad thing. There is an important role in advocating a generational politics that Greens are fulfilling. It is important that we are joined by the rest of the left. It is important to build generational solidarity to address the generational injustices of neo-liberalism.

Greens and power

Greens continue to formulate their approach to power. This has focused upon a number of areas. The first is on increasing participation in democracy. Instead of the old municipal model of power, where elected officials create a barrier between themselves and those they are elected to represent, Greens have sought to bring people into the heart of decision making. In Edinburgh, this has been manifested through the *£eith Decides* participatory budgeting programme. *£eith Decides* allows the community to make decisions on up to £17,000 of community grants for voluntary sector programmes in Leith. While this is a relatively small sum of money, it has attracted up to 600 members of the public to the events where funding decisions are made. It is the first step in a process Greens hope will lead to one per cent of non-statutory Council spending being decided by the people. This builds confidence in public spending and returns people to the heart of the democratic process.

Greens have tried, wherever possible, to give more power to people and communities. Where other parties have done this in order to avoid the responsibility for making cuts, Greens have done it to ensure that people are more a part of the political process. This has extended to making the argument for a renewal of local democracy in Scotland (see Andy Wightman, *Bella Caledonia* website 2012). By reinvigorating town and district councils, Greens hope to be able to create more effective governance.

Asset taxes and universal services

In two of the key debates around taxation and public services, Greens have taken distinctive and radical stances. Greens are the party most committed to asset taxes as a way of achieving a fairer society. While traditionally progressive parties have sought a focus on taxing income, Greens recognise the vital role played by asset wealth in preserving privilege. Greens are, therefore, committed to land value taxes as a way of ensuring a tax on assets. As a tax on all land assets this is unique to Greens. Greens have also committed to supporting universal public services. This is of fundamental importance at a time when the Labour Party has chosen to abandon universal public services free at the point of use, believing it to constitute a 'something for nothing culture'. The very clear evidence from around the world is that public services only for the poor quickly become poor public services. The most fundamental manifestation of the Green belief in a universal public services is the policy of a universal citizen's income. This would be paid to everyone, avoiding the benefits trap and allowing an end to poverty. At a time when welfare claimants are under attack as never before a citizen's income would create an easily supported central plank of our welfare state.

Conclusions

The Scottish Green Party finds itself in a position that is both difficult and loaded with promise. While the party's work over the past seven or eight years in parliament has largely bypassed the electorate, there are huge opportunities ahead to deliver our policies and to help transform Scotland. We can lead the independence debate by mobilising a radical vision of an independent Scotland. We can resist the neo-liberal order's demand for cuts to public services. We can be spokespeople for a new generation, most damaged by neo-liberalism. But to do so we must move on from talking about our comfort zone issues of transport and waste. Too often we seem to be chiding people for making difficult life decisions out of necessity. Instead we need to stand with and for people in their daily struggle - a daily struggle imposed by a plutocratic elite determined to destroy our planet and our society through greed and for individual gain. Green politics is vital in the century ahead. It is our job to place it at the centre of Scottish public life.

Chapter 20

An enemy of the state

Gordon Morgan

You have not only the right to choose, but the duty to choose and if you are not surrounded by poverty, by war, by oppression, by cruelty - that is what you have chosen. (Jean-Paul Sartre The Roads to Freedom)

The UK state is one of the mainstays of world capitalism and a major barrier to any developments towards a socialist world. Scotland separating from the UK would weaken the residual state's ability to engage in aggressive wars and hopefully fatally undermine its nuclear capability. Prospects for socialism would be enhanced not only in Scotland but ultimately in England and elsewhere. On these grounds alone all socialists in Scotland should vote 'yes'. I have not always held these views.

I spent my first years in rural 1950s Ayrshire, where my father a Labour supporter, teacher and local historian regaled me with tales of Roundheads playing football with Covenanter's heads along Galston Road; Bruce being cured of leprosy at Prestwick well; Wallace and other romantic individuals; the Enlightenment; as well as the benefits of the welfare state and by implication the Union. This syllabus was also reflected in school history books. For most of my school-days, I identified myself as a Scot who was British and remained in ignorance of wider social history or the true nature of Britain. My political awakening came with television pictures of the Prague Spring and Vietnam. Going to university in 1968, I joined protests against the Vietnam War then joined the Young Liberals and was elected to their national executive. In 1969, I helped organise protests against the South African Springboks team at Murrayfield. To my shock a female student next to me was beaten bloody and unconscious by a special policeman deliberately and without provocation, smashing her head against a steel scaffold. Peter Hain and I had to stretcher her out. Other friends had limbs broken in police vans. Fortunately, against the orders of an inspector, my police arrestors only twisted my arms and threw me out. This was my first encounter of the state as Marx described it as 'a body of armed men' being used for political ends, i.e., the defence of representatives of Apartheid, and marked the beginnings of my progress from liberalism to Marxism.

Over the next years, I developed as a student then community then union representative and read more history and theory. The effect of Heath government's economic and social policies - rising unemployment, the UCS work in, the 1972 miners' strike (at Longannet picket line, getting my legs severely bruised taught me why all the miners had brought newspapers and wrapped them round their legs as shin-guards) and 'Bloody Sunday' and its aftermath - all made me acutely aware that the government and wider state could deliberately create confrontation between classes for ideological purposes. The idea the state was a neutral servant of the people was frankly laughable.

In the autumn of 1972 at a Scottish Actuarial Society meeting I made a criticism of the speaker for ignoring the chaotic effect politics could have on investments. I was then invited to join four heads of Scottish Life Insurance companies for a pint. Their concern was the ineptitude of the Heath Government and all of them agreed that 'we need a Labour government to sort the unions out'. The following week the *Financial Times* took the same line. The casualness of this encounter and its real effects (Labour won) made me aware how subservient the media and the British establishment were to the interests of finance capital and also how they believed they could and, indeed, had manipulated the Labour Party e.g. blocking nationalisation of insurance during the earlier Wilson government.

Around then I determined to oppose the UK capitalist state and attempt to change things. I joined the International Marxist Group (IMG) and was elected to its Central Committee (CC) and Scottish Committee. In 1972-1973 apart from union activity and Vietnam, the IMG's main campaign was support for those struggling for civil rights in Ireland. This had developed into a war between the nationalist population and the British army and many British troops were being killed, some based in Stirling. Alongside Pat Arrowsmith and Finlay Binning, I spent months issuing leaflets and talking to soldiers telling them how to defect to Sweden to escape returning to potential death in Ireland.

Inevitably, in 1974 some Scottish IMG members demanded we also fight for Scottish independence. However, before the discussion had begun they left to form the Scottish Workers Republican Party (SWRP). Some peripheral supporters, who we suspected of being police agents, suggested a violent campaign. This resulted in my refusing to talk on the phone to these individuals, the phone being bugged and all mail to the house being opened by the post office and delivered without envelopes. My attitude to the UK state appeared to be reciprocated.

Lest I seem paranoid, note that as well as an ongoing Irish war, Allende's government had just been overthrown in Chile, the Greek colonels were still in power, as was Salazar in Portugal and Franco in Spain, the IMG's sister organisation, the Ligue Communiste, had been outlawed in France in 1973 for opposing fascists; Kevin Gately was killed by police on an anti-fascist demonstration in London; and many other IMG members houses were being raided and papers seized but no arrests. At this point, we notice that a 'grain silo' on Colonel Stirling's lands outside Stirling was being protected by armed men with Alsatian dogs. Shortly thereafter, tanks encircle Heathrow airport in what we were later told was an exercise. We now know plans for a military coup were in place with Lord Mountbatten to replace Wilson (see BBC documentary *The plot against Harold Wilson* 16 March 2006). Democracy in the UK is optional for the ruling class!

A Scottish road

I consider capitalism the most infamous, bloody and evil system that mankind has ever witnessed. (John Maclean, High Court, Edinburgh, 9 May 1918)

Marx and his followers held that whilst socialism cannot be achieved in one country, a break from capitalism can happen in a state (e.g. Russia, Cuba) or even city (e.g. Paris 1871, Petrograd 1905 and 1917). A decisive break Lenin, Trotsky and Gramsci believed requires a party with 'hegemony' over a major portion of workers. Creating or controlling such a party at the correct place in time is the hard part as well as the little matters of strategy and internal democracy. However, a break from capitalism in an advanced economy could spark a series of other breaks. Could Scotland prove the catalyst?

The debate started in the Scottish IMG by the SWRP led to a re-looking at the works of John Maclean and other Communists as well as a debate with the likes of John Foster and the Keynesian views of Gordon Brown in his Red Papers in 1975. A series of IMG pamphlets were produced under the banner Scotland, Labour and Workers Power. These analysed Scotland's wealth - people and oil - as well as our rich tradition of strikes/workers councils and community support and Labour/communist electoral history. Whilst disagreeing with Maclean's historically inaccurate view that primitive communism existed under the clans, we fully endorsed his call for a Scottish Workers Republic based on workers control and public ownership. The question was how to get there.

All agreed Scotland had the right to self-determination and most disagreed Scotland was 'an oppressed nation'. In a wider context, there were differences in relation to the Labour Party - could it be used as a vehicle for entry-ism and influencing unions or should a party be created by a break from Labour. There was also the matter of the EU (then the EEC) - to join or not. Much of the debate related to the then situation of international capital and the union movement which has now changed significantly.

The majority view which I supported was to support a Scottish Workers Republic, campaign against the EEC, work for a Scottish Assembly, work in trades councils and unions and look for a break from Labour to the left. After a relatively successful Labour campaign against the bosses' EEC despite losing the referendum in 1975, a major opportunity to present our views arose with Jim Sillars breaking from Labour to form the Scottish Labour Party (SLP) in 1976. All members of the IMG joined the SLP. I became secretary of Pollok Branch. The SLP tapped into a rich seam of opinion that wanted a radical social democratic agenda allied to a demand for Scottish Independence. Although there were differences in approach, Rowland Sherret and I pushed for the IMG to constructively build the SLP and saw its potential to replace Labour as the representative of unions and the wider labour movement in Scotland. Unfortunately, Sillars demanded everyone agree with him that Scotland should be in the EEC. Most disagreed so we were summarily expelled without a debate and the SLP was destroyed (see Henry Drucker's *Breakaway: The Scottish Labour Party* (1978) for more).

Having seen the possibilities of a pro-independence left social democratic/socialist party in Scotland, constructing such a party has been for the last thirty five years and remains my goal. The rest - denied a parliament in 1979 despite winning the referendum; founding the *Scottish Socialist* magazine on a cross-party basis; fighting for the parliament; founding the Scottish Socialist Alliance with the 'Independent Socialist Scotland' slogan; winning the 1997 referendum; the SSP, the split, Solidarity, the independence convention and now the independence referendum - are all as they say history. But thirty five years on, what do I now think socialism is and are we closer to getting there?

Socialism and capitalism

Communism is socialism plus electricity (shortened from 'Communism is the power of soviets plus the electrification of the whole country!', Lenin, Eighth Congress of the Soviets, 1920)

Engels and Marx's anticipated socialism coming into being after the replacement of capitalism worldwide when the state 'withers away' and all human needs are met through public ownership and democratic cooperative management of production. Would money then be used as a medium of exchange or of (labour) resource allocation? The productive forces and automation would need to have reached a point where all material needs/wants for each individual could be met without restricting another's needs/wants. We are a long way from realising that ideal of socialism, and should take the lesson from the Stalinist regimes of Eastern Europe that in Lenin's words 'democracy is indispensable to socialism'. But can we replace capitalism with something better? There are positive signs!

Capitalism has greatly expanded the world's productive forces and population, lifted billions out of poverty and ignorance, created a world intellectual and technological culture undreamed of by Marx. The means for democratic control over decision-making have been created. Governments and large corporations use computer techniques for forward planning and allocating resources which would have amazed the Soviet Gosplan and could be used to end poverty and hunger forever. Yet we are at best two bad harvests from mass starvation, global warming threatens our survival, wars for resources and over religion and ethnicity are endemic and a small group of billionaires control an unparalleled share of resources and monetary wealth. Marx predicted that at least!

The problem remains a world order of privately owned wealth and money as a means of exchange rather than use value, i.e., capitalism. But capitalism has, indeed, changed over recent decades and that has to be taken into account. In the mid-1970s, Keynes' views of actively managed capitalism began to be replaced by Friedman and Hayek's monetarism - no state intervention in the market. Within a few years, most academic economics espoused these dogmas and current day politicians were taught this new orthodoxy which has everywhere failed. The motivations for this ideological shift amongst academics at that time have been inadequately studied. In a contrary move in 1971, the US abandoned the gold standard. However, the US dollar largely remained the world reserve currency, so effectively the US could print money without inflationary effects. This role of the dollar was only partially threatened by the development of the EU and Euro-dollars then the Euro. In effect, Europe and the UK learned they also could print money without inflation.

The collapse of the Soviet Union and the development of kleptocracies in Russia, China and other states extended capitalisms hubris and the development of financial services and growth of debt rather than investment and production became the main forces for economic growth in the developed world until the crunch of 2007. This era of globalisation, i.e., American dominance and integrated markets, seems to be coming slowly to an end. Nevertheless it hugely influences UK policy. The week after 9/11, I was working in the City of London. At least 50 per cent of those I was dealing with had been in the Twin Towers in the last two months. This brought home to me how closely Wall Street and London were integrated at a social level and why traders refer to the Atlantic as 'the pond'. Nor should it surprise us that UK and US foreign policy have been closely aligned on Iraq, Afghanistan and on nuclear weapons. Remember the Falklands and the assistance the UK received from the US! A retired submariner told me he was in a nuclear submarine in the River Plate during that war. Does anyone doubt Thatcher would have bombed Buenos Aires if the Ark Royal had been sunk?

Crisis and change

In financial markets, the idea of 'value' has limited value. (Benoit Mandelbrot *The (Mis)behavior of Markets*, 2004)

The boom in derivatives which led directly to the credit crunch was based on the idea that you could manage financial risk using mathematical formulae - CAPM, MPT and particularly Black-Sholes (Sholes won a Nobel for his work). Financial institutions were legally obliged to value investments using these formulae, typically using credit agencies to do the calculations. Mandelbrot, mainly known as the inventor of chaos theory, for decades had been highly critical of these formulae believing the data showed they massively underestimated risk and investment values were largely chaotic. In 2007, he was proven correct, but credit agencies live on.

World GDP is approximately $70 trillion, derivatives in 2007 were priced at 11 times world GDP. All these derivatives were valued by credit agencies, held on banks' balance sheets and treated as equal in worth to other assets such as factories or materials. With the collapse of confidence in 2007, much of banks' balance sheets were wiped out, i.e., their derivative assets had no 'exchange value' so banks stopped lending to each other or companies. Every bank in America and Europe was technically bust. Credit and other financial instruments, described by Marx as 'fictional capital', had actually become on a world scale 'fictional' and were unavailable.

Monetarism had no answers and instruments not used since the 1930s were exhumed by central banks. The UK and the US embarked on creating money from nothing, i.e., 'quantitative easing', and guaranteeing bank (worthless) debt at face value. Close to one year's world GDP in money terms has been created in this way. Politicians have been miss-educated in monetarism. Most continue to believe in the clear separation of monetary and fiscal policy and, in the face of credit-led recession, espouse balanced budgets and 'austerity'. Countries in the Euro-zone have been worst affected. These countries have given up the ability to devalue and print money and the Bundesbank and Angela Merkel refuse to hand over policy to the ECB or the European parliament, conscious that it benefits from exploiting the peripheral European countries. Unless fiscal austerity is abandoned by the Euro-zone, leaving the Euro or breaking from capitalism are the only options for Greece and other relatively undeveloped Euro-zone countries.

The UK can print money and through investments in the 'real' economy boost spending and consumption and GDP, but its politicians, Labour, Tory and sadly most of the SNP, remain wedded to failed policies such as hoping to resurrect zombie banks and looking to the private sector for recovery.

Other spokespersons for capital realise the risks of on-going recession and are examining even more radical options. When the governor of the Bank of England can in October 2012, openly discuss, but reject the merits: of simply writing off all Government debt; of ending the separation of fiscal and monetary policy; of handing out fivers outside the bank and using helicopters to dump money on poor areas - we can conclude they know not only monetarism but Keynes plan a), b) and c) have failed and 'we ain't in Kansas anymore' as Toto was told in the Wizard of Oz.

New revolutions, new strategies

*We must confront the privileged elite who have destroyed a large part of the world. (*Hugo Chavez, 4 September 2002)

Struggles of the poor and indigenous people of Latin America against corrupt elites tied to the US are not new. However, the achievements of Chavez's Bolivarian revolution since 1999 are unique. Elected on a capitalist social reform programme to be financed by oil revenues, his government has moved steadily to the left despite US coup attempts, building close ties with Cuba, nationalising foreign companies, redistributing wealth to the poor, banning sexual discrimination, introducing a shorter working week and promoting community organisation. Since 2007, Venezuela has provided medical help and finance across Latin America and supported socialists and indigenous campaigners as well as setting up a Bank of the South in opposition to the IMF. Increasingly, Venezuela is showing that an alternative social model to free market capitalism is possible in large parts of the world.

The Arab Spring has been as yet confined to a liberation struggle against corrupt elites initiated by largely educated, unemployed youth. Increasingly bloody, it has already shown dictators have no hiding place in the digital age and has thrown up new forms of self-organisation via social media which are being copied across the world. The struggles against austerity across Europe have shown once again the unstable nature of a currency union which unites countries with widely divergent economies. The forces of combined and uneven development are accentuated and the weaker countries impoverished. Only radical wealth redistribution between rich and poor and rich country to poor country can save the Euro.

Across Europe, nationalist parties seeking to break from their existing states are seen as an alternative to austerity. Basque nationalist parties now have a majority in the regional parliament; Catalonia's parliament is seeking an independence referendum; and both Walloons and Flemish seek the breakup of Belgium. Scottish people are not alone in seeking to control their destiny.

In October 2008, Alistair Darling, then UK chancellor, used anti-terrorism legislation to freeze £4bn of assets of Iceland's banks including its central bank, in effect, holding the Icelandic people to ransom for the credit crunch. The Icelandic government capitulated but the Icelandic people sacked their government and refused to pay the UK compensation for the actions of private banks. They have since in a uniquely democratic fashion rewritten their constitution enshrining people's rights and become a rapidly growing economy, largely debt free. Increased affluence, literacy, new technology and an increasingly multipolar world, have created new opportunities for social liberation across the globe. Latin America is one example but if Iceland with a population of 320,000 can be affluent, independent and democratic, why can't Scotland?

Socialism in the UK?

Labour's never been a socialist party, but it's always had socialists in it. (Tony Benn, Radio 4, 10 February 2006)

I was in the Labour Party for 16 years, having joined when we were attempting to turn Labour to the left, by electing Tony Benn as deputy leader, in order to better fight the Tories. That failed. We then attempted to democratise the party and in Scotland to make the Scottish Labour Party autonomous. That also failed. What we got was less democracy, removal of conference power, keeping of Trident, abolition of Clause 4 - a symbolic act but the last token of Labour's homage to socialism - and finally the Iraq and Afghan wars and the Labour Party embracing austerity. Labour has failed to abolish the Lords, failed to embrace voting reform, failed to tackle unemployment and poverty - but embraced billionaires like Ecclestone and city bankers. There is not a scintilla of evidence that Labour can be reformed, that significant forces wish it to be reformed or that any UK socialist party can emerge to replace it. One thing that may force left realignment in England is the loss of any prospect of a Labour government when Scotland leaves the UK. A yes vote in 2014 would necessarily bring to the fore a discussion about a democratic road to socialism in England.

A socialist Scotland

Democracy is the road to socialism (attributed to Karl Marx)

All supporters of independence, irrespective of their vision for Scotland, should unite to win the referendum on a simple message of scrapping

Trident and providing hope - for the future, for peace, prosperity and tackling unemployment, poverty and deprivation. Alex Salmond is right! Scotland has a similar GDP to the rest of the UK; it has abundant renewable energy which can be developed to make Scotland a green beacon within Europe; it has some of the best universities and research establishments in the world and a well educated population; it has successful companies and unique brands like whisky and exports across the world. For these reasons, Alex Salmond is right that without changing very much an independent Scotland can become a prosperous left social-democratic but capitalist nation. But Salmond's vision is not of a truly democratic or socialist Scotland and these visions must also be presented to the Scottish people in the 2016 Scottish Parliament elections alongside his.

There are obvious inconsistencies in Salmond's vision:

- How can we remain a monarchy and claim to be a true democracy?

- Why should a newly autonomous Scotland seek continued membership of the EU, an organisation which demands the interests of multinationals take precedence over Scottish workers and Scottish laws? As a non-member we can still embrace laws and projects that benefit all.

- Why should we commit to retaining the pound even if England and Scotland's economic interests diverge? Economic autonomy is essential for independence and a separate Scots pound could better meet our needs.

- Why when we are committed to a Green Scotland and the fight against climate change, do we promote continued exploration for oil and gas in Scottish waters?

A socialist vision would also say:

- Unemployment is immoral! Provide jobs and training to all who need them, for all who need what they could do or produce. Cut the working week appropriately.

- Ensure those who can contribute and those who need get! Tax income, land and large mansions appropriately and prevent Scottish residents from using tax havens. Ensure the vulnerable are cared for and no one is in dire need.

- Take back into public ownership essential services! Nationalise transport, electricity, gas and telecoms companies. Introduce rules restricting foreign ownership of strategic resources.

Any socialist programme for Scotland needs discussion and extension, however, rejection of 'the inconsistencies' listed above must be shared by many in the SNP, Labour and Green party.

A new party for a new Scotland?

*As the present now, Will later be past, The order is Rapidly fadin',
And the first one now, Will later be last, For the times they are
a-changin'. (Bob Dylan, 1964)*

The SNP has always argued for an independent Scotland but encompassed many visions for how a 'free' Scotland should develop. Can free marketeers and socialists survive in the same party when choices have to be made? The Labour party in Scotland has always contained both nationalists and unionists, social-democrats, socialists and opportunists and had its policy decided by London. Can it reinvent itself as a left party in Scotland or will it seek to re-unite the UK - something with no successful precedent in other countries? Those of us who have consistently argued for a socialist Scotland have every expectation of a new socialist party rising phoenix like from the ashes of the Union.

Chapter 21

Scotland 3.0

Mike Small

In the face of the austerity measures sweeping Europe, and the inevitable and formidable resistance it has evoked, the question of a socialist response has returned, not just in Scotland but across the world. But the nature of the debate has changed. Two things have altered fundamentally the stakes of what we are discussing. One is the more naked aggressive and exposed conduct of late capitalist society, its brutal inequalities, its obscenely commodified relations and its manifestation in Westminster social policy characterised as punishment of the poor and extended elite rule. The debate is no longer between capitalism and socialism: it's between democracy and authoritarian kleptocracy. The second is the reality of climate change and the unfolding ecological crises. With these two driving forces - come two counterbalancing forces, the relentless inferiorism of Scottish society, daily reinforced by those whose interest it serves, and in ecological terms, the endless addiction to materialism that we are all part of.

So what grounds have we to believe that any sort of change is possible here, and what would that change process look like? It might not be about replacing one system with another, it might not be about 'one great heave' and it might not draw upon some pure cultural root of Caledonian collectivism. It's likely to be chaotic, unexpected, diverse in motivations and outcomes and to draw on a much wider set of impulses and experiences. Alongside these tensions - between the drive for self-determination and the Scottish cringe and the cycle of consumerism and productivism - lies a profound disillusionment with the political process itself. The collapse of faith in political processes, governance and conventional forms of leadership could feed into a positive loop of more radical and far-reaching changes, focusing on not just the economic goals and ends but the structures and processes too.

From Sheridan to Blair, the outmoded icons of conventional political leaders have been exposed. After Peter Capaldi, the contrived, compromised, born-to-lie structures and systems of power need no further satire-isation. They are bare as bones before a world-weary electorate. The counter-factual of the Obama-moment crushed in its absurdity and summed up in the pitiful (but tragically accurate) slogan of Sarah Palin's 'How's that hopey-changey stuff working out for you?' lies as a warning to anyone wanting to try and envisage a better Scotland. So the question we are all faced with, set against this backdrop of political failure is: can we aspire for better? Would we believe anyone who told us we could? The answer is probably not, and yet we all know in our heart of hearts that 'continuity' is not an option. The option remains 'socialism or barbarism'.

If we could imagine a renewed Scotland, one that exemplifies a new set of standards, that would be Scotland 3.0. It's one that's created collectively, relies on open source social programming and crowd sources a new republic. We can imagine this sequence:

- 'Scotland' as covering the period from the rise of Cínaed mac Ailpín (Kenneth McAlpine) to 1707;

- 'Scotland 1.0' as covering the period of Union 1707-1999;

- 'Scotland 2.0' covering the brief period of devolution 1999-2014; and

- the subsequent emergence of Scotland 3.0 following independence.

Why will any of this happen? Why would change come to deeply-conservative Scotland which sometimes feels like its blighted by generations of inertia?

Paul Mason, BBC *Newsnight* economics editor and author of *Why It's Kicking Off Everywhere*, has written:

> *There is something in the air that defies historical parallels: something new to do with technology, behaviour and popular culture. As well as a flowering of collective action in defence of democracy, and a resurgence of the struggles of the poor and oppressed, what's going on is also about the expanded power of the individual. For the first time in decades, people are using methods of protest that do not seem archaic or at odds with the contemporary world; the protesters seem more in tune with modernity than the methods of their rulers. Sociologist Keith Kahn-Harris calls what we're seeing the 'movement without a name': a trend, a direction, an idea-virus, a meme, a source of energy that can be traced through a large number of spaces and projects. (Guardian 3 January 2012)*

We're not immune to this process, we are, as perpetual innovators lost in post-industrialism in a great place to explore this new landscape.

Deindustralialisation, decentralisation and democracy

Any Scottish manifestation of socialism would need to look beyond productivism and consumerism towards ideas of being and living. And, if the fires of industrialism fed the furnace of John Maclean, John Wheatley, Michael McGahey and Jimmy Reid, the wind and sun of post-industrialism need to power the new socialist movement. The task is not, as Salmond would have it, the 'reindustrialisation' but the 'deindustrialisation' of Scotland. The structural consequence of re-imagining political systems that do not lend themselves to corruption, secrecy and the self-delusion of power and the practical consequences of deindustrialisation are the same: a decentralisation of bodies, institutions, organisations and systems into smaller units and confederations. Democracy, economics and technology recast at a town, city and regional level as appropriate. The scale, structure and technology of a socialist Scotland will be profoundly shaped by the reality of the networked age.

It may take us time to awaken to this. At the moment there are few icons of Scottish identity that we cling to more tightly than our industrial past: 'Clydebuilt'. Perhaps only our military past is held as dear to us as the idea of Scotland as industrial nation. One motivation for this process to kick-off is the spectacular re-framing of the national question into one of class war and society versus the state by the leaders of Labour and Conservative parties in late 2012. The 'new realism' of Lamont and Davidson may have a combustible effect when mixed with the flammable material of mockery that finds expression through the pages and screens of a feral union press and the Anglosphere.

Too poor?

What's emerging is a response to the Bullingdon Club politics that asserts a 'independence without nationalism', a response that is becoming more open to possibility as the Unionist parties haemorrhage credibility. But there's still a massive task to overcome the inferiorism that blights Scottish culture. While this culture is fed daily by the forces that wish to protect vested interests and the establishment values, there's also a palpable growing sense of possibility emerging as forces merge in the prospect of fundamentally disturbing the British state. There's a growing realisation that while we are a country of huge potential scarred by inequality but this is not a poor nation:

• Scotland contributes 9.6 per cent of total UK tax revenue, yet only 9.3 per cent of total public spending is spent in Scotland (GERS)

- Scotland generates over £1,000 more tax per person than the UK average

- Over the past 30 years, Scotland has a cumulative relative surplus of £19bn

- 95 per cent of North Sea oil reserves and revenue are situated in Scottish waters; North Sea oil has been estimated by scientists to have over 60 years of production left

- Scottish North Sea oil and gas is an asset worth over £1 trillion

- In the next five years alone, North Sea oil revenues will be £54bn

- Trident cost approximately £15bn and continues to cost over £2bn annually; removing Trident from Scottish waters would save billions which could be spent on hospitals, schools and the police

- A Scottish Defence Force would save Scottish taxpayers at least £1.5bn; independence would reduce our spending on defence from £3.3bn annually in the UK to £1.8bn under independence

- The war in Iraq cost the UK nearly £10bn; an independent Scotland would not take part in such expensive, destructive and potentially illegal wars

- Scotland has an exceptionally strong exporting sector, including whisky and renewable energy sustaining thousands of jobs and livelihoods

- Scotland has 25 per cent of the whole of Europe's renewable energy potential; fully harnessing this great asset could create 28,000 quality jobs and attract £30bn of investment to Scotland

These facts sit at odds with the daily diet of economic miserabilism and the extraordinary idea put forward that what Scotland really needs is to host weapons of mass destruction made in another country for the defence needs of a different century.

The emerging realisation is that Scotland needs to be liberated from the mindset and the dogma of neo-liberal Britain, and it needs to be creative about new economic models and social experiments to lead us out of the darkness of Union. People quite rightly point out that a yes or a no vote should not be cast solely on the exquisitely attractive option of permanently ridding this country of Tory rule. It's about far more than that. But the attacks on the gains of devolution, on the fabric of society, on the concept of univeralism and on the poor are not confined to the current Coalition Government in Westminster, or that 'new' Labour manifesto. They are built into the structure of the British state and the structure of power relations within it.

This is what needs to be understood about Britain, that it is structurally incapable of being progressive. Why? Because of the concentration of power and privilege in the south-east and in the City of London; because of the power of the military establishment; and because of the wholesale capture of government by private interests. The reality is that south of the Severn-Wash line, outside London, Labour holds just ten of 197 seats. This is why, if Labour wants to win some of these back, Labour must be according to Ed Miliband: 'the party of the private sector as much as the party of the public sector' and the party of the 'squeezed middle' as well as those of those in poverty.

This is getting worse. As the Tory party begins to shed its veneer of respectability and organise around the far-right agenda of *Britannia Unchained: global lessons for growth and prosperity* (2012), its authors MPs Kwasi Kwarteng, Priti Patel, Dominic Raab, Chris Skidmore and Elizabeth Truss call for a Britain of extreme economic liberalism in which, in the words of Labour's Jon Cruddas, 'their ideal worker is one prepared to work long hours, commute long distances and expect no employment protection and low pay'. The *Financial Times* called it 'shock therapy for the country', a quote the publishers, Palgrave, apparently took as a compliment.

Is this all the preserve of right-wing think-tanks of London and the chattering classes? Not at all. This is co-ordinated and is unleashing a new throwback to a new Thatcherite policy surge. As the Reid Foundation (9 October 2012) has outlined:

We should not mistake the onslaught for the passing thoughts of a few individuals on the back of the announcement that Scottish Labour is to review what its leader calls 'something for nothing' benefits. This is a political programme actively supported by a number of groups. Right wing think tanks (and especially the David Hume Institute) has been gnawing away at the principle of the welfare state for ages, mainly using 'public sector accounting' as its method of attack. Likewise many parts of the Scottish media have been curating a story about 'affordability' and 'maturity' for ages, absolutely confident in their belief that accountants are the most valuable members of society when it comes to defining political ideology. What you don't see is the use of the expensive lobbying budgets of organisations like SERCO or A4E or Atos Healthcare which are being used at all times to pressurise government to carry out more and more means testing (it's one of their main sources of profit after all).

There is an extraordinary attack coming. The carving up of the NHS is one travesty, now in the hands of the private sector. The extension of a tax system staggering in its inequality is a central part of rip-off Britain. This is the future we have to avoid being drawn into.

Scotland 3.0

As the date for the liberation poll is announced, clarity is needed. Liberation from what, for what? A replica mini-state is not what we need from this process. We need a new operating system, not a new computer. What social software do we need? What political apps are required? What could Scotland 3.0 look like?

Number one on my list - and I suspect the vast majority of us, is a response to the crisis in child poverty outlined recently as figures suggest 13 Scottish councils have wards where more than 30 per cent of children live in pockets of severe poverty. Equality needs to be hard-coded into the new Scotland. The 'worst areas were in Glasgow, the west of Scotland, Edinburgh, Dundee, Fife, Aberdeen and Stirling', in other words right across the country. The Campaign to End Child Poverty warned inflation, unemployment and cuts could see levels of deprivation spiral. The group has produced a map of child poverty for every ward, council and constituency. It's not a pretty picture. In fact, it's a national disgrace. The figures are matched for old people suffering from fuel poverty and the results of this poverty are seen in our disgraceful record of ill-health. This is a union dividend that needs to end. This isn't going to change with new policies or a new constitution. Instead, it's going to change with a new economics.

Second, we need to create an open-source politics. This needs to be the new operating system, contrasting with Britain's closed, elitist, feudal stratification. It needs to be an operating system called 'Scotland SD'- Scotland self-determination. Self-determination is about new emerging forms of democracy - forms that reflect the kind of society we might want to create, ones that might be inclusive, participative and creative. So let's build new systems where people want to participate in forming and shaping policy and running their towns and cities and communities. And that process itself has to be open to all. Crowd-sourcing our new constitution should be a key aim of the wider independence movement.

Third, we need to download a Peace App. We can start by scrapping the British state's Weapons of Mass Destruction, and we can continue by withdrawing our troops from whatever theatre of war they are currently engaged in. Then we can offer a better option to our young men than the 'adventure' in Belfast, Helmand or Iraq as has been dangled by recruitment officers for hundreds of years. It's a sick farce from Tory-Liberal and Labour alike to be opposing the extension of the vote to 16 and 17 year olds whilst young people have died in Blair's Wars in Iraq and Afghanistan.

Fourth, we need to upgrade the anti-virus software that has affected our culture and leaves it marginalised, degraded or abandoned. Finally, this - like all upgrades - needs to be part of global network. The network is the thing. It's not just about us. And there is no doubting that there are geoplitical consequences for what's going on. Scotland is home to 5m UK citizens, five per cent of UK GDP, Europe's sixth largest finance sector in Edinburgh, four Trident submarines (with around 200 nuclear warheads and 58 ballistic missiles), four regular British Army garrisons, three frontline RAF bases and six Royal Navy bases. On its North Sea coast lie oil reserves perhaps amounting to 30bn barrels. So, it's important not just for us. Scotland has been the military playground, a place where the British elite are educated and where fossil fuel extraction has made oil barons rich and propped up 30 years of neo-liberalism from Maggie T to Tony B to Dave C. All that's got to go! Install Scotland 3.0 now. *Warning this may take two years to download.*

Chapter 22

Many possible roads

Dave Watson

My political philosophy probably starts with Rousseau's proposition in his *Social Contract* (1762) that human beings are inherently good, but are corrupted by the evils of society - or, in more modern terms, our environment. In that context, I cannot deny the influence that my own environment has on my approach to a Scottish road to socialism. I was born in Liverpool. My dad's family were Scots and my mum's English. I have worked in several parts of England and Wales before moving to Scotland in 1990. My oldest friends and relatives live and work across the globe and regard national boundaries largely as irritations to be crossed - with the possible exception of sporting affiliations!

I joined the Labour Party on my fifteenth birthday, founded a Young Socialist branch that year, became a Constituency Labour Party secretary at sixteen and spoke at my first party conference at seventeen. In political terms, it has probably been downhill ever since! One of my early political influences was a former Welsh miner who had been to Spain to fight against fascism. He argued strongly that democratic socialism was an international cause, a movement for freedom, social justice and solidarity. His emphasis was on solidarity, as he believed that socialism could not simply be achieved in one country alone. I still believe he was right. We live in an increasingly globalised society in which the dark forces of the Washington Consensus seek to influence and direct national economies across the world. The fate of people living in many different parts of the world is more interlinked than ever before and, therefore, as socialists we must work together.

So, my environment leads me away from nationalism. This doesn't mean I reject the politics of national identity. I am simply not drawn to it. Paradoxically, it also means that I am relaxed about the prospect of Scottish independence. If I could be convinced that it will, not could, lead to greater social justice, then I would indeed support it. By the same token, Unionism has no hold on me either.

In this chapter, I will be taking the reader on my personal journey, examining the prospects for the Scottish road to socialism. I am a lawyer by training, so I am drawn to evidence. I am also a pragmatic - some might say hardnosed - union official who takes his responsibilities to the members I work for seriously. The advice I give, and decisions I take, impact upon the lives of members as well as others. This doesn't mean that I reject deeply held beliefs - I did after all start with Rousseau - but I will need more than flights of fantasy.

Scotland and socialism

Let's start our journey here in Scotland. This is a country long claimed to have an egalitarian tradition. As William McIlvanney put it, the most appropriate motto for a Scottish flag would be: 'Hey - that's no' fair!' This tradition is arguably based on the democracy of the Kirk and the Scottish education system. While Burns was too early to be described as a socialist, the democratic and nationalistic strains in his poetry influenced later socialists, including Keir Hardie. As Bob Holman (2010) explained: 'Hardie absorbed Burn's example of the low born making good and his insistence on the basic equality of mankind. He rejoiced in 'A Man's a Man for a' That'. Hardie was a supporter of home rule and Ramsay MacDonald, Labour's first Prime Minister, was Secretary to the Scottish Home Rule Association that was formed in 1886. And, Scotland's place in the vanguard of socialism in the UK is the stuff of leftist lore. The Scottish Labour Party was founded in 1888, followed by its subsequent merger with the Independent Labour Party in 1893. This led the labour movement in Scotland to move away from the Liberal Party and into the formation of the Labour Party in Scotland in 1906. Red Clydeside may have been viewed by the government of the day as a possible Bolshevik uprising but, in fact, the organisers had more modest industrial goals.

Nonetheless, communism was strong in Scotland, leading to the formation of the Communist Party of Great Britain (CPGB) in 1920. While Willie Gallacher took most of the Red Clydesiders into the CPGB, there was a strong nationalist element led by John MacLean who formed the separate Scottish Communist Party. Home rule remained an important part of Labour policy after Hardie's death. In 1918, Labour in Scotland fought the general election on a programme of 'self-determination for the Scottish people' and put home rule bills before parliament in both 1924 and 1927. The Scottish National Party was formed in 1934 in a merger that included the left of centre National Party of Scotland, led by John MacCormick, who came from an Independent Labour Party background. The harsh realities of the depression and World War Two marginalised the home rule tradition. Although Churchill appointed Labour home ruler Tom Johnston as Secretary of State in 1941, it was administrative centralism that dominated post war thinking through nationalisation and the foundations of the welfare state.

Before we get too carried away with our socialist tradition, it is worth remembering that the only political party ever to gain a majority of the Scottish vote (50.01 per cent) was the Conservative and Unionist Party in 1955. This was largely achieved by capturing the Protestant Orange Order portion of the working class vote but it did not mean that the socialist tradition had died away. The Communist Party had 10,000 members in Scotland in the 1950s and was particularly influential in the union movement. The STUC adopted support for home rule in 1969, although it was not until 1979 that the Labour Party in Scotland fully supported that position.

The 'egalitarian myth' is not without its critics, including David McCrone's (1992) assessment. He argued that patterns of social mobility are substantially similar throughout the UK. His study concluded that the 'myth' appears to be more ideological than 'social structural'. Others have pointed to social attitudes survey data. On issues like public ownership, taxation and the welfare state, opinion between Scotland and England usually diverges by only a few percentage points. Still, even a few percentage points can matter and it is indisputable that, in modern times, Scotland consistently votes for parties which make a left of centre pitch. The leafy suburbs of Scotland, which in England would be safe Tory seats, return Labour MPs to Westminster. Some argue that this is less a desire for socialism than a reflection of 'a corporatist conception of Scotland's welfare, stemming from the strong integrative role of dominant bureaucratic institutions' (Hearn 2000:153). This ethos even spills over into broader social policy. For example, a recent YouGov poll found over half of Scottish savers and investors say they want at least some of their money invested according to green and ethical criteria. The finding was well above the 45 per cent recorded for the UK as a whole (*Herald* 12 October 2012). Interestingly, for me at least, the notion of Scottish egalitarianism appears to be adopted by the largest immigrant community in Scotland, the English. Murray Watson (2003) having interviewed English immigrants for his book concluded: 'The majority of English migrants came to adopt many of the values and perspectives of their host communities and country of adoption. In this sense there was a discernible Scottishing effect'.

My conclusion is that, although I accept it can be subject to exaggeration, there is a recognisable egalitarian ethos in Scotland. This is not to imply, as some do, that we are the only part of the UK with a radical tradition. So at the end of the first stage of my journey, there would appear to be at least the building blocks for a Scottish road to socialism.

Independence

So let's not mess about, if there is a Scottish road to socialism that must include consideration of independence. Radical groups (like the Radical

Independence Conference network) campaign for independence. Colin Fox, in the *Morning Star* (19 September 2012), made this pitch: 'for the Scottish Socialist Party independence means that Scotland will be free from the neo-liberal stranglehold of the financial speculators that dominate the world economy today'. As a blog post on UNISON Active rather harshly put it: 'For his next trick presumably he will make the burns run with whisky and create big rock candy mountains' (*Scots Wha Hae?* 24 September 2012). This is an amazing claim from a political party that has no elected representatives and no explanation as to how this seismic political change is going to happen. Radical independence does at least include the Scottish Green's and Patrick Harvie's claims for independence are a little more rooted in reality. He argues for independence to bring about a 'transformation in our society, our economy, and our politics'. His vision has much that I can agree with on energy, a more equal society and even some of the green economics. However, this vision is not really socialism and many Greens view of how we should live are the opposite of collective. Patrick's pitch is summed up in his statement to the launch of the Yes Scotland campaign on 26 May 2012: 'Does anyone really consider the UK capable of this transformation? I can't see it happening'. Maybe not, but this is hardly a positive case for independence.

The harsh political reality is that independence will be defined by the SNP, not by those of a radical independence persuasion. As Bruce Crawford MSP put it at the 2012 SNP conference in the NATO debate: 'There are of course others with a legitimate view of how an independent Scotland would look. We should respect their views, give them the space to articulate them but make no mistake. It will be the SNP view that will predominate, and it will be the SNP view that the vast majority of the people will hear'. The SNP, particularly in the west of Scotland, has many socialists within its ranks. On most issues, I would be hard put to find policy differences between the latter and people like me on the left of Scottish Labour. The question I have to ask, is it their vision that drives SNP policy? With regard to social policy, the SNP may have a left of centre approach. As Alex Salmond himself said: 'I think that people are looking for a political party which is collectivist in terms of its view of social provision'. However, on economic policy he famously said, Scotland 'didn't mind the economic side' to Margaret Thatcher, but disapproved of the 'social' implications of her policies.

I examined the economic case for independence in my contribution to the Red Paper Collective' (2012) publication, *People Power*. It appears that John Swinney's post-independence strategy is to keep the pound within a Sterling zone including financial services (and possibly consumer) regulation. A VAT cut for tourism and construction coupled with a Corporation Tax cut to give Scotland a 'fiscal edge'. I struggle to follow this strategy as handing over monetary policy to the rest of the UK limits the scope of fiscal policy. We only have to look at the Eurozone crisis to see the link between monetary and fiscal policy. For an SNP government to support regulation from London, which will very much be in the interests of City institutions, is bizarre. If the key economic levers are in hands of another country, then there is less influence on monetary and fiscal policy than under devolution.

However, my biggest difficulty is with the concept of a 'fiscal edge'. It appears that SNP policy is still wedded to the Celtic tiger strategy. Even if desirable, you simply cannot replicate Ireland of the 1990s. Neither is the marginal tax differentials used in some EU countries, as argued by SNP strategist Stephen Noon (on his blog 'Scotland uniquely incapable?' 7 September 2011), a solution. Multi-national companies are not interested in paying marginally less Corporation Tax - they want to pay no tax. Other small countries like Denmark, Norway, Sweden and Finland all have higher Corporation Tax and better performing economies. The evidence that tax cuts pay for themselves (Laffer curve) is simply not there. Any saving goes into profit, not investment and many of our companies are sitting on vast cash reserves already. There will certainly be a huge hit on public finances that is unsustainable. A better way is actually higher taxation to fund investment in people, plant, infrastructure and research. The Laffer curve theorists that promote this view would also apply it to personal taxation. In particular, they oppose progressive taxation and promote the flat tax approach. Like so many issues, the SNP leadership has been less than clear on where they stand on personal taxation.

We must also judge politicians on what they do, not just on what they say. The SNP in government has done many things I have happily acknowledged as positive. However, there is also an underlying centralisation creeping into their actions, undermining local democracy and that's not a vision of Scotland that I share.

So does all this look like the road to socialism? So far, I'm afraid not. Nor am I prepared to leap into the dark on the basis that we can turn it all around post-independence. At its worst, it looks like a strategy of Scotland the tax haven. Far from freeing Scotland from the 'neo-liberal stranglehold', it looks like we would be a welcoming home for that ideology.

Devolution

Devolution is at least an actual destination on our journey. Labour, to its great credit, delivered quickly on its 1997 election manifesto, resulting in the *Scotland Act 1998* which created the Scottish Parliament. This institution is now so well established that it is hard to imagine Scottish politics without it. While devolution may not have delivered Scotland from neo-liberalism, it has enabled Scottish solutions to Scottish problems. In particular, the collectivism I discussed above has been maintained through our public service structures, rejecting the marketisation that has overtaken England. The Scottish Parliament has also energised our engagement with the political process through its work, giving an access that simply did not exist pre-devolution.

So while the structures of political engagement have improved immeasurably, what about the outcomes? Here the picture is not so good. In key outcomes such as income, employment, health, learning and safety, the gap between top and bottom is much wider in Scotland than in other European countries. Worse still, most of these negatives are inter-generational and often clustered in small areas. There have been improvements since devolution but, on most key dimensions, inequalities have remained unchanged or become more pronounced.

There are some positive outcomes. Healthy life expectancy and household income have, in general, improved as have some learning outcomes, and the overall risk of being a victim of crime. However, income inequality has widened since devolution because the richest 30 per cent has got richer and the bottom 30 per cent has remained static. In education, the gap between the bottom 20 per cent and the average in learning outcomes has not changed at all since devolution. The gap in healthy life expectancy between the 20 per cent most deprived and the 20 per cent least deprived areas has increased from eight to 13.5 years. Thirty two per cent of adults in the most deprived areas in Scotland report a long-standing illness, disability or health problem compared to 14 per cent in the least deprived areas. Half of all young people in Scottish prisons have been in care. This rises to 80 per cent when looking only at those convicted of violent offences. This is despite just one per cent of all Scottish children having been in care. We lock up more people than in most European countries and politicians compete to be tougher on crime. The link between deprivation and the likelihood of being a victim of crime has also become stronger.

There are broader social factors that can affect outcomes in a city such as Glasgow. Carol Craig, in her *Tears That Made the Clyde* (2010), highlights that even after taking account of deprivation, Glasgow's indicators are worse than comparable cities like Liverpool and Manchester. She cites family breakdown rates and men detached from family life, together with a culture of violence and an unhealthy relationship with alcohol.

I spent around six months in 2011 looking closely at outcomes as an Expert Advisor to the Christie Commission. While that Commission made many positive recommendations on how public services might respond to these challenges, I recognised that more radical political action was required. Does that more radical political action require further powers for the Scottish Parliament? This was, of course, examined by the Calman Commission. Sadly, given the breadth of membership, it was doomed to propose only limited reforms. The politics of the time, particularly the views of MPs, made progress difficult. As Secretary of the Scottish Trade Union Labour Party Committee, I well remember the difficulty we had even getting the principle of a review of powers into the 2007 Scottish Labour manifesto. I subsequently chaired the Scottish Labour Party's Calman Working Party - not one of my easier tasks!

Nonetheless, Calman did result in the *Scotland Act 2012*. While the transfer of responsibilities in the Act was minimal, it will give the Scottish Parliament significant new fiscal powers such as: a Scottish income tax to replace part of the UK income tax; the devolution of stamp duty land tax and landfill tax; the power to create or devolve other taxes to the Scottish Parliament; new borrowing powers (although only a consultation on bonds); and a Scottish cash reserve to manage fluctuations in devolved tax receipts. So let's examine the extended devolution options.

Devo-Max (Hughes-Hallett and Scott 2010) proposes that all revenues would be raised in Scotland and the cost of reserved services would be paid to London out of these revenues. The mechanisms for this have been set out in some detail. What is less clear is the purpose or the economic benefit. In addition, this model in full is untested anywhere in the world and, therefore, there must be a real risk of unintended consequences.

Then we have Devo-Plus (2012). This proposal argues that most revenues would be raised in Scotland to pay for devolved services with VAT and National Insurance retained at UK level to pay for reserved services. Again, the mechanisms have been worked out in some detail, but the purpose of this devolution is somewhat vague. For that we need to look at the report's backers, Reform Scotland, objectives that are the apparently 'traditional Scottish principles of limited government, diversity and personal responsibility'. I obviously missed these principles in my description of Scotland's egalitarian tradition above! In the Red Paper Collective publication, I translated Reform's objectives as small state, privatisation and blame the poor. Not much hope for socialism there. The Liberal Democrat's federal proposals are similar to Devo-Plus, with the addition of some interesting ideas around local government.

While these proposals have adequate mechanisms, they do not meet the key test of devolution for the purpose of creating a more equal society and investment in our people. And, of course, they ignore issues of class and class power. Does this all mean that devolution can't provide a road to socialism in Scotland? I would argue that there is scope for a further transfer of powers to Scotland based on the principle of subsidiarity - the idea that matters should be handled by the smallest (or, the lowest) competent authority. This principle also applies to the Scottish Parliament in its dealings with local government because decisions should be taken as closely as possible to the citizen. In this context, I think there is a strong case for devolving a range of reserved powers including data protection, aspects of immigration, safety, competition law, franchise, drugs and energy policy. In the Red Paper Collective publication, I also set out the case for further fiscal devolution including full control of income tax, National Insurance, all property taxes and borrowing powers that are only limited by a prudential code.

While I believe there is the possibility of getting broad support for extended devolution, this in itself does not constitute a Scottish road to socialism. Devolved powers could just as easily be used for nefarious purposes. However, there is potentially a political consensus in Scotland to exploit these powers to tackle the underlying inequalities in our society.

Political will

That leaves us with the final part of my journey, political will. Many of the powers we need to create a more equal society in Scotland are already devolved. So if we had more through devolution or independence - would we have the political will to use them? As Wilkinson and Pickett have highlighted in *The Spirit Level* (2010), inequality is about more than income. It requires action on education, health, criminal justice and just about every aspect of social policy. Most of these are already devolved, yet arguably government has been better at producing glossy strategies than solid action.

Material inequality requires income redistribution, largely a function of the tax system. An independent Scotland would have greater control of these levers but would there be the political will to use them? Apart from the modest 'Penny for Scotland', no serious proposal, let alone use, has been made of ability to vary income tax by three pence in the pound. This arguably only applies to the basic rate. But will the 10 pence power in the *Scotland Act 2012* be used? Labour is wary of being labelled as 'tax and spend' and the SNP appear wedded to a low tax model in its approach to Corporation Tax and the regressive Council Tax freeze. Preventative spending illustrates the lack of political will. Just about everyone accepts the logic of preventive spending, including the Finance Committee and the Christie Commission, but the doing is much more challenging. Targeting resources on the bottom 10 per cent, as Christie recommended, makes sense even to the right wing, given the impact on public expenditure. Christie estimated 40 per cent public spending in Scotland goes on failure demand. But actually delivering it has got bogged down in a puerile political slanging match around universalism. Some still seem to believe Scandinavian levels of public services on US tax rates is possible.

I believe that extended devolution or independence could bring important levers to help address these issues and provide a Scottish road to socialism. I think a consensus could be developed, but our politicians need a bit of help. It is unrealistic to expect political parties to lead unless we have created a groundswell of public opinion. If we have not won over the people of Scotland, then we need to try harder. So let's start the debate, not from constitutional mechanisms, but from the sort of Scotland we want. Only then look at what type of constitutional change can deliver that vision. Initiatives like the Red Paper Collective, UNISON's *For a Fairer Scotland* and the STUC's *Just Scotland* (see appendix) provide the building blocks for such an approach. These set out a range of principles and policies that would create a better Scotland.

Conclusion

At the end of my journey, I must conclude that there are many possible Scottish roads to socialism. Those roads must be about building on our traditional egalitarian ethos to develop a civil society consensus around the sort of Scotland that we want to live in. As a socialist, I believe that should be a Scotland which is rooted in social justice with a real commitment to tackle inequality. However, I accept that I have to do more to persuade my fellow citizens of that cause. Only then can I reasonably expect our political parties to adopt the necessary and often challenging policies to deliver better outcomes for everyone.

Appendix

A Just Scotland Interim Report, November 2012

STUC

Introduction

At its Annual Congress in April 2012, STUC agreed to undertake a wide ranging consultation with its members and across Scotland's communities on Scotland's constitutional future. This reflected its view that there is a duty on civil organisations to ensure that it is not left to elected politicians alone to frame and conduct the debate on Scotland's future.

Historically, STUC and its affiliated unions have had a major part to play in the debate over Scotland's relationship with the rest of the United Kingdom. As one of the architects of the Constitutional Convention and having campaigned for the establishment of a Scottish Parliament, STUC is widely recognised as being a progressive force in Scotland's democratic development and a champion of devolution.

However, things do not stay the same. Scottish unions have changed significantly in the past two decades. The same is true of Scotland's communities. Activism manifests itself in different ways. Community empowerment and democratic accountability have diminished. New communities of interest have been formed and communication methods have changed. However, a strong ethos of solidarity and collectivism remains.

The starting point for the discussion was to allow individuals, trade union members and their families to be empowered to consider Scotland's constitutional future within the wider context of the collective values we hold. Thus, for STUC, the referendum debate needs to be seen, not just as a means of discussing the form of Scotland's constitutional arrangements, but as an exciting opportunity to reawaken a debate on social justice and equality, to talk about the sort of Scotland we want to see.

A Just Scotland was launched in August 2012. STUC published 12 discussion papers on the A Just Scotland website, considering a range of key policy areas. In addition to collecting the views of online respondents, STUC held five discussion events in Glasgow, Dumfries, Inverness, Edinburgh and Dundee which included members and also those in the wider community. As well as trade union speakers representatives from a number of campaigning and community organisations made presentations or otherwise contributed to the events. At the time of the A Just Scotland discussion, the process for the referendum had yet to be agreed. Anticipating two potential outcomes on the number of questions to be posed, STUC asked participants to consider the issue of 'enhanced' devolution along with the status quo and independence.

A Just Scotland is the starting point rather than the end point of that process. STUC has not reached a point where it is able to definitively recommend a Yes or No answer to the independence question.

It was never imagined that at this stage it would. There are, however, some key questions which STUC believes will help to shape the views of its members and some major challenges which both sides of the debate must meet.

Challenges

The first is a general challenge. To hold a full and frank debate, we need more information and less sloganeering. A minority within the STUC discussion process were both clear about how they intended to vote and what they believed the economic, social and democratic consequences would be. A greater number, whether or not they leaned towards a yes or a no, voiced frustration at the level of information and analysis currently available and the overall poor quality of the debate.

The second challenge, again for both sides of the debate, is to persuade us that social justice is more achievable as a consequence of their chosen constitutional option. Inevitably the focus should be on Scotland, but the impact of change on the countries within the rest of the UK, as well as Europe and wider world can also be part of that discourse. Neither side of the debate can claim with authority to be the 'voice for social justice'. The Yes Campaign derives considerable support from sections of the business community which aspire to a low tax, low regulation economic and social model with diminished social protection. The 'Better Together' campaign includes the Scottish Tories. In both campaigns there is a tension between the desire to project a vision of social justice and the view that policies are a matter for the post-2016 elected governments. STUC recognises that the policies of elected Scottish Governments cannot be wholly predicted, however, it is not enough to 'wait and see'. The result of the referendum will in large part be conditioned by what people expect will be achieved and the post-referendum future direction of Scotland in the short and long-term, whether independent or devolved, will be influenced by how the debate develops between now and October 2014.

The third challenge is for the Yes Campaign or to the political parties which support it. A Just Scotland participants cited concern at mixed messages emanating from the campaign. A central argument for independence has been rejection of the UK approach to taxation, welfare and a range of Coalition policies relating to social justice. The First Minister said at SNP Conference in October 2012 that only independence could protect the social fabric of Scotland. However, on other occasions, a low tax economic model with 'growth at all costs' has appeared to be the approach with current or increased spending imagined to flow from increased GDP not redistribution. It is fair to say that our members will need to hear of a more detailed vision for fairness in an independent Scotland if the Yes campaign is to succeed.

The fourth challenge is for the 'Better Together' campaign and specifically for the Scottish Labour Party. There was concern and, on occasion, outright anger at some of the economic, social and international policies which have been pursued by government, particularly at the UK level. 'Not being the Tories' and negative messages about the SNP will not suffice and members will require a clear steer on how economic and social justice will be achieved at all levels of government and to be convinced that the Scottish Labour party intends to play an active and radical role in achieving this. Equally, whilst not necessarily convinced of the 'Devo Max' model as broadly outlined by the Scottish Government, there is clear support amongst those who are opposed to independence (or undecided) for significant additional powers for the Scottish Parliament. Detailed attention to this must be given by the 'Better Together' parties in the next period and meaningful proposals brought forward.

In addition to posing these challenges to the campaigns, this interim report, leaning heavily on views gleaned from those involved in the *AJS* discussion, looks at the key areas which will impact upon a socially just future for Scotland. The report also references the developing Scotland wide debate and views received both from affiliated organisations and a range of other organisations.

STUC hopes that the interim report will provide a basis for further public discussion. For its part, STUC will organise a range of further discussions, reports and events concentrating on the detail of some of the issues raised whilst continuing to focus on the social justice as the outcome we aim to achieve. It will also participate in events organised by other community and campaigning organisations which share our approach.

For richer or poorer?

Notice has been served that the debate over Scotland's fiscal position will be a key battleground for the two campaigns. Somewhat surprisingly, few AJS contributors concentrated on arguments that Scotland would become dramatically better or worse off through achieving full independence. This may be due in part to the wildly differing and poorly argued positions adopted by the two sides of the debate. It may also reflect the view that the resource question should focus less on absolute figures and more on how wealth is shared.

The 'Better Together' campaign has focused on an interpretation of the General Expenditure and Revenue in Scotland account (GERS)1 account which shows both the UK and Scotland to be in deficit with Scottish public spending exceeding its Gross Domestic Product (GDP) by a significant amount - amounting to £1200 per household. Whilst the campaign is correct to point out that comparisons between Scotland and the UK are between relative deficits (to be clear, even if Scotland were independent it would still be borrowing heavily at this moment in time), it singularly fails to recognise that an independent Scotland's GDP would include around 90 per cent of current UK oil tax receipts. The £1200 deficit figure is flawed and the 'Better Together' campaign should not be using it.

The 'Yes campaign' has spent considerable time and resources to convey the impression that post-independence, Scotland would be better off to the tune of over £1000 per household. Whilst it is true to say that in 2010-2011, Scotland's net deficit (including a geographical share of oil and gas revenues) compared to the rest of the United Kingdom (rUK) was £2.7 billion better, the campaign has failed to clearly point out a) that this is a comparison between deficits rather than surpluses and b) that 2010-2011 was a year of high oil prices and that past and future oil revenues vary considerably. Scotland's net fiscal position within the UK is likely to be healthy for the next couple of years, but most experts predict a falling of oil revenues from the date that Scotland would become independent. There is also some uncertainty over the interest rate an independent Scotland would be charged for its sovereign debt. Therefore, the £1000 figure is not a reliable starting point for calculating the relative fiscal position of Scots post-independence and the Yes campaign should not be using it.

A more sensible analysis draws the conclusion that Scotland's income against expenditure has been reasonably balanced when the effects of a geographical share of North Sea oil are taken into account and higher public spending are factored into the equation. In the future Scotland's relative fiscal position under independence would be initially heavily reliant on the tax revenues derived from oil and gas and, as that resource dwindles, *on the success or otherwise of wider economic development.*

A further factor for an independent Scotland would be the price paid for servicing its debt. As a new nation with no 'credit history' and most probably a comparatively high deficit and stock of debt, Scotland might find difficulty in convincing the markets that it should enjoy interests rates at the same level of rUK, through its income stream from oil revenues and the extent to which, if at all, the rUK Government and Bank of England would guarantee Scottish sovereign and bank debt would both also be factors. It should also be noted, however, that a number of people at the AJS seminars argued for an independent Scotland which would nationalise the oil and gas sector and in turn, significantly impact on revenue streams and Scotland's choice of currency.

It remains the case that, whilst informed analysis of the relative positions of an independent Scotland and rUK is to be welcomed the debate, it will be difficult to resolve on this basis. AJS participants were most interested in how wealth is shared. Evidence from Wilkinson and Pickett (*The Spirit Level*, 2010), shows that it is the division of resources in a society rather than their absolute level which impacts health and happiness. AJS participants heard from the Scottish Poverty Alliance whose discussion paper highlights some key issues following this theme as well as from the Church of Scotland on its project to examine the purposes of economic activity.

The question therefore is not about absolute economic wealth, but how best to reduce economic inequality. Equally we should ask not whether Scotland could be a viable independent nation, it could. But which constitutional settlement provides best scope for Scotland to flourish?

Sustainable economic growth

Scotland has prospered marginally since devolution compared to the UK, improving our performance somewhat on employment levels and GDP. However this modest improvement sits within the context of a systemically weak and unequal UK economy.

There has been near consensus at each of the AJS events that current economic orthodoxy has led to policy which has undermined the economic security and living standards of workers in Scotland. Privatisation, deregulation (particularly of finance), business tax cuts, attacks on the welfare state, the undermining of workers bargaining power and of workplace health and safety has not led to a fairer and more prosperous society.

These processes have produced a society that is less equal, fair and democratic and an economy more unstable and much more prone to systemic crises. It is vital that Scotland's politicians start to embrace new economic thinking as part of the constitutional debate.

A consistent theme throughout the AJS has been the question of economic growth and its purpose. Respondents are sceptical of the claims and counter-claims assuming automatic advantages and disadvantages of the various constitutional scenarios.

Major constitutional change could have significant consequences for specific industrial sectors. The STUC will develop its thinking in this area over the coming year but it is reasonable to assume that defence, financial services and energy could face particular challenges. The drivers of defence procurement will change due to naked politics and issues around technology ownership. Financial institutions could face a new regulatory system and questions over lender of last resort facilities and deposit guarantees. The scale and nature of investment across energy sub-sectors will depend upon the subsidy available and the regulatory regime.

Given that renewable energy is widely regarded as Scotland's greatest industrial opportunity, the potential loss of subsidy from the UK market could be a constraint on development. However, the UK electricity market is in the process of fundamental reform; a process which may not have concluded by the time of the referendum. The consequences for the Scottish energy industries pre and post independence are therefore far from clear.

Attempts to privatise the Royal Mail have foundered on the basis that the Universal Service Obligation (USO) has dissuaded private companies from purchasing the asset. Current moves to water down the USO could see the fragmentation and piece by piece sell off of the service. Independence would not necessarily provide a satisfactory Scottish solution to this and the existence of a UK-wide service would appear to be at threat under any constitutional scenario.

Whilst the STUC accepts that constitutional change either through enhanced devolution or independence offers the prospect of potentially developing better policy more effectively aligned with additional economic levers (i.e. industrial and tax policy) and building more effective institutions, we are profoundly sceptical that better policy and more effective institutions will lead to growth rates akin to those of developing nations. Indeed, we believe that the notion that the long-term growth rate can be significantly improved by, for instance, cutting corporation tax, is misguided, damaging and wrong. The assumption that policy alone can achieve such outcomes is poisonous to the debate about Scotland's economic future.

Under any constitutional scenario, the successful long-term development of the Scottish economy will depend on the quality of both policy and institutions. There are no simple policy levers which if pulled will ratchet Scotland's growth rate up to levels of the BRIC countries. In any case, the STUC believes that it would be impossible to seriously reconcile growth rates of eight or nine per cent with the Scottish Government's climate change targets. What should be the aims and objectives of economic development and in what ways might Scotland's constitutional position become a key determinant of future success?

Monetary policy

There was a degree of uncertainty amongst AJS participants over the implications of proposals for currency post-independence. In terms of the three options available, no-one argued for a policy of adopting the Euro. For some the optimum solution is an independent Scottish currency allowing monetary and fiscal policy to operate together, however this was not examined in depth given that the version of independence currently promoted by Scottish Government ministers would see Scotland remain part of a monetary union with the rest of the rUK.

This would entail Scotland continuing to use Sterling, the Bank of England (BoE) continuing to set interest rates for the whole of the UK, and UK institutions (BoE, FSA and Treasury) continuing to regulate the financial sector on a UK wide basis. These arrangements will inevitably include some kind of fiscal compact limiting the independent state's ability to borrow and spend.

It should be noted that the First Minister (and some others) has recently argued that such arrangements would be fairly loose given the similar productivity of the Scottish and UK economies. Learning from the recent crisis and ongoing events in the Eurozone it is hardly feasible that the dominant partner in the currency union would facilitate such arrangements without stipulating the smaller partner's fiscal envelope. The degree to which Scottish Ministers would have flexibility within that envelope to develop radically different tax policies is also highly uncertain. Whilst recognising that this is but one model of an independent Scotland it is the one that has to be taken most seriously as it is proposed by the current Scottish Government. And the STUC has major concerns over the model as currently described.

An unavoidable conclusion is that the successful long-term development of a sustainable and fair Scottish economy would be heavily reliant on the macro-economic direction of the UK irrespective of Scotland's constitutional position. Would Scotland be in a better or worse position to influence this if independent?

Fiscal policy and social justice

In the context of opposition to wrong-headed austerity measures, participants were keen to explore the potential for fiscal levers which might be available to an independent Scotland or under enhanced devolution.

An independent Scotland would be expected to assume responsibility for its own debt and within the limits of prudence be able to adopt different approaches to challenges such as the current economic crisis. The two main political parties in Scotland have both made clear their opposition to the austerity approach of the Coalition Government, and whilst future conditions are difficult to predict it can be assumed that in certain scenarios, the capacity to borrow to invest would be a likely feature of progressive governance in Scotland.

As discussed earlier, it is unlikely that the dominant partner in the currency union would not seek to limit the smaller partner's fiscal envelope, particularly if the interest rate on Scottish debt demanded by the markets was reliant on implicit expectations of rUK underwriting of Scottish debt.

It is certainly feasible that an independent Scotland could establish a separate borrowing capacity with which to undertake alternative spending and capital investment policies at points during the economic cycle. What is the likely extent of this capacity (compared to the new borrowing provisions contained within the Scotland Act), and what are the implications for credit rating, interest rates and conditions placed upon Scottish fiscal policy by rUK?

Tax policy

A substantial majority of the advocates of independence at AJS seminars have stressed that their position rests on the opportunity independence provides to establish a fairer economic and social model. Awareness of the iniquities of the current taxation system and of the degree of tax avoidance formed a major part of the discussions. There was a regular assumption during AJS that an independent Scotland could and would wish to make use of progressive taxation to meet social justice and redistribution ends. An alternative view given was that the reality of 'tax competition' would actually drive Scottish taxes down and limit or undermine progressive measures.

Once again, potential limitations arising from the currency union emerge. Would rUK seek to negotiate to limit the potential for tax competition through limiting corporation tax variation for instance? Membership of the EU would certainly open the possibility of objections from countries such as Germany and France which dislike the low corporation tax policy adopted by Ireland. Equally, and particularly given Scotland's fairly high levels of GVA per capita, rUK and particularly its less productive regions and countries might itself seek to limit the variability of corporation tax. In any case, AJS participants argued strongly against the use of lower corporation tax and it is fair to say that its potential use in an independent Scotland will dissuade rather than persuade a yes vote amongst union members.

There is strong support for the potential use of income based taxes to support services and welfare transfers. It was recognised by some that the integrated economic and currency framework would place practical limitations on the extent to which any Scottish Government would be likely to vary income based taxes upwards, indeed some made the argument that the most likely direction for income related taxes would be downward with a view to increasing the tax base through offering lower rates. In terms of other taxes, the EU limitations with respect to VAT were recognised along with practical limits to the variation of 'behaviour taxes' such as tobacco and alcohol duties.

Notwithstanding the limitations, a Scottish tax system would be able to more easily consider new approaches to local taxation. It could potentially make income based taxes more progressive and increase overall taxation to fund public services, although, the converse is also true. The capacity to look at taxes as they interact with the welfare system would also be a potential feature of independence.

Whilst some flexibility would exist, are there any guarantees that the fiscal and monetary arrangements outlined as the most likely to be negotiated following independence would facilitate higher social spending; or is the opposite true?

Taxation and further devolution

There was a general acceptance that the tax powers currently held by the Scottish Parliament (including those proposed by the Scotland Bill) are too narrow, limiting the capacity to create a more progressive tax system and impacting accountability. At present revenue from devolved taxes in Scotland is one of the lowest in Europe at 13.8 per cent, just over £4bn. After the Scotland Act 2012 is implemented that will rise to 30.8 per cent, just over £9bn.

No single proposition for devolving additional taxes emerged. Few actively promoted the Devo Max option wherein all taxes would be devolved and a grant paid to Westminster in lieu of services provided. This is largely seen as independence without some of the advantages and a number of contributors including the Devo Plus campaign highlighted it as the worst of the three options.

Far more support was evident for enhanced devolution. It was widely agreed that the new powers of the Scotland Act do not go far enough. Frustration was voiced that the pro-union parties have yet to bring forward tangible proposals for enhanced devolution. That said, no single scheme was proposed by respondents though note was taken of the Devo Plus and Red Paper Collective proposals. The discussion predated the findings of the Scottish Liberal Democrat Home Rule Commission. Enhanced tax devolution would see taxes raised in Scotland in a general range between 50 per cent and 100 per cent of overall Scottish spending, which equates to 30 per cent and 60 per cent of the combined Westminster and Holyrood spend.

The taxes most favoured for devolution were income tax (all bands) and all property based taxes. Some also favoured the devolution of National Insurance. Fuel, alcohol and tobacco taxes were also supported though there was a degree of greater scepticism on the potential for varying these. The devolution of Corporation Tax was not supported as it was identified as the most likely to lead to tax competition. In all of the aforementioned scenarios a continued, but reduced block grant was supported on the grounds of UK-wide redistribution and stability.

Under independence, we anticipate negotiated limits to Scottish tax powers as a consequence of currency union and practical limits as a consequence of the integrated nature of the UK economy. There is a particular risk of tax competition around corporation tax and policy limitations imposed by potential tax flight.

There was surprisingly little support for Devo Max amongst participants but a genuine interest from some in the various enhanced devolution proposals, will the pro-union parties come forward with detailed proposals for the devolution of additional tax powers?

The labour market

There is widespread anger at the attacks on employment rights, equalities and trade union rights at Westminster and this is not a view confined to active trade unionists. Participants from key social justice campaigns identified labour market regulation and pay in particular as a primary driver of poverty and income inequality.

Incredibly, in a nation where the main parties on either side of the constitutional debate claim to be of social democratic bent, there has been virtually no discussion at all on the likely structure and regulation of the labour market in different constitutional scenarios. The assumption appears to be that the UK labour market will continue to be regulated as it is now or that a new Scottish state would simply replicate the current regulatory framework.

The STUC is clear that the orthodoxy of flexible labour markets has led to an economy where work is less well paid, less secure and less permanent. The human and social consequences are severe and reasonably well understood but the macroeconomic consequences are almost completely overlooked. If the wage share in the economy of an independent Scotland continues to fall then the only way in which the products and services the economy produces can be consumed is through rising debt. This hardly provides for the foundations of a stable, prosperous society.

The issue of trade union freedom is central to this question. Strong unions which are able to bargain effectively and, as a last resort, undertake industrial action without undue impediment, play a key role in ensuring better wage distribution and share. Thus a vision of an independent Scotland which committed to more equitable trade union laws and which enshrined democratic participation of trade union members in the economy would be an attractive proposition for many members and trade union reps. The question of whether, in an integrated economy such as would still exist post independence, progressive reform would be enacted, is harder to answer.

The European Union has always been a matter of debate within the trade union movement. However, there is a shared criticism of the historic failure of UK Governments to sign up to all of the labour protections accepted by most other EU nations and a concern that in any case, the EU has moved unambiguously towards a deregulatory agenda in which the single market overrides all other considerations. Thus the current debate over automatic membership, or otherwise, of the EU has allowed a narrative to emerge in which no side of the debate has been challenged to say what the EU should be doing differently and how each would work within their stated constitutional preference to protect and enhance regulated labour markets. Proponents of the status quo have given our members very little reason to believe that improving labour market regulation is on the agenda.

Beyond general opposition to the deregulatory agenda of the current Government, the Labour Party both at UK and Scottish level has failed to convince members that, even on election, it would pursue a positive reform agenda on labour market issues. In this context it should not be surprising if many trade union members feel that there is little to be lost in pursuing a 'Scotland alone' approach to regulation. That said, the current SNP Government and the YES campaign have had almost nothing to say about an alternative vision for the labour market in an independent Scotland. What does either side of the debate have to say about fair employment and pay as the basis of a sustainable and fair economy?

Public services, universalism and welfare

There was a widespread view amongst participant in *AJS* events that public services are fundamental both to sustainable economic recovery and achieving social justice outcomes. Thus, the debate about Scotland's future cannot be separated from how future services will be funded and how they will be designed. There was a wide recognition that the Scottish approach to public service delivery is distinct from south of the border. Criticism of UK public service policy was not confined to the actions of the current Coalition Government with many blaming 'new' Labour for initiating many of the reforms including the creation of Foundation Hospitals, privatisation of local authority services and education reform south of the border. In each case, an overwhelming majority preferred the Scottish approach, highlighting the record of successive governments in Scotland in resisting NHS privatisation, limiting the contracting out of local authority services and committing to free and accessible education.

There are a number of caveats:

- Widespread anger at the level of cuts to public services did not focus solely on the UK Government with a number of respondents highlighting the failure of Scottish Governments to use revenue raising powers or maintain taxation levels to fund public services.

- Deep concerns exist about the drift towards less accountable public services through the diminishing role of local government and the creation of arms-length delivery companies.

- Empowering service users and properly involving public service staff in service design was recognised as an imperative though many speakers recognised the tension between this and providing a universal quality of care and for strategies such as personalisation not to be used as cover for budget cuts.

- The use by successive governments of private finance mechanisms to fund capital investment was a focus for critical comment.

In public services which are currently devolved, the likely employment impact of independence would depend on overall public spending commitments of the Scottish Government, which would in turn be reliant on revenue. There are however issues for those who currently deliver reserved services for the other parts of the United Kingdom but are based in Scotland. Government departments such as the Department of Work and Pensions, HM Revenue and Customs, and the Driver and Vehicle Licensing Agency do not necessarily distribute staff evenly on a regional basis.

Overall, 9.4 per cent of civil service employment is in Scotland which is above the Scottish population share but consistent with its 2010-2011 share of GVA and UK public spending in Scotland. Further detailed analysis in this area is likely to undertaken by civil service unions.

Another key area of discussion relates to demographic change. The ageing population across the United Kingdom and much of the western world is understood to provide significant challenges for public service delivery as well as the provision of state and occupational pensions. The most significant questions in relation to independence surround the question of whether Scotland's current demographic trends are more challenging than those of the UK and the extent to which such trends as can be identified can be addressed.

An independent Scotland would require to negotiate with rUK arrangements for sharing existing and future state pension responsibilities. There are certainly ways in which this could be achieved though not without some complications. Equally, the liabilities or assets of the unfunded public service pension schemes which include the NHS, teachers' and civil service schemes would require negotiated separation using actuarial valuation where possible but using other criteria in the case of the Civil Service scheme.

The extent to which Scotland's population is ageing more rapidly than that of the UK, the generally earlier mortality rates north of the border and the extent to which independence might encourage inward migration are all subjects which will require further analysis.

Whilst the record of political parties in Scotland would suggest an approach more founded in the public service ethos, what can the proponents within the Yes and No campaigns offer in terms of a vision for future public services which goes beyond rejection of aspects of the UK model and towards a more complete vision of public services which are democratically accountable, free at the point of delivery and of consistent quality?

Universal services

The debate over universal services intensified towards the end of the AJS process. Throughout the AJS discussions we heard of strong attachment to those services which are provided universally in Scotland but not down south. These include free travel, free tuition, free personal care etc. This reflects an understanding that universalism supports a philosophy of social solidarity in which all who are able contribute and all benefit irrespective of income. It also reduces inefficiency and transaction cost.

For many, the current public spending cuts being driven by Westminster put such services in potential jeopardy and make a strong case for independence. However, if the prize of the maintenance, or even extension of universal services is to be a convincing persuader for independence, a much clearer vision of a just taxation system will be required. There is a clear divergence of opinion between members who believe that Scotland could and would introduce more redistributive taxation and those who believe, either that the scope of an independent Scotland would be severely limited and/or the political will is not currently manifested by any major party. Issues around tax competition and progressive taxation have been covered in depth in another area of this report.

The ability to provide some universal provisions and to adopt different approaches to public service delivery is a cherished feature of devolution.

The effect that constitutional change would have on the delivery of education in Scotland was not given considerable attention at the AJS debates as education is primarily a devolved area, where a uniquely Scottish system already exists. There was, however, some discussion over how education could better support participation in the democratic process and many participants believed that citizenship education has a valuable role to play in Scottish schools and there was general support for lowering the voting age to include 16 and 17 year olds for all elections. There were, however, also general concerns raised about the need for better funded early years education and childcare provision and increased funding for further education colleges.

Participants identified higher education as an area where constitutional change could make a difference due to the globalised nature of this sector. Potential positive benefits of independence could come from the creation of a Scottish specific immigration system which would allow Scottish Universities to become more attractive to overseas students. A range of AJS participants cited that recent changes to the immigration system made by the Westminster Government are already making Britain less attractive to students from outside the EU and making it more difficult for universities to attract staff. These changes present a challenge to the Better Together campaign as many believe that current aspects of Government policy are having a negative impact on the international reputation of British universities.

Equally, however, independence would almost certainly create a short term funding crisis in higher education in Scotland. RUK students, who currently pay fees to Scottish institutions and add significantly to the funding available in the Scottish system, would be classed as EU students in an independent Scotland and therefore no tuition fees could be charged as long as tuition remained free for Scottish students. Some participants felt that this funding crisis could potentially endanger the long term future of free tuition in Scotland, and felt that the Yes Scotland campaign had not given sufficient detail on how funding for higher education would be maintained.

Maintaining universal provisions and improving the quality of services in general requires a commitment from all parties to use existing or new powers to increase tax revenues if required.

Welfare

Discussions about the welfare system at A Just Scotland events have taken place in the general context of cuts in welfare payments and the specific move towards the Universal Credit. In straightforward cash terms, the creation of a Scottish welfare system would be by far the largest shift in resources from UK to Scotland whether under independence or enhanced devolution.

In political terms both major parties in Scotland are openly opposing the current benefit cuts and some of the features of the new Universal Credit system. This was reflected by overwhelming opposition amongst those involved in the AJS discussions. Labour was criticised by many for its own approach to welfare reform and its refusal to signal a commitment to reversing all cuts. Differences of opinion emerged around the extent to which assumptions of Scottish people having a markedly more progressive attitude to welfare could be substantiated.

Thus the question of what sort of welfare system we might have is integral to the debate. A better welfare system would be simpler to claim and administer, would rely less on means testing and remove barriers and disincentives to work but would also move away from the extreme focus on conditionality. This would come at some cost. Long term predictions of the cost of welfare are difficult given its sensitivity to employment and inactivity levels as well as health and wider demographic factors. A simple if crude approach would be to assume that an independent Scotland would wish, at the very least to spend as much on a welfare system as was spent by the last Labour Government prior to the Coalition cuts. This would be around £2 billion a year, around four per cent of the predicted tax revenue of an independent Scotland - a very significant sum.

The legislative separation between welfare services and the devolved areas of health, education and housing continues to provide major challenges for supporters of the status quo. Irrespective of critiques of some aspects of the policy, the 'employability' agenda seeks to bring together the various interventions which will improve access and ability to work. There is a clear logic to all such interventions being fashioned by the same tier of government. The separation of these powers can also lead to negative incentives whereby the financial benefits of particular policy initiatives fashioned and paid for at a devolved level are accrued by the UK Treasury rather than in Scotland.

Participants were asked to consider the potential for devolution of the welfare system or elements thereof. It was recognised that this is a difficult process which has been complicated by the introduction of Universal Credit. Short of the full devolution of tax and welfare as imagined under Devo Max, the most coherent partial devolution proposal is forwarded by the Devo Plus campaign which imagines a system in which approximately £1 billion of additional expenditure is devolved covering primarily Attendance Allowance and Job Centre Services with the main elements of the benefit system including all pensions and the Universal Credit reserved. Additional payments could be made at the expense of the Scottish Government and passported benefits would remain devolved.

A more integrated relationship with the DWP can be imagined under enhanced devolution in which specific programmes undertaken by the Scottish Government with demonstrable savings to the UK welfare budget, such as direct interventions to create jobs for the long-term unemployed or additional childcare support linked to back-to work strategies could give rise to compensatory adjustments to the block grant.

It would not be reasonable or practical to ask of proponents of independence or enhanced devolution to describe a system which would be in place immediately following constitutional change. It is however reasonable to elicit views on what kind of system is aspired to and, crucially, is there an expectation that tax increases would be used to fund a more humane and effective system?

There are difficult questions too for those opposing the current direction of policy on welfare but who also oppose constitutional change. By any measure, UK public opinion is no more well-disposed to welfare than in Scotland. It is the case without question, that UK political parties are considerably less sympathetic to claimants. In this context what can those within the Better Together campaign offer to convince people that change is possible? Is serious consideration being given to further devolution of aspects of the welfare system?

Community empowerment and regeneration

Participants in AJS are overwhelmingly negative about the state of local democracy and community empowerment. Power has been centralised and there is a drift away from local public services, accountably delivered. Whilst the redistributive role of central government funding for local councils is recognised many felt that the balance between Holyrood funding (approx. 80 per cent) and local funding (approx. 15 per cent) is wrong. There are differences of opinion on the Council Tax freeze, but few doubted its role as a driver of further centralisation.

A range of contributors pointed to the size of Scottish local authorities and the number of electors per elected members, contrasting this with smaller councils across Europe. The Community Council system is widely considered to be broken and there is widespread cynicism about the 'voluntarist' approach to community engagement. Regeneration strategies centring on property ownership, debt finance and rising land prices came in for particular criticism as did the failure of successive governments to adequately invest in social housing. Questions were raised over community land ownership at all events, but noticeably in Inverness and Dumfries. On the positive side a number of community regeneration projects around renewable energy were highlighted as positive examples of asset based approaches to regeneration. Contributors consistently returned to the failure of previous 'trickle down' models of regeneration highlighting the importance of investing in communities through local employment and decent jobs paying a Living Wage. In this area the currently devolved areas of procurement and other government 'encouragement' were seen as key.

Promoting genuine community empowerment and sustainable models of regeneration are certainly not an alternative to debating constitutional change. Nevertheless a vision of a devolved or independent Scotland would be incomplete without a new approach to communities and local democracy. What additional powers should be devolved FROM Holyrood towards more local levels of government?

Equality and human rights

There was a high level of support for the principle of equality and for equalities law in the UK and a general agreement that the law as it exists at present is the minimum that we expect in our society. Many participants also acknowledged that the commitment to continued EU membership by the Yes Scotland campaign suggests that the floor for equality law and practice would continue to exist in an independent Scotland. Some participants were, however, sceptical of the role the EU and questioned the need to stay inside Europe, even in the context of discussing European minimum protections.

On the whole, however, conversation focused on where provisions could be improved with participants recognising that legal protections alone are not enough to achieve an equal society. Ultimately there was an acknowledgement that culture change within organisations and the wider community was needed to bring about real improvements in people's lives and that Government policy and the signals it sends through its own practices and decisions on funding levels, very much set the tone. This suggests that there is scope to change the general approach to equality, including how easy it is to enforce equalities law, which would lead to real, meaningful and positive outcomes in people's lives without significantly changing the legal framework.

There were also suggestions around improving equality outcomes in the private sector, including introducing a private sector duty, similar to the public sector duty, and making use of provisions like equal pay audits and quotas for boards. While no consensus was reached on how best to achieve these aims there was a general desire to see the private sector taking more seriously its ethical responsibilities and doing more to promote equality.

There was, however, general concern about the current UK Government's approach to equality. Many participants cited the swingeing cuts that are currently being made to the EHRC and the repeal of certain sections of the Equality Act as examples of where this Government is attempting to water down protections and the effectiveness of the law. This presents a challenge to the Better Together Campaign as it creates a negative context for this debate and calls into question the commitment of certain parties to achieving a more equal society.

Support for Human Rights came through strongly in the discussion and many saw this debate as an opportunity to improve the Human Rights requirements that currently have a justiciable basis in UK law. Participants were particularly keen for economic and social rights, including the right to join a trade union, to be enforceable under domestic law and saw this as a possible benefit of independence. Equally, however, there was some concern that independence could reduce the ability of Scottish people to enforce their rights and assurances are needed from Yes Scotland that the

Scottish people will not be left without domestic remedy, reverting back to a situation where the Strasbourg court is the only place for Scottish citizens to challenge a breach in their convention rights.

Immigration

There was general agreement that the approach taken by the British Government to immigration policy is extremely negative. Participants felt that recent changes to the points based system, including the move to place a cap on migration, were detrimental to the Scottish economy and to Scottish communities and that the Westminster Government tended to play on the legitimate insecurities of workers about their jobs in order to score cheap political points. There was also a general concern that the limited flexibility that existed in the system previously, to account for the different economic contexts across the UK, was being stripped back by the Government in Westminster, creating a system that is even less likely to work for Scotland.

Asylum seekers and refugees were repeatedly cited as groups that suffer under the current approach. Child detention, dawn raids and the forced destitution of asylum seeking families were all highlighted as shameful practices that mar the current system. The majority of participants felt that an independent Scotland would almost certainly approach the issue of asylum in a more humane way, offering dignity to those who have sought sanctuary in our country. There was a clear desire to hear a commitment at this stage from the Yes Campaign that an independent Scotland would restore the right to work for asylum seekers, allowing them the ability to support themselves and begin rebuilding their lives in this country.

International affairs and peace

AJS participants were almost unanimously opposed to the possession of nuclear weapons and the UK's involvement in wars such as Iraq. Equally, there was scarcely any support for continued membership of NATO, a position which has now been debated and narrowly defeated at SNP conference in October 2012.

Despite the generally negative view of UK foreign policy, many pointed out that the Scottish people's part in the British fight against fascism in the Second World War remained a matter of pride.

Critics of the UK's current foreign policy role and possession of Weapons of Mass Destruction were broadly in three categories.

'Break the British State' was a frequent theme and is associated with the views of a particular section of the Scottish Left. This articulates the view that the act of 'breaking Britain' will have significant international implications and serve to undermine rUK foreign policy in so doing damaging US foreign policy. This is presented as a general case although the forced removal of Trident from UK shores is a key factor.

An alternative view sees the removal of Trident as a good thing to campaign for on a UK basis but without the enthusiasm for the 'break the British State position'. In this view, there is little evidence that rUK as part of NATO would play a significantly diminished international role. A number of participants questioned the morality of remaining under a nuclear umbrella whilst removing nuclear weapons from Scottish soil and a degree of uncertainty exists as to the terms of any deal which saw Scotland remaining as part of NATO.

The support for removal of Trident is also enhanced by perceived savings to public expenditure. There was though a tendency to overestimate the actual savings (£200 million a year is a reasonable actual estimate).

There was also interest in the potential for a peace 'dividend' available from reduced conventional defence spending in an independent Scotland. Estimates of the levels of public spending released by a lower defence spend are of course reliant on the imagined size and scale of an independent Scotland's military scope. The Scottish tax base currently spends £3.3 billion per year on its share of UK defence spending and estimates of future spending have ranged between £1.8 billion8 and £2.5 billion.

There would of course be employment and procurement considerations which is of concern to many members and the YES campaign should be seeking to make some very clear commitments on defence diversification if they wish to pursue the 'peace dividend' position. Equally, a more detailed assessment of the likely size of the military capacity of an independent Scotland is required if an accurate assessment of the impact on local communities of potential base closure and reduced defence contracts is to be made.

Whilst there are concerns about the actual impact of the policy of removing Trident in the context of remaining membership of NATO, the most important question for the SNP, as part of the YES campaign, to answer is what vision it has for the role and size of a future Scottish defence force and what actions it might take to ameliorate the impact on Scottish industry of a reduction in defence contracts? Given that Scottish trade unionists appear to strongly support the removal of Trident, the question of the 'Better Together' parties is how else can Scotland and the UK be freed of Trident other than through a vote for independence?

References

Baird, S., Foster, J. and Leonard, R. (2007) 'Scottish Capital: still in control in the 21st century?' *Scottish Affairs,* No.58, Winter.

Bevan, A. (1952) *In Place of Fear*, London.

Dahl, R (1989) *Democracy and its Critics,* Yale.

Devo-Plus (2012) *A Stronger Scotland within the UK: first report of the Devo-Plus group*, Edinburgh.

European Commission (2007) *Employment in Europe Report 2006*.

Foulkes, G. (1981) *Socialist Arguments for Devolution,* Labour Campaign for a Scottish Assembly.

Scottish Government (2011) 'Table 3: Number of registered enterprises and their total Scottish employment & turnover by sector and country of ownership' March, wwwscotland.gov.uk website.

Scottish Government (2012) *Global Connections Survey 2010* wwwscotland.gov.uk website.

Gustavsson, P. (2005) Speech to Campaign for Socialism & Morning Star Conference Glasgow June 2005 Reprinted in *The Citizen* Autumn 2005.

Hearn, J. (2000) *Claiming Scotland: national identity and liberal culture*, Edinburgh.

Holman, B. (2010) *Keir Hardie: Labour's greatest hero?*, Oxford.

Hughes-Hallett, A. and Scott, D. (2010) *Scotland: A New Fiscal Settlement*, St Andrews.

Ibec Technical Services Corporation (1952) *An Appraisal of Ireland's Industrial Potentials*, New York.

McCrone, D. (1992) *Understanding Scotland: The Sociology of a Stateless*

Nation, Edinburgh.

McKinlay, A. and Morris, R. (1991) (eds.) *The ILP on Clydeside 1893-1932*, Manchester.

Red Paper Collective (2012) *People Power: The Labour Movement Alternative for Radical Constitutional Change*, Glasgow.

Reid, J. (1984) *As I Please*, Edinburgh.

Rohac, D. (2012) 'Scandinavia is a showcase of free market reforms' *City AM*, 26 October.

Scottish Business Insider (2012) Insider Top 500 Companies, January.

Shaxson, N. (2011) *Treasure Islands: Tax Havens and the Men Who Stole the World*, London.

Therborn, G. (2000) 'Social democracy in one country?' *Dissent: a quarterly of politics and culture,* 47/4.

Trichet, J.-C. (2005) 'Asset price bubbles and monetary policy', MAS lecture, 8 June 2005, Singapore.

Watson, M. (2003) *Being English in Scotland: a guide*, Edinburgh.

Williams, R. (1988) *Keywords*, London.

Wolfe, W. (1973) *Scotland Lives: The Quest for Independence*, Reprographia